AMAZONS OF BLACK SPARTA

D0168611

To all my womenfolk:
my wife Frances,
my daughters Jennifer, Jamie and Mary,
my sisters Rozzy and Dorothy,
my granddaughter Kari,
and to the memory of my mother Belle,
and my mother-in-law Marie

STANLEY B. ALPERN

Amazons of Black Sparta

The Women Warriors
of Dahomey

With a New Preface

NEW YORK UNIVERSITY PRESS
Washington Square, New York

First published in the U.S.A. in 1998 by
NEW YORK UNIVERSITY PRESS
Washington Square
New York, NY 10003
www.nyupress.org

Library of Congress Cataloging–in–Publication Data

Alpern, Stanley B. (Stanley Bernard), 1927–
  Amazons of Black Sparta : the women warriors of Dahomey : with a new
  preface / Stanley B. Alpern.
    p. cm.
  Originally published: 1998.
  Includes bibliographical references and index.
  ISBN-13: 978-0-8147-0772-2 (pb)
  ISBN-10: 0-8147-0772-6 (pb)
  1. Women soldiers—Benin—History—19th century. 2. Women, Fon.
  3. Benin—History, Military—19th century. I. Title.

UB419.B46A48 2011
355.3'1082096683—dc22

                          2010049597

∞

CONTENTS

PREFACE

West African history intrigued me early on; I remember doing a college paper half a century ago on the founding of Liberia by freed American slaves. Sustained study was spurred in 1963 by participation in Martin Luther King jr.'s march on Washington. I wanted to know all I could about the origins of American blacks, and focused on the Ghana-to-Nigeria region, which sent more slaves to the New World than any other part of Africa (though Congo/Angola ran a close second). Nearly five years' service in West Africa during a career with the U.S. Information Agency fortified my interest, and when I took early retirement at age 50 it was to devote myself full time to research and writing on the area's pre-colonial history. *Amazons of Black Sparta* is a fruit of that decision.

No history book can be written without a greal deal of help: I am indebted to many people. First among them are friends and relatives who supplied me with photocopies of magazine articles and theses, library books, translations of words or phrases from other languages, or simply moral support. I am particularly grateful to Thomas V. Atkins, Frances Alpern, Jamie Lovdal, Albert P. Burckard jr., Peter Lubin, Monique Tavano, Ursula Timmermans and Hope Martin.

Some professional custodians of knowledge have also been especially helpful: Joy Fox, archivist of the Methodist Missionary Society in London; Philippa Bassett, keeper of the Church Missionary Society records in Birmingham, England; Bernard Favier, archivist of the Società delle Missoni Africane in Rome; Jean-Louis Bartoli and Maria Biro of the Bibliothèque Municipale of Nice; Josette Rivallain of the Musée de l'Homme in Paris; Marie-Thérèse Weiss-Litique of the Centre des Archives d'Outre-Mer in Aix-en-Provence. Thanks, too, to Betty Thomson, who found documents for me at Britain's Public Record Office in Kew.

I am beholden to several fellow Africanists: John D. Fage and P.E.H. Hair, who read the manuscript and made valuable comments; Amélie Degbelo, who gave me a copy of her important master's dissertation on the amazons of Dahomey and clarified certain points; Selena Winsnes and Finn Fuglestad, who encouraged me to persevere.

Finally, I would have gotten nowhere without the help of my private heroes: the amateur ethnographers and historians who, for whatever reason and however subjectively, took the trouble to write down their observations and impressions of Dahomey in the eighteenth and nineteenth centuries, and the twentieth-century scholars who have worked at organizing and expanding our knowledge and understanding of the kingdom. The names of outstanding members of both groups will appear again and again in the text and notes; I have not stinted in giving credit where it is due, or in letting sources speak for themselves when I felt I could not improve on the original. But of course I assume full responsibility for all opinions not explicitly attributed to others.

Villefranche-sur-Mer, France   STANLEY B. ALPERN
February 1998

PREFACE TO THE SECOND EDITION

I have the late Swedish crime novelist Stieg Larsson to thank for the second edition of *Amazons of Black Sparta: The Women Warriors of Dahomey*. As every fan of the genre knows by now, his posthumous Millennium trilogy has swept the world, at last count selling thirty million copies in more than forty languages. And it has begun to beget feature films.

I first heard of Larsson a couple of years ago when a Danish friend phoned from Copenhagen to my home in France to tell me that in the third volume of the trilogy the Swede made glowing mention of my book. It was of course nice to hear, but as far as I knew the book had appeared only in Swedish and Danish and the plug was unlikely to have much influence on sales of *Amazons of Black Sparta*.

Some months later, a neighbour photocopied the pertinent passage of the French translation of Larsson's third volume and left it in my mailbox. Not long after, a German friend called to give me the same news from the German edition. Then a Norwegian friend wrote me about it. Finally an English edition came out in London in the fall of 2009 with Larsson's third volume titled *The Girl Who Kicked the Hornets' Nest*, and there it was on page 447:

"Despite the rich variety of Amazon legends from ancient Greece, South America, Africa and elsewhere, there is only one historically documented example of female warriors. This is the women's army that existed among the Fon of Dahomey in West Africa, now Benin.

"These female warriors have never been mentioned in the published military histories; no romanticized films have been made about them, and today they exist as no more than footnotes to history. Only one scholarly work has been written about these women, *Amazons of Black Sparta*, by Stanley B. Alpern (C. Hurst & Co., London, 1998), and yet they made up a force that was the equal of every contemporary body of male elite soldiers from among the colonial powers." Larsson went on to summarize my findings in two paragraphs.

Well, mine was not the only scholarly work on the Dahomean women warriors. A Beninese scholar, Amélie Degbelo, submitted a 198-page master's thesis, "Les amazones du Danxomè, 1645–1900," at the University of Benin in 1979. In 1994 I tracked Amélie down in Cotonou and was rewarded with a gift copy of her dissertation (see p. vi). It is rich in detail and was an important source for my book, but unfortunately it was never published.

A French Africanist, Hélène d'Almeida-Topor, published a book in Paris in 1984 titled *Les amazones: une armée de femmes dans l'Afrique préco-loniale*. I cite it several times in my own work. (I must say that when I found her sources for two amazon poems to be in error [see endnotes 100 and 101 for Chapter 13], I wrote her to determine the correct sources, in vain.)

For a while I thought a Dutch writer had published a book on the amazons. *De amazone van Dahomey: verhalen*, by Conny Braam, came out in Amsterdam in 1998, the same year as mine. It is very hard to find out-side Holland, but finally a Dutch friend, Annelies Speksnijder, read it and reported that it is pure fiction—*verhalen* means stories—with hardly a reference to the female soldiers of Dahomey despite the title.

A solid work of research and interpretation, Edna G. Bay's *Wives of the Leopard: Gender, Politics, and Culture in the Kingdom of Dahomey* (Char-lottesville & London), also came out in 1998, but only intermittently focused on those women (see especially pp. 198–209 and 226–33).

Two years later, however, the American anthropologist Robert B. Edger-ton did produce a scholarly book on the subject: *Warrior Women: The Ama-zons of Dahomey and the Nature of War* (Boulder, CO, 2000). In his acknowledgements, he very graciously (and modestly) wrote: "Mr. Alpern's detailed treatment of the Amazons made it possible for me to reduce much of the detail in my book that was not directly relevant to the issues I wanted to emphasize. Interested readers are encouraged to refer to Alpern's book for a broader discussion of the Amazons than I provide." But Mr. Edgerton certainly enlarged our understanding of Dahomey's female troops.

In *Amazons of Black Sparta* I devote only two pages to the question of why the amazons arose in Dahomey and nowhere else. The Victorian traveler Richard F. Burton thought the answer lay in their sturdy phy-siques, but there is no evidence they were any sturdier than other West African woman. I credited the need to compensate for the manpower discrepancy between the Fon of Dahomey and their main rivals in the eighteenth and nineteenth centuries, the Yoruba of what is now south-western Nigeria. The Yoruba outnumber the Fon by at least 10 to 1 today and probably did in the past. I reiterated this point in an article, "On the origins of the amazons of Dahomey," published in *History in Africa* (25, pp. 9–25) the same year as the book.

Edgerton (see especially pp. 122–3 and 146–8) noted that losses of male soldiers in battle, plus the fact that substantially more men than women were shipped across the Atlantic as slaves, would have widened the gender gap and might have encouraged the training of female soldiers. But he suggested that the best explanation for Dahomey's use of women warriors was their loyalty to the king. To protect themselves from possible coups, Dahomean monarchs did not allow men into their palaces at night and so came to depend on women guards. The guards proved so loyal, so adept at military arts and so hardened by physical training, that they evolved into elite troops.

In my 1998 article, I assembled evidence for the use of female palace guards by the time of King Agaja (1708–40), and of royal female body-guards outside the palaces during the reigns of Tegbesu (1740–1774) and Kpengla (1774–1789). I also made a case for the use of those women in warfare during the same reigns. There is no doubt that the armed females of Dahomey came of age as superior fighters under Gezo (1818–1858).

Evidence brought to light by Robin Law in 1990 for Agaja's use of female palace guards (see p. 27 of *Amazons*) was confirmed by him in 2002 (*History in Africa*, 29, p. 266) through the discovery of a second version of the king's 1726 letter to George I of England. It appeared in the *Pennsylvania Gazette* in 1732. The first version was found in the House of Commons proceedings for 1789. In 2004 Law added greatly to our knowledge of the kingdom of Dahomey with a meticulous work on its principal slave-trade outlet, *Ouidah: The Social History of a West African Slaving 'Port', 1727–1892* (Athens, OH, and Oxford), but it contains no references to the amazons.

As I and other writers have noted, celibacy was imposed on the amazons so that pregnancy would not disrupt their martial regime. According to Edgerton, this ban was enforced by apparently mandatory consumption of an herbal concoction thought to be a contraceptive (see pp. 24, 119 and 152). This disputes Melville J. Herskovits, who in his ground-breaking two-volume study, *Dahomey, an Ancient West African Kingdom* (New York, 1938), said that despite repeated efforts he had found no information indicating Dahomeans had "knowledge of contraceptive measures" (I, 268 n. 3).

On the other hand, I may have erred when I wrote (p. 46) that abortion was unheard of in Dahomey. In a passage I overlooked, Herskovits (I, 268–9) said a drink based on lime juice was used (in the early 1930s, at least) to bring about an abortion after the first or second month of pregnancy. It was thought to be useless three months after conception. Herskovits did not suggest, however, that the potion was known in amazon times. (His main references to the female troops are to be found in II, 46–7 and 84–90.)

A book titled *King Guezo of Dahomey, 1850–52: The Abolition of the Slave Trade on the West Coast of Africa*, was published in London in 2001. Edited by Tim Coates but lacking an editorial apparatus, it is a compendium of official British documents dating from the period when the amazon corps reached its maximum strength. References to the women, all by familiar sources—John Duncan (on pp. 18–9), Frederick E. Forbes (30–2, 57–62, 65–77, 91) and Henry Townsend (131–4)—add little to our knowledge.

All in all, not a great deal has been written about the amazons of Dahomey since 1998. A pity since, as Larsson recognized, they are unique in world history.

In this second edition of my work, a few errors have been corrected but otherwise nothing has been changed. The first edition received only one negative review, by Edna Bay in the *Journal of African History*, 40 (1999), 485–6. She acknowledged that "the first book-length study in English devoted solely to the Dahomean women's army" was "meticulously researched" and "painstakingly documented," showing "good judgement about…sources." But the review contained more than a few critical comments. In a letter, Ms. Bay explained: "Although I admired the depth and quality of your research, I criticized your use of language that makes the women soldiers seem very exotic. I suppose you can call it simple differences in taste (or maybe my feminist background), but I've always wanted to distance our contemporary thinking about them from the Victorian visitors' visions of amazons of antiquity." I leave it to the reader to judge.

Stanley B. Alpern
Villefranche-sur-Mer, France
May 2010

ILLUSTRATIONS

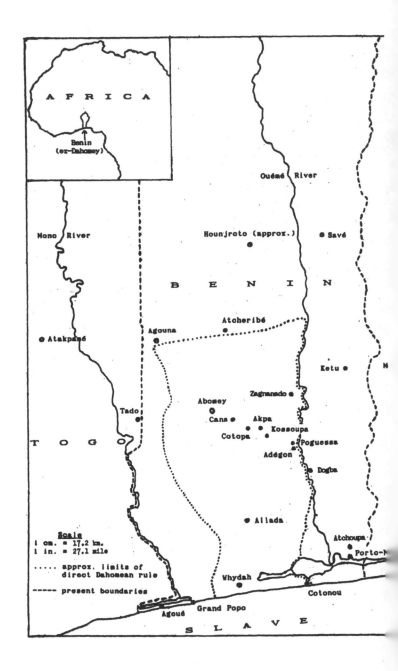

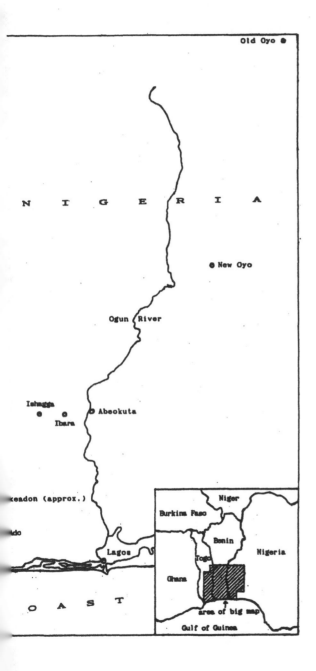

THE KINGS OF DAHOMEY

Dako (*ca.* 1620–5 -*ca.* 1640–50)
Wegbaja (*ca.* 1640-50 – *ca.* 1680-5)
Akaba (*ca.* 1680–5–1708)
Agaja (1708–40)
Tegbesu (1740–74)
Kpengla (1774–89)
Agonglo (1789–97)
Abandozan (1797–1818)
Gezo (1818–58)
Glele (1858–89)
Béhanzin (1889–94)
Agoli-Agbo (1894–1900)

INTRODUCTION

World history and historical legend are strewn with references to fighting women. Some were warrior queens, who both ruled and waged war: the semi-mythic Semiramis of Nineveh who carved out an Assyrian empire; Tomyris of Central Asia who reputedly defeated and killed Cyrus of Persia; Artemisia of Halicarnassus who helped Xerxes against the Greeks; Virgil's Camilla of the Volscians, an Italic princess who fought to the death against Aeneas and his Trojans; Cleopatra VII of Egypt, familiar to us all; Boadicea of the Iceni who led a blood-soaked British rebellion against Rome; Zenobia of Palmyra who over a much longer spell humbled Rome; Matilda of Canossa, armed champion of two popes; Tamara of Georgia who gave her homeland its golden age; Catherine the Great of Russia, Voltaire's "Semiramis of the North"; the Rani of Jhansi, heroine of the Indian Mutiny. Antonia Fraser, who has catalogued warrior queens for us, submits Golda Meir, Indira Gandhi and Margaret Thatcher as latter-day examples.[1]

Africa had its share of warrior queens. One, Candace (or Kandake) of the Nubian kingdom of Meroë, fought the Romans in southernmost Egypt in the first century BC. Classical authors tell us she was mannish and blind in one eye, and little else. Her name was actually a title meaning queen-mother.[2] A later Candace is mentioned in the Bible: Philip the Evangelist baptized her chief treasurer, a eunuch who had made a pilgrimage to Jerusalem.[3]

We know much more about another African warrior queen, Nzinga of Matamba, a dominant figure in seventeenth-century Angola. Nzinga (a.k.a. Jinga, Xinga, Zhinga,

1

Zingha and Singa) ruled for forty years, moulded a strong (male) army and fought several wars against the Portuguese. During the 1640s she had Dutch support; a Dutch officer sent to give her assistance saw her when she was probably in her sixties. Nzinga was "a very stouthearted virago", enjoyed fighting, and dressed like a man. Before going to war, she danced in animal skins, a broadsword suspended from her neck, an axe stuck in her belt, and a bow and arrows in her hands, as nimble as a young man. Then she sacrificed a male prisoner, beheading him and taking a great swig of his blood. At the same time, according to the Dutchman, Nzinga kept a harem of fifty or sixty male concubines who dressed like women.[4]

History also informs us of inspired women patriots who were military leaders without being rulers. Joan of Arc is a classic example. Another teenaged French heroine is Jeanne Hachette, who defended Beauvais against Charles the Bold of Burgundy. In *Childe Harold's Pilgrimage* Byron immortalizes the Maid of Saragoza, María Augustín, who fought French besiegers in the Peninsular War. Vietnam honors the memory of three such women, the sisters Trung Trac and Trung Nhi in the first century AD and Trieu Au in the third, who led uprisings against China.

Armed women appear many times and in many places as royal or palace guards. Candra Gupta, the first Hindu king to unite most of India, and an interlocutor of Alexander the Great, is said to have boasted a guard of giant Greek women. Two millennia later, the nizams of Hyderabad in the Deccan also had female guards. The kings of Kandy in Sri Lanka were protected by archeresses. And women are reported to have guarded the kings of Persia.

When King David quit Jerusalem to avoid being captured by his rebellious son Absalom, he left ten concubines in charge of his palace. Presumably they were armed, although one wonders how they were expected to stand up to Absalom's army. They did not, and Absalom lay with them "in the sight of all Israel". David later punished them with celibacy for life.[5]

In the nineteenth century the king of Siam was guarded by a battalion of 400 women armed with spears. They were chosen, it is said, from among the most robust and beautiful girls of the country, performed drills better than male soldiers and were crack spear-throwers. But kings found them too precious to send off to war. In the same century two battalions of spear-women were found protecting a king among the Beir people on the White Nile.[6] A similar phenomenon was reported in a Javan princedom.

By far the most common martial women have been those who fought alongside their menfolk, whether by custom, or in moments of communal peril, or out of personal inclination. Time and again the Romans, who would never countenance females in their own ranks, found themselves fighting Celtic or Germanic tribes in which wives stood shoulder to shoulder with their husbands. Tacitus quotes the Roman general who defeated Boadicea as saying contemptuously that she had more women under her than men. An Irish law of AD 697 *excluded* females from the army, implying they had previously served. Byzantines reported women soldiers among the Slavs. The horse-borne nomadic tribes of Eurasia – Scythians, Huns, Mongols, Tatars, Uzbeks, Tajiks – had female warriors riding beside males. Graves of such women belonging to two such tribes, the Sauromatians and Sarmatians, have recently been found. Igbo (Ibo) women in southern Nigeria shared combat duty with men c. 1750,[7] and Fulani women in northern Nigeria did likewise in the 1820s.[8] The roster of peoples known to have relied on women as fighters at one time or other or at one place or other includes Scandinavians, Arabs, Berbers, Kurds, Rajputs, Chinese, Indonesians, Filipinos, Maori, Papuans, Australian aborigines, Micronesians and Amerindians. Well before women were integrated into the armed forces of Western societies in the twentieth century, they were signing up in male disguise. "Many a fair form", it has been recalled, "was found stark on the field of Waterloo."[9] An estimated 400 women enlisted in the American Civil War.[10]

Beginning with the ancient Greeks, there have been reports of fierce fighting women who lived apart from men, were trained from girlhood in martial and athletic skills and to endure hardship, were led into combat by their own kind and often bested males on the field of battle.

The Greeks called them "amazons", meaning literally "without a breast". It was explained (quite fallaciously) that to make it easier to draw a bow or hurl a javelin, their right breast was either seared with a red-hot iron or excised in childhood. The two greatest names in Greek medicine, Hippocrates and Galen, agreed that the operation would not only remove a hindrance to the use of weapons but divert nourishment to a woman's right arm and so strengthen it. The question of left-handed women was never raised.

The word amazon[*] has been variously traced to Phoenician, Armenian, a Slavic language, Kalmuck (a Mongol tongue), Scythian or even to Greek terms with other meanings. It has been suggested that the initial "a" meant not "without" but the opposite, designating big-breasted women. The ancient Greeks themselves were not sure of the etymology, and their artists obviously did not take the standard explanation seriously: not one of the many surviving representations of amazons in sculpture and painting (on vases and other ceramic vessels) shows a breast missing.

Amazons appear in Greek literature with Homer's *Iliad*, first written down in the sixth century BC. He and many subsequent Greek authors locate the warrioresses in Asia Minor. The same women are also the subject of all Greek artists who treat the amazon theme. However, an historian

---

[*] In all probability, the word itself produced the rationale. It is not uncommon for people encountering a mysterious foreign locution to deform it into something intelligible to them. From my home in France I see a hill known as the Tête de Chien (Dog's Head) and a promontory called Cap d'Ail (Garlic Cape). Neither geographical feature lives up to its billing because both names are French distortions of words in the local patois that meant something else.

of the first century BC, Diodorus of Sicily, describes another group who lived in Libya (a term then used for much of North Africa west of Egypt) and antedated those of Asia Minor. Classicists regard both Diodorus and his acknowledged main source, Dionysius of Alexandria, as untrustworthy, but neither pretends that his own story is anything but myth.

Libyan Amazonia was a gynecocracy: women alone did military service and held all political and judicial offices. Men kept house, reared children and obeyed their consorts. Exceptionally among amazons, *both* breasts of young girls were cauterized (fathers fed babies sheep's or goat's milk). From a base on an island in a lake, a queen named Myrina sallied forth on a career of conquest with a female army of 30,000 infantry and 3,000 cavalry, armed with swords, spears and bows. After defeating all neighboring peoples, including that of Atlantis, Myrina led her forces through Egypt, Arabia, Syria and Asia Minor to islands of the Aegean Sea, among them Lesbos and Samothrace. Eventually the queen was killed and her army shattered by male soldiers from Scythia and Thrace. The amazon survivors withdrew to Libya, where ultimately they were wiped out by Hercules.[11]

Greek stories about the amazons of Asia Minor vary with each telling, but a rough consensus emerges. Two Scythian princes were expelled from their homeland north of the Black Sea with their families and followers and migrated to the Caucasus region. They subdued and oppressed local peoples, who rebelled and slew all the males. The Scythian women took up arms, successfully defended themselves, and formed a manless, militaristic nation. Eventually they settled in northern Anatolia, on a rich plain bordering the Thermodon River, which runs into the Black Sea. At the river's mouth they built their capital, Themiscyra.

The new state was on a perpetual war footing. Girls were brought up rigorously, accustomed to fatigue and privation, trained to fight equally well on foot and horseback. They became expert archers, equestrians and hunters. Besides bows and arrows, the amazons were armed with darts, javelins, lances, swords and single- or double-edged axes, and carried small shields shaped like phases of the moon. They could pole-vault on to horses using a spear, and, riding bareback, feign retreat, then swing around to face backward and rain arrows on the foe.

Their basic garment was a tunic tied at the left shoulder, cinched by a girdle, or sword-belt, and reaching almost to the knee. It left the right breast bare, the one that had purportedly been burnt off in childhood but that Greek artists would not remove. After contact with the Greeks, the amazons began wearing Greek armor – plumed helmets, cuirasses, cuisses, greaves – sandals with ankle straps and more voluminous robes. When the Greeks engaged in the Persian Wars, artists began putting amazons in oriental trousers and long sleeves.

The amazons renounced marriage as servitude. When they were not fighting, they farmed the land and tended livestock. For procreation they took two months off every year to couple with men of a neighboring tribe, at random and in the dark. Only women who had killed a man in battle could give up their virginity. Girls born from such unions were reared as amazons; whereas boys had various fates – some were returned to their fathers' community; some were deliberately crippled and kept as slaves to do such menial jobs as spinning wool; some were sacrificed, presumably to the gods of war.

The amazons of the Thermodon conquered many peoples but finally met their nemesis in the Greeks, and particularly four Greek heroes: Bellerophon, Hercules, Theseus and Achilles. Bellerophon, who had slain the fire-breathing Chimera by flying above it on the winged horse Pegasus and sending a spear into its mouth, routed the amazon army by raining down arrows and boulders from his steed.

The ninth labor imposed on Hercules was to seize the golden girdle of the amazon queen, a gift of Ares (Mars). He sailed to Themiscyra and invulnerable in his lion's skin, slew twelve amazon champions, led his men to total victory and obtained the girdle. Theseus, king of Athens, either then or later carried off the queen, Antiope, or her sister-queen Hippolyte, as a bride. Another sister, Orithya, who had been off on a military campaign, pursued the Greeks to Athens itself, and was defeated by Theseus in a famous struggle.

The amazons made a last appearance toward the end of the Trojan War when the gorgeous Queen Penthesilea and twelve stalwart warrioresses joined forces with King Priam. They killed many a Greek captain but died one by one till only Penthesilea, swinging a battle-axe, was left to face Achilles, unaware of his only vulnerable point. He drove his spear through her and into her horse – then, remorseful, fell in love with her corpse.

Despite the abundance of detail in Greek literature and art about the amazons of Asia Minor, there is no conclusive proof, indeed no real evidence, that they ever existed. Since their putative forebears the Scythians did not appear on the Greek horizon till the seventh century BC, a Scythian connection to the women is anachronistic. A gap of more than half a millennium separates the Trojan War from the first depictions of the female soldiers. A Turkish port, Terme, would seem to be on or near the site of Themiscyra, but no trace of the amazon capital has ever been found, nor have any other ruins or buried artifacts been attributed to the women. In a region where contemporary peoples kept records on cuneiform tablets, none seem to have been left by them.

A tantalizing theory links the women to the Hittites, who lived in the same general area at about the same time and could eventually have been confused by the Greeks with Scythians. The theory is encouraged by the knowledge that the Hittites had double-edged axes and wore boots with turned-up toes like those seen in some amazon representations. The Hittite empire collapsed toward the end of the thirteenth century BC under blows from Assyrians to the south and Greeks to the west. It may be that the Hittite army was off battling the Assyrians when the Greeks invaded, and that Hittite women fought in self-defense. This, it is suggested, could have given rise to the amazon myth. An alternative speculation is that the Greeks mistook Hittite males for females because the latter shaved off their beards whereas they did not.

Today's classical scholars see the amazon myth as an elaborate cautionary tale. Greek males viewed their patriarchal society as natural, orderly, civilized. It was normal for men to rule, fight, hunt, farm, exercise outdoors and control marriage and reproduction. It was normal for women to obey, marry, keep house, rear children, for girls to be virginal and wives to be chaste and modest, constant and tame. For Greek males, who monopolized public discourse, amazon society was a topsy-turvy world, unnatural, disorderly, un-civilized, barbaric, even bestial – and therefore doomed. It was an object lesson in what could happen if Greek gender roles and values were reversed and women took charge.[12]

Many centuries after the women soldiers of Greek legend were supposed to have died out, they briefly reappeared in an anecdote about Alexander the Great. An amazon queen named Thalestris, learning of Alexander's military prowess, traveled twenty-five days with 300 horsewomen to meet him in what is now northern Iran. She offered to give him an heir, and shared his bed for thirteen days, but died soon after returning to her country in the Caucasus region. One of Alexander's top generals, hearing the story much later, smiled and asked, "And where was I at the time?"[13]

A millennium and a half passed before Europeans, in the first flush of the Age of Discovery, would again locate, or hear about, or imagine amazons in far-flung places. Marco Polo prefigured the trend with a tale of two Indian Ocean islands some 30 miles apart, one inhabited by men, the other by women. Masculina's residents joined their wives for three months every year on Feminea; sons were sent to their fathers, girls stayed with their mothers. But these women made love, not war.[14]

Columbus was told on his first trans-Atlantic voyage about a Caribbean island named Matinino where women dwelt alone. They "employ themselves", he reported, "in no labor suitable to their own sex, for they use bows and javelins...and for defensive armor...have plates of brass." But he never found the place.[15]

Not many years later the Portuguese navigator Tristan da Cunha reported that the women of the island of Socotra off the Horn of East Africa were "so manly that they go to war", and in order to have children coupled with strangers.[16]

Two Portuguese priests who visited Ethiopia separately in the early sixteenth century heard about a province where the women were suspiciously like those of Greek legend. Their right breast was branded to prevent growth, they were constantly armed, were expert archers, and devoted their lives to war and hunting. They fought on bullback rather than horseback. Unlike their precursors in Asia Minor, they married at least sometimes but were much bolder and more martial than their husbands. Children, once weaned, were given over to the men.[17]

Later in the same century southern Africa yielded *its* echoes of the Greek myth. The Portuguese traveler Duarte Lopez related that the emperor of Monomotapa, inland from Mozambique, had a big army that was constantly at war to maintain his realm. "Amongst his warriors", said Lopez, "those most renowned for bravery are the female legions, greatly valued by the Emperor, being the sinews of his military strength." Their *left* breast was burnt off so as not to hamper their archery. They were "extremely agile and rapid", fought with "great daring and courage", and showed "wiles and cunning" in pretending to retreat then turning round (but not on horseback) and slaughtering the prematurely elated foe. As a result, they were "held in great dread in those regions". The emperor gave them lands where they lived alone, but they mated with men of their own choice at certain times. Baby boys were sent to their fathers, girls were "kept apart by themselves, and brought up in the arts of war".[18]

California takes its name from a Spanish romance of 1510 about an island peopled solely by cave-dwelling black amazons. "They were of strong and hardened bodies, of ardent courage, and of great force." They wielded gold weapons, rode wild beasts they had tamed, and sailed ships on raiding voyages. Their queen savaged enemy "knights" like a raging lioness.[19]

The only sighting of amazons claimed during the whole century after Columbus was the one that apparently led to the naming of the Amazon River (although an Amerindian etymology is not excluded). A Dominican friar named Gaspar de Carvajal accompanied a Spanish expedition from Quito to investigate reports of an enormous river, and wrote an account. In June 1542 the expedition, riding in boats on the river, was attacked by Indian men led by ten or twelve very white, big and robust women. The women had long plaited hair wrapped round their heads, and were naked except for a *cache-sexe*. Each fought "as much as ten Indians" with bows and arrows; they also carried clubs to kill any Indian who turned tail. The Spaniards slew seven or eight of the women and routed the attackers.

One Indian was captured. Questioned about the women, he said they lived seven days' journey from the river but had come to defend the local chief, who was one of their many vassals. They were very numerous in their homeland, he said, dwelling by themselves in stone houses in at least seventy villages. They captured Indian men from a neighboring country, kept them "long enough to satisfy their caprices", then let them go home when they became pregnant. Boy babies were killed or sent to their fathers, girls "reared with great solemnity and instructed...in the arts of war". (It was not explained how with Indian fathers the women stayed white.) Carvajal's story was never contested by any of the sixty-odd members of the expedition, but neither was it corroborated by any later explorer.[20]

In truth, the only thoroughly documented amazons in world history are the subject of this book. Their uniqueness was recognized as early as 1793 when Archibald Dalzel, in *The History of Dahomy, an Inland Kingdom of Africa*, wrote: "Whatever might have been the prowess of the *Amazons* among the ancients, this is a novelty in modern history, which ought not to be slightly passed over."[21] European visitors generally began referring to the women soldiers of Dahomey as amazons in the 1840s. By 1850 the Dahomeans themselves were aware of the institution's uniqueness: Frederick Forbes heard a male bard sing praise of King Gezo as "the only monarch in the world who held an amazon army".[22] For Aristide Vallon, a French visitor in the 1850s, Dahomey was "assuredly the only country in the world that offers the singular spectacle of an organization of women as soldiers, captains, generals and ministers!"[23] After the event, the Larousse publishing house had no doubt that "the only historical Amazons known are the Amazons of Dahomey."[24]

Remarkably, the fantasized amazons of antiquity and the real amazons of Dahomey share a good number of attributes. From an early age both were taught to fight, to handle weapons, to be strong and swift and hardy, to withstand suffering. Hunting, dancing and instrumental music were among their skills. Their basic purpose in life was to make war. They lusted for battle, rushed into it with blood-curdling cries, reveled in it, and fought with fury and valor, seemingly immune to fear. In victory they were pitiless. They terrified their neighbors. Men regarded them as worthy, implacable adversaries.

On the other hand, there were notable differences. The amazons of Dahomey never rode horses or any other animal. Instead of bows, spears and axes, their main weapons were muskets, clubs and machetes. They rarely used shields. Their breasts were intact. They were vowed to celibacy, and thus did not produce their own replacements. Like their ancient forerunners they lived by themselves, but in royal palaces, not off somewhere autonomously. They fought in an army with a male majority. Though they had their own officers, they were ultimately ruled by men. They were, in fact, completely devoted to their king, and would die for him – which they often did.

A word about the title of this book. The British traveler Richard F. Burton called Dahomey "this small black Sparta"[25] for its militarism and subordination of the individual to the state. Its amazons resembled the women of Sparta in one respect: their bodies were hardened from childhood by physical exercise. Footracing, wrestling and spear-throwing were sports they probably shared; the Greek girls also threw the discus. (The African girls were more demure: they did not compete naked in public.) Spartan women kept in shape to breed male warriors, Dahomean amazons to kill them.

Here, then, is the amazons' story.

1

A MOCK BATTLE

Toward noon on Saturday, November 30, 1861, Father Francesco Borghero was called to the parade ground in Abomey, capital of Dahomey, by his host, King Glele (pronounced Gleh-leh). The monarch's female warriors, the priest was told, wanted to put on a show for him.

Across a huge open space, a barricade 400 meters long had been erected. It was composed of bundles of acacia branches with needle-sharp thorns. The pile was 2 meters high and 6 wide. It represented the outer wall of a town.

Forty paces beyond, and parallel to the barricade, was the frame of a house of equal length, 5 meters wide, and roofed over. The ridgepole was 5 meters high, and the two slopes of the roof were covered with a thick layer of the same thorny branches. The structure represented a citadel bristling with defenses, the space before it a ditch.

Fifteen meters beyond the linear pseudo-house was a row of huts simulating the town.

At some distance from the barricade were about 3,000 armed and uniformed women. Two or three hundred of them carried giant straightedge razors folded into wooden handles. It was said that these weapons, wielded with both hands, could cut a man in two at the middle with one swipe. All the other warrioresses were equipped with flintlock muskets and swords.

The women wore battledress: a half-sleeved rust-colored tunic cinched at the waist by a cartridge belt, and shorts of almost knee length. Narrow white headbands were tied at the back. Some amazons wore copper or gemstone bracelets and anklets. All were barefoot.

At a signal from the king, the amazons began reconnoitering the enemy's defenses. First they moved forward bent over, almost crawling, to avoid being spotted. Their weapons were held close to the ground. They advanced in total silence.

A second reconnaissance was made standing up, heads high.

The female soldiers then massed in battle array, muskets raised, razors open, along the 400-meter front. Glele, a tall, handsome, bronze-black man of athletic build, stepped forward to harangue them and fire them up. Then, at an order, the attack began.

The amazons rushed with indescribable fury at the thorny barrier, climbed over it in a flash, charged across the make-believe ditch and up the first roof slope. At the top they were beaten back by imaginary defenders.

They returned to their starting point, regrouped, and repeated the attack. Again they were repulsed by a hypothetical counteroffensive.

A third assault was launched. The women moved so fast that Borghero's eye had trouble following them. They scrambled over thorns, he observed, as easily as a *danseuse* gliding across a parquet floor.

This time they were successful. They scaled the nearer roof slope, streaked down the other side, stormed the huts and captured the "town", then hauled make-believe prisoners to the feet of the king.

Early in the spectacle, an amazon who had reached the rooftop of the makeshift house tumbled five meters to the ground and remained seated, writhing in pain. Her comrades' words of encouragement were having no effect when the king himself intervened with a stern look and a shouted reproof. The women sprang up as if electrified, rejoined the battle and distinguished herself. Military valor, Glele told Borghero, was Dahomey's first virtue.

The battle won, a young female general who had controlled the action made a speech directed at Borghero, a Genoese who headed a newly-established French Catholic mission at Whydah (Ouidah), Dahomey's port, and was on his first visit to Abomey.

She was aged about thirty, slender but shapely, proud of bearing but without affectation. With her figure, European-type features and vivacious movements, the priest mused, one might have taken her for a Virgilian huntress...had it not been for her deep black color.

The general talked for more than half an hour, comparing the valor of her warrioresses with that of white male soldiers, and suggesting that good relations should always exist between equally brave peoples. Both Dahomeans and Europeans, she said, were rich enough in glory to seek no other conquests but mutual friendship. She concluded by pronouncing Borghero an honorary chief of the amazons and presenting him with her commander's baton to the applause of the massed army.

The baton, 60 centimeters long, had the carved figure of a shark at the free end. As this fish destroys men, Borghero was told, so did the warrioresses in combat.

The priest watched the amazons head for their barracks in the immense royal palace enclosure, their legs all torn and bleeding. Those who excelled in the pantomime wore crowns or belts of thorns as their prizes. Borghero suspected they could hardly wait to take them off.

The whole scene unfolded, as he reported, under dark, threatening skies, a storm rumbling in the distance, that made it seem even more animated and altogether unreal. But nearly every detail of his account rings true.[1]

2

ORIGINS OF DAHOMEY

The origins of the women warriors of Dahomey, as of the former West African kingdom itself, are lost in the shades of unrecorded time.

According to oral traditions of the Fon, the people who founded the kingdom, their ancestors came from a village cluster called Tado in what is now eastern Togo. Estimates by mainly French scholars of when Tado was founded range from before the tenth century AD to the fourteenth, but in the absence of archeological evidence all the datings are pure guesswork.[1] From this area successive streams, or rivulets, of migrants went out to populate most of southern Togo and southern Benin (ex-Dahomey).

The ancestors of the Fon went southeastward. At least ten different myths try to explain why they left Tado. Most versions are totemic: they begin with a leopard, often a royal symbol in Africa. Usually, in these stories, a male leopard lies with a daughter or wife of the king of Tado and a son results. In one variant the leopard is a female who changes into a woman and marries the king. Either the leopard or his (or her) son is named Agasu, and their descendants are called *Agasuvi*.

Sooner or later the Agasuvi make a losing bid for the throne of Tado; they are led by one Ajahuto who kills the king, or the crown prince, or simply his enemies, after which the clan must flee. Although these myths are related by people who regard the Agasuvi as their founding heroes, they generally concede that the Agasuvi claim to the Tado throne was weak because the clan belonged to the local tribe through descent from a woman. Conceivably this folk

16

memory recalls a time when the patrilineal principle prevailed over the matrilineal.[2]

The Agasuvi wandered for some years and ultimately settled at Allada, only about 50 miles southeast of Tado. The age of Allada, like that of Tado, is unknown. Authors suggest it was founded in the fifteenth or sixteenth century but they have little to go on. Eventually Allada became a kingdom.

The name appears early in European records on West Africa. The Fon and their near relatives, collectively known as the Aja, are among those peoples who, like the Chinese and Japanese, mix up the L and R sounds. And so do the Portuguese, who, for example, say *branco* for white in contrast to the Spanish *blanco* and "*Obrigado*" ("Obliged") for "Thank you". Thus in the old accounts Allada comes out Arda, or variations on it. A place named "Alhadra" is marked in roughly the right location on a Portuguese map of the 1480s.[3] A Portuguese letter of 1539 refers to the ruler of "Arida" who had sent an envoy to the king of Benin in what is now south-central Nigeria.[4] A Portuguese map of 1570 shows the "Costadarida" ("Coast of Arida") and another from about the same year shows "Arda".[5] In 1590-1 an English shipmaster, James Welsh, captured and burned a Portuguese caravel "thwart of Arda".[6] By 1602 the Dutchman Pieter de Marees could report:

Rio de Ardra [not a river but a coastal lake]...is much navigated by the Portuguese, and is well known everywhere...because of the multitude of Slaves who are sold and bought there in order to be transported elsewhere, to St. Thome [São Tomé] and Brazil, in order to work there and refine Sugar; for they are very stout and steadfast Men, well suited to heavy labour.[7]

The Slave Coast, a label that would not be affixed to the area between the Volta River in what is now Ghana and the Lagos area in southwestern Nigeria till the end of the seventeenth century,[8] was already earning its reputation.

Europe's first contact point with the kingdom of Allada was a coastal community that Europeans called Petit Ardra or simply Ardra. The capital, an inland town 23 miles from the sea, was called Grand Ardra, or Allada. It was there, in around 1610, that a royal succession dispute between brothers is believed to have sparked an exodus by the losing party. The migrants went north to the plateau of Abomey, 60-70 miles from the coast. About 1620-5 another succession dispute ended with the victory of Dako, considered the founder of the Dahomey dynasty.

Dako began a state policy of conquering neighbors that would make Dahomey the premier power of the region a century later. Territorial expansion accelerated under his son Wegbaja, who is thought to have ruled from about 1640-50 to 1680-5. It was Wegbaja who is said, after killing a rival chief named Dan, to have built his palace on the victim's grave and dubbed it Danhomé, meaning "in the belly of Dan". This is the most common explanation of the name Dahomey. The palace site was Abomey, which became the country's capital.

Wegbaja strengthened royal authority over kin groups, arrogated the sole right to punish criminals and impose the death penalty, regularized the collection of tribute from his subjects and in general created a Dahomean version of the "divine kingship" found in many parts of old Africa. He is also said to have introduced pre-dawn surprise attacks as the Dahomean military tactic *par excellence* and to have begun importing firearms from European traders on the coast.

It was toward the end of Wegbaja's reign that the Fon appear in history, if by history we mean the written record. They are first mentioned in a Spanish manuscript of 1675 as a kingdom named "Fo" that had won its independence from Allada.[9] This information seems to have come from Spanish Capuchin missionaries who spent a year in Allada in 1660-1.[10] The Fon are "Fumce" in a Dutch document of 1680.[11] They make a more formal literary debut in the journal of a French naval officer, Jean-Baptiste Ducasse, who visited the then-independent slaving port of Whydah in 1687-8. He reported that Whydah traders were having "some differences with the King of Fouin", who was blocking their passage upcountry.[12]

Dahomey itself does not enter the written record until 1716, when the name appears in French correspondence.[13] The first eyewitness account dates from 1724, when a British Royal African Company agent, Bulfinch Lamb, being held captive at Abomey, sent a plaintive letter to his superior.[14] From then on the history of Dahomey is well documented by sub-Saharan African standards, particularly so in the kingdom's last half-century, from the 1840s to the 1890s.

3

ORIGINS OF THE AMAZONS

THE ELEPHANT HUNTRESSES

Some oral historians of Dahomey trace the amazons back to a band of women who hunted elephants for King Wegbaja, presumably to supply him with ivory as well as meat for royal feasts. They were called the *gbeto*, and in the nineteenth century were regarded as the oldest amazon unit. J. Alfred Skertchly, a British entomologist who spent eight months in Dahomey in 1871-2, has left us the most detailed description of the huntresses. He watched forty-eight of them parade before the king:

They were all tall well-proportioned women dressed in dull-brown petticoats, and indigo-dyed tunics, with black sashes, profusely ornamented with magic relics. Round their waists they wore a curious affair composed of strips of hide with the hair on dangling from a belt, and a fillibeg [kilt] of leather ornamented with cowries in front. Their guns were heavy, wide bore muskets, and their ammunition was carried in black leather pouches. All wore their hair cut close, save a circular patch on the top of the poll, where it was combed out like a brush. They are renowned for their prowess in the chase...[1]

A decade and a half earlier, a French naval surgeon, Dr A. Répin, had seen about 400 *gbeto* at a military fete in Abomey. His observations on their appearance differ somewhat from Skertchly's, details no doubt having changed over time. Répin's huntresses were clad all in brown, carried long, heavy carbines with blackened barrels and wore powerful curved daggers at their belts. Two antelope horns sprouted from above their forehead, "fixed...on an iron hoop circling the head like a diadem".

Répin watched some *gbeto* mime their hunting technique:

They formed a circle, and crawling on their hands and knees without abandoning their carbine, they converged on a point where the elephant herd was supposed to be... [T]he latter, deceived by those false horns [on the women's heads], think they see and hear a peaceful herd of antelopes, and remain unsuspectingly exposed to the huntresses' fire. Arriving near the elephants, they all rose up together at a signal from their chief, discharging their carbines; then, knife in hand, they sprang forward to finish them off and cut off their tails, trophy of their victory.[2]

During a royal audience, Répin saw a messenger arrive with three freshly-cut elephant tails, proof of a successful hunt.[3] A French naval officer who attended the same audience (the Vallon quoted in the Introduction) adds the details that twenty huntresses were involved, that they attacked a herd of thirty to forty beasts and killed the three with a single point-blank volley.[4] Répin heard that these expeditions always cost the lives of some *gbeto*, gored or trampled by wounded beasts.[5] Skertchly was told of a hunt fatal to twelve Dahomean Dianas.[6] One author says the *gbeto* were disbanded before the kingdom's final reckoning against France in the early 1890s for the simple reason that elephants had been hunted to extinction in the area.[7] But more persuasive testimony indicates that they were among amazon units who fought to the end.[8]

It seems plausible enough that women capable of killing elephants would sooner or later be viewed as capable of killing enemy warriors. An apocryphal tradition relates that when King Gezo (pronounced Ghézo – 1818-58), perhaps Dahomey's greatest monarch, praised his elephant-hunting wives for their courage, they replied that "a nice manhunt would suit them even better".[9] But there is no solid evidence that the one led to the other.

THE ROYAL TWINS

Another theory of amazon origins is also rooted in unprovable oral tradition. It involves Wegbaja's son and successor, Akaba, who reigned from *c.* 1680-5 to 1708. Akaba had a twin sister named Ahangbé (or Tassin Hangbé).

Twins were very special individuals in precolonial West Africa, and were either abhorred or revered, depending on the ethnic group into which they were born. Some peoples, like the Igbo, Ijo and Ibibio of southern Nigeria, killed twin infants and punished the mother. They regarded single births as the exclusive human norm and multiple births as bestial or demonic, hence taboo. Other peoples, like the Bini of old Benin and most of the Yoruba of southwestern Nigeria, welcomed twins as the most desirable offspring, sometimes to the point of worshiping them. The Fon were among the latter. Their twins had a special guardian spirit, and were thought to maintain relations with the spirit world and to have the ability to die and come back to life at will. The Fon insisted that twins be treated equally well, even those of different sexes.

Therefore, according to legend, Ahangbé was named co-sovereign with her brother Akaba, had her own palace and court, and theoretically reigned jointly with him. In fact, goes the story, she was content to stay in her palace and indulge her passions. These included copulating with any man she fancied, a privilege customarily accorded Dahomean princesses, who were exempt from the strict prevailing laws against adultery.

In 1708 Akaba is said to have died of smallpox while leading his army against a people living along the Ouémé River east of Abomey. Ahangbé's close resemblance to her brother was purportedly exploited to keep the news of his death from Dahomean troops till the final victory. If she did take his place in the field, it might qualify her as the only possible Dahomean candidate for the title of warrior queen (see Introduction).

Ahangbé may then have been named regent because the heir to the throne, Akaba's son, was still too young to rule. Her regency lasted only three months, according to one version, three years according to another. What was permitted a Dahomean princess ill became a reigning queen, but Ahangbé refused to change her bacchanalian life-style. Widespread opposition developed, and extremists assassinated Ahangbé's son to force her to abdicate.

The dénouement came at a public session of the throne council. Ahangbé, decked out in all her finery, sat majestically on the throne, flanked by ministers and other dignitaries of the realm. Suddenly she rose, descended from the dais, and was met by a woman servant with a vase of water. In a gesture of supreme contempt, Ahangbé stripped and proceeded to wash her most intimate parts while cursing indiscriminately the high and low of the country. Ahangbé predicted a great misfortune for Dahomey (interpreted two centuries later as the French conquest). Then she resigned, to be succeeded not by her nephew, the legal heir, but by her younger brother Dosu, the name given to the first male child born after twins. As Agaja he would become one of Dahomey's great kings. Ahangbé's regency is generally ignored in Dahomean oral tradition; it has been suggested that Agaja tried to erase her memory because she opposed his seizure of power.[10]

A few slender clues link amazon origins to Akaba and Ahangbé. Oral traditions of the Ouéménou, the riverine people conquered by Dahomey in 1708, speak of facing women soldiers.[11] An amazon song tells of defeating Yahazé, king of the Ouéménou, with swords under Akaba's leadership.[12] Another seems to have amazons setting down roots in the shallows of the Ouémé River, just like native mangrove trees.[13] A unit of male warriors created under King Akaba was known as the "Company of Queen Angbé", according to a French officer who collected data on the Dahomean military in 1894[14] (a clue not to amazons but perhaps to the combat role of Ahangbé, whose very existence has been questioned by a leading modern authority on Dahomey, the British historian Robin Law).[15] King Agaja confirms, in a letter to George I of Great Britain dictated to Bulfinch Lamb in January 1726, that Yahazé and his Ouéménou forces were destroyed in Akaba's time.[16] And there is one clue that links the amazons to any or all monarchs from Wegbaja to Agaja. In 1850 a British naval officer, Frederick E. Forbes, witnessed sacrifices in Abomey at the grave of Agaja's mother, Adono, and was told that hers was "one of the titles of royalty held by the amazons".[17] Adono was Wegbaja's wife and the mother of Akaba and Ahangbé as well as Agaja, but the fact that she was referred to as the latter's mother suggests it was he who conferred the honor on the women soldiers.

(If nothing else, the story of the defeat of the Ouéménou in 1708 illustrates the remarkably long oral-historical memory of the kingdom. Nearly two centuries later, in 1890, Béhanzin, the last king of independent Dahomey, sent a letter to a French admiral indignantly rejecting complaints about Dahomean attacks on Ouéménou villages. As justification, he cited the war during Akaba's reign, which he blamed on the Ouéménou, and claimed that Yahazé had burned down the royal palace at Abomey.)[18]

The Akaba-Ahangbé twinship may have given rise to one of Dahomey's most extraordinary institutions, a dualism that pervaded many areas of life and possibly furnished the rationale for the amazon corps. From at least the time of Gezo, all male officials had female counterparts who lived in the palace. The women's duties were to memorize the assignments and commitments of the men, inspect their performance and monitor their expenditures, all for the king's benefit. This neatly solved the problem of record-keeping in an illiterate society. Alongside the male-female dichotomy was a left-right dichotomy, every office being paired with another. The dualism extended to the military: male officers had their female counterparts, warriors their parallel warrioresses, fighting units their right and left wings. It is said that in making these innovations Gezo revived a "concept that dual nature is the condition of completeness" dating back to the period of the royal twins,[19] but evidence is scanty.

POLICEWOMAN TO SOLDIERESS?

One of the common elements of Africa's divine kingships was a ban on men touching royal wives (and sometimes even looking at them). The most powerful state on the Slave Coast in the late seventeenth and early eighteenth centuries was Whydah, where kings turned the ban to ingenious effect. The Dutchman Willem Bosman, who visited Whydah in the late 1690s, tells us how:

[T]he King's Wives...are sometimes made use of by him as Executioners of the Sentences he pronounces against Offenders: Which is only done by sending three or four hundred of them to the Habitation of the Malefactor, to strip his House and lay it level with the Ground; for all Persons being forbidden on pain of Death to touch the King's Wives, they are enabled to execute his Commands without the least interruption.[20]

Bosman, who put the number of royal wives in Whydah at four to five thousand, had a local contact who had been falsely accused of a crime. The man was determined to stand his ground instead of fleeing his home, as was customary. When the king's wives arrived, he threatened to ignite a heap of gunpowder "and sail thus with a *hot arse* together with them to *heaven* ". Frightened off, they decided to inform the king, but the accused reached the royal ear first with clear proof of his innocence, and was acquitted.[21]

An anonymous Frenchman who spent some time in Whydah a dozen or so years after Bosman offers a somewhat different version. The king, he says, dispatched his wives whenever he wanted some house plundered. They went in a group, all carrying long poles or switches for hitting the residents if need be. Anyone who resisted would suffer the retribution of king and nobles however high his rank.[22] The king also sent his wives, armed with big sticks, to break up any "little wars" between villages or provincial authorities and bring the antagonists to the palace for royal arbitration.[23]

A French slaving captain, Jean-Pierre Thibault Des Marchais, who visited Whydah in 1725, adds some details.[24] He says the king's wives were divided into three classes. The first were the youngest and most beautiful. The second were "those who have already had children by the King, or whom age or some sickness have made unfit to serve [his] pleasure".[25] In the third class were women brought into the harem to serve the others as well as the king. Though they never shared the monarch's bed, they had to remain celibate. It was these third-class wives who were used as law enforcers. When sent to punish someone in the capital, each carried a stick or long pole, and they proclaimed the king's sentence to the culprit before devastating his home. Des Marchais also heard that the king sometimes intervened in armed disputes between grandees, and if one side did not accept his proposed solution he sent two or three thousand third-class wives to ravage their lands and oblige them to make peace.[26]

Since the Whydah people were related to the Fon ethnically and culturally, it is not hard to imagine the women soldiers of Dahomey originating in a similar use of royal wives as armed police. But again, there is no evidence for it.[27]

GUARDS OF KING AND PALACE

In public ceremonies, favorite wives of a divine African king shaded him from the sun with his umbrellas, cooled him with his fans, shooed flies away from his body with his whisks, served him drinks, dabbed his mouth, wiped his nose or mopped his brow, neck and armpits with his handkerchiefs, kept his spittoon handy, filled his pipe with tobacco and lit it, played his musical instruments, and paraded his most prized possessions in a show of wealth.[28] Wives of Dahomey's king also displayed his *weapons*. We have Agaja's word for it, in his aforementioned letter of 1726. At military reviews, he said, some wives held his "armes, as guns [muskets], pistols, and sabre, &c."[29] This passive role, perhaps sometimes mistaken by early European observers as that of bodyguards, could well have evolved into just that.

In the 1820s British explorers saw royal females carrying spears in two towns northeast of Dahomey. When the king of Kaiama, in the country of Borgu, approached the British visitors on horseback, he was accompanied by six naked girl-wives (or slaves) who danced round his horse singing their husband's (or master's) praises and brandishing their weapons. When they followed the king into the visitors' lodgings, they left their light spears outside and "for decency's sake had wrapped a piece of striped cotton round their delicate waists". And when the visit was over, they doffed their sarongs.[30] Later, in the Yoruba city known to posterity as Old Oyo, when the king came calling, he was accompanied by 500 "half-dressed" wives, each holding a light spear in her left hand. As they sang, the weapons were "flourished over their heads with inconceivable animation and rapidity". Their song exhorted the Yoruba to smite the enemy (in this case the Muslim Fulani to the north, not the Fon), but there was no suggestion that these women, or those at Kaiama, were soldiers or even guards. Their spears seemed pure show.[31]

There is no doubt, however, that in Dahomey armed women guarded both the royal person and the palace during the eighteenth century. It could hardly have been otherwise since men other than the king could not inhabit the palace. The only possible exceptions were eunuchs, some castrated in the palace at the age of eighteen or twenty,[32] who shared guard duty with the women.

In his 1726 letter, Agaja spoke of palatial "dore-keepers and thare assistants, who are always a robusk sort of women slaves".[33] English slaver William Snelgrave, at an audience with Agaja in 1727, saw four women standing "behind the Chair of State, with Fusils [muskets] on their Shoulders".[34] A Dutch trader, Jacob Elet, spotted two of the same in 1733.[35] Antoine-Edmé Pruneau de Pommegorge, who headed the French fort at Whydah in 1763-4, said the king's palace at Abomey was "guarded within only by his wives, who number two or three thousand".[36] Archibald Dalzel, director of the English fort at Whydah in 1767-70, said a "very substantial" quadrangular clay wall about 20 feet high surrounded the royal palace at Cana, near Abomey. In the middle of each side was a gate with a guardhouse occupied by armed women and eunuchs.[37] The English slaver Robert Norris visited the Abomey palace in 1772. "In the guard house", he wrote, "were about forty women, armed with a musket and cutlass each; and twenty eunuchs, with bright iron rods in their hands."[38] Later Norris saw the king (Tegbesu, who succeeded Agaja in 1740) march in a procession "followed by a guard of twenty-four women armed each with a blunderbuss".[39]

Two years later Tegbesu was succeeded by Kpengla, who maintained the distaff guard. French visitors in 1776-7 saw gunwomen on duty at the palace.[40] John M'Leod, a British slave ship's surgeon who stayed at Whydah in 1803, heard that the king of Dahomey had "from three to four thousand wives, a proportion of whom, trained to arms, under female officers, constitute his body guards".[41]

It appears that discipline broke down among palace guards when a king died, and that sometimes they fought each other until a new king was enthroned. It's not clear why. Traditionally an interregnum, usually lasting only a few days, was a time of anarchy when some people took advantage of the power vacuum to settle scores, steal and commit mayhem. Within the palace were scenes of carnage. According to Norris, 285 royal wives were killed by other royal wives on the death of Tegbesu in 1774.[42] Dalzel heard that 595 were murdered when Kpengla died in 1789.[43] Since palace guards were nominally wives of the king, had weapons and knew how to use them, they presumably played leading roles in the slaughter.

One possible explanation has to do with the custom in divine kingships for a certain number of wives to accompany a dead king to the other world for which, as both Norris and Dalzel indicate, the slain wives automatically qualified by being killed.[44] Though it is said that royal wives often went willingly to their deaths to be able to attend their master in the beyond, one can speculate that most were reluctant to depart this life. Killing other wives may have been the best way to assure one's own survival.

Robin Law suggests instead that royal wives fought each other because they supported rival claimants to the throne. A Portuguese priest, Vicente Ferreira Pires, heard of fighting in the palace after Kpengla's successor Agonglo was assassinated in 1797. He said that more than fifty persons perished in a factional "war" over the royal succession.[45] The next king, Adandozan, was ousted in a palace coup in 1818 that brought his brother Gezo to power. According to Dahomean tradition, an amazon detachment that was not in on the coup fought for Adandozan in a palace wing until it was wiped out.[46] Répin heard that Gezo owed his victory to amazons rebelling *against* Adandozan.[47]

AS TROOPS

The first definite use of women as soldiers by the kingdom of Dahomey was in 1729. Two years earlier Agaja had conquered Whydah. Its king, Huffon, had fled with the remnants of his army to islands in the lagoon west of the port. The Fon, unused to canoes, could not follow them. Subsequently the Dahomean army suffered heavy losses fighting an invasion by the great Yoruba empire of Oyo, and left Whydah unguarded. Encouraged by Charles Testefolle, director of the local English fort, Huffon returned to Whydah at the head of an army put at 15,000 men. They camped near the English and French forts. Dahomean traders reported the news to Agaja, who resolved to recapture Whydah despite his serious manpower shortage. Snelgrave tells us that Agaja

....ordered a great number of Women to be armed like Soldiers, and appointed Officers to each Company, with Colours, Drums and

Umbrellas [symbols of rank], according to the *Negroe* Fashion. Then ordering the Army to march, the Women Soldiers were placed in the Rear, to prevent Discovery. When they came in sight of the *Whidaw* Army, the latter were much surprized to see such Numbers of *Dahomè* Soldiers, as they supposed them all to be, marching against them...[48]

Part of the Whydah forces panicked and fled, allowing the Dahomean army to outflank and rout the rest. Huffon, "a very fat unwieldy Man", was conveyed to safety over the wall of the English fort by two of his sons. Testefolle, afraid of Dahomean retribution, persuaded the monarch to leave during the night. Huffon managed to elude the Dahomeans and make it back to his islands.[49]

The Englishman was not so lucky. Soon thereafter he was captured by Dahomeans who, after obtaining a ransom for Testefolle from the English fort,

....seized his Person, and made his Body fast to Stakes drove in the Ground: Where, spreading him on his Belly, they with sharp Knives cut open his Arms, Back, Thighs and Legs in several places, and filled the Wounds with a mixture of Limejuice, Salt and Pepper...; which put him to inexpressible Torment. However, they soon after put him out of his pain, by cutting off his Head. Then they cut his Body in pieces, broiled them on the Coals, and [ate] them...[S]ome of them...have been since so audacious, as to tell several *Portuguese* Gentlemen...'That *English* Beef was very good' [if cannibalism there was, it was highly unusual for this part of Africa].[50]

(In another version of Testefolle's torture, circulated by the French, it's said that each day a piece of his flesh was cut off, roasted on coals in front of him, and then *he* was forced to eat it.)[51]

There is no suggestion in Snelgrave's account that Agaja's women soldiers actually took part in the fighting. But some commentators have sensed the origin of Dahomey's amazons in the king's ruse. They include the anthropologist Melville J. Herskovits, father of African studies in the United States, who specialized in Dahomey.[52] A late-nineteenth-century British army officer-cum-ethnologist, Alfred Burdon Ellis, wrote that "the women-soldiers behaved with such unexpected gallantry that [Agaja] determined to maintain a permanent corps of women," but he gave no source for this information and may have invented it.[53]

Nevertheless – and despite a judgment by Robin Law that the amazons did not serve as a fighting force outside the palace during the eighteenth century[54] – scattered evidence points to the use of the king's bodyguards in that century as real troops in the field. Law himself has unearthed and published a four-page manuscript by a French ship's captain named Ringard who happened to be in the Whydah kingdom during Agaja's initial invasion in March 1727. After a decisive Fon victory, Ringard was told by a Whydah commander that his army, though far bigger and better armed, had been beaten by a Dahomean force of "no more than 3 thousand persons of whom half were women & children".[55] In Law's opinion, the women were probably "camp followers", not soldiers,[56] but he offers no hard evidence for it and could be wrong. The children were most likely boys apprenticed to male warriors: Agaja's spokesman told Snelgrave "the King allowed every common Soldier a Boy at the publick charge, in order to be trained up in Hardships from their Youth." The Englishman saw the acolytes following troops and carrying their shields.[57]

Several decades later Pruneau described King Tegbesu's armed wife-guards "comme enregimentées", which suggests that they were formed into military units.[58] In what may be the earliest written observation of Dahomean dualism, he reported that "their female chiefs bear the same name as the chiefs of the male warriors".[59]

Pruneau witnessed the king's "customs" at Abomey, the annual ceremonies in honor of the royal ancestors. Female troops paraded past Tegbesu in five or six groups of about eighty to a hundred young women each, "all...hardly older than sixteen or seventeen except for some of their commanders". Each carried a small musketoon and a short sword, usually sheathed in a crimson velvet scabbard. They were bare-breasted, wearing only a knee-length silk pagne, and marched four abreast, at a slow pace. Each unit carried two or three silk flags that were dipped three times in salute as they approached the king. Then they performed identical drills, which, if done well, earned presents from the monarch.[60]

Historians are fairly sure that in 1764 occurred the one and only military clash between Dahomey and Asante (Ashanti), by then the most powerful state in what is now Ghana. It was won by the Fon, who may have been supported by Oyo. An Asante tradition about fighting female soldiers has been linked to this battle.[61]

A few years later Norris saw a parade in Abomey involving, first, "a guard of ninety women, under arms, with drums beating", then six "troops" of seventy women each, all led by "a distinguished favorite" [commanding officer] walking under an umbrella, then seven more units of fifty women each, all preceded by two English flags – a grand total of 860 women. Every contingent sang and danced as it passed the king.[62] Four dancers in particular caught Norris's eye. Their dress, he wrote,

....was too extravagant to be described; and each had a long tail fixed to her rump, which seemed to be a slip of leopard's skin, sewed up and stuffed; which, by a dexterous wriggle of their hips they whirled round with surprising velocity, like a sling.[63]

More than three-quarters of a century later Auguste Bouët, who led a French mission to Abomey in 1851, marveled at a performance by tailed women adorned with little bells who repeatedly threw their muskets high in the air and caught them while whirling around and at the same time twirling their weighted tails with a pelvic grind.[64] And two decades after that, Skertchly saw about twenty of these "tail-dancers" in an amazon procession and described their get-up. They

....wore pink skirts reaching down to the knee, and open-throated tunics of white calico embroidered with scarlet. Round their waists they wore broad scarlet sashes, to the back of which enormous

"Armed Women, with the King at their head, going to War"–the first, highly fanciful attempt to depict the amazons, late 18th century. They are topless save for crossbelts, and carry muskets. The hollow log being handloaded in the foreground is a war drum. The king, presumably Kpengla, wears a plumed hat and carries a sword; an umbrella symbolizing high rank is held over his head. Subjects kowtow on their bellies, left foreground. (A. Dalzel, *The History of Dahomy*, 1793, reprint London, 1967, opp. p. 54)

Tail dancers, as seen by J.A. Skertchly in 1871. (*Dahomey as It Is*, London, 1874, p. 264)

Amazon elephant huntresses, the Gbeto, in action. The women wear antelope horns and approach their prey through high grass. One elephant has been killed by their muskets. Another is goring a Gbeto with its tusks, and a third gripping one in the air with its trunk. (A. Répin, "Voyage au Dahomey", p. 89)

bustles were attached. From the back of these proceeded a short stick, from which depended a long tail of alternate black and white horse-hair, as thick as a man's arm, and just clearing the ground.[65]

The dancers stood in a row with their backs to the king, arms uplifted, and

....began a see-saw movement of the gluteus until their tails acquired sufficient momentum to swing completely round like a sling. They then commenced to waltz in a circle, still keeping up the rotary movement of their tails, thereby eliciting thunders of applause from Amazons and warriors.[66]

Skertchly was told the tail-dancers were "invented" by King Glele (1858-89), which recalls equally subjective efforts to credit the amazons as a whole to Glele's father Gezo.[67]

In 1777 the head of the French fort at Whydah, Olivier de Montaguère, traveled north to pay his respects to King Kpengla. In the palace at Cana he saw "a great number of armed women, forming a sort of square battalion.[...] [They] lined up 15 by 15, and...as they paraded, they fired a musket volley; soon they formed into two lines, and kept up a general fire which was very well executed."[68] Clearly these women were not simply bodyguards.

Another clue was found after the French conquest of 1892 in Kpengla's own palace (each king having one built for himself on his accession). This was a clay bas-relief – an art form that enabled the Fon to record their history – on a palace wall. It showed two amazons boiling enemy corpses in a large kettle resting on a skull, presumably to strip the flesh off the crania, jaws and other bones, which served as trophies and ornaments.[69]

As noted above, Dalzel, who published his book on Dahomey in 1793, was the first author to liken its women soldiers to the amazons of old. He wrote that among no less than 3,000 women "immured" in the various royal palaces, "Several hundreds...are trained to the use of arms, under a female general and subordinate officers, appointed by the King... These warriors are regularly exercised, and go through their evolutions with as much expertness as the male soldiers. They have their large umbrellas, their flags, their drums, trumpets, flutes." Dalzel said the king sometimes took the field, "on very great emergencies, at the head of his women".[70]

Relying on information from Lionel Abson, long-time governor of the British fort at Whydah, Dalzel dates one such emergency to 1781. From the 1730s or '40s to the 1820s, Dahomey paid an annual tribute to the Yoruba empire of Oyo. Dalzel tells us Oyo envoys happened to be in Dahomey in 1781 to collect the tribute when Kpengla's second-ranking minister, the *Meu*, died. The envoys saw a chance to increase the payment: they demanded 100 of the Meu's women. Kpengla reluctantly handed over some of them to get rid of the Yoruba, but three months later the king of Oyo threatened an invasion if he did not receive the rest.

Unwilling to give up more Dahomean women, Kpengla sent troops to the neighboring country of Agouna to seize the requisite number of females. The local leader repulsed the Dahomean forces, inflicting heavy losses. "This news being brought to the King of Dahomy at mid-day", Dalzel relates, "he immediately got up, girt on his cartouch-box [cartridge case], shouldered his firelock, and marched toward Agoonah, at the head of eight hundred armed women". The foe was routed and pursued; Kpengla received some enemy heads, apparently severed by his female soldiers. He then returned home, perhaps with his amazons, because operations were now entrusted to the *Gau*, commander of male troops. The enemy was hunted down and defeated, and 1,800 were captured.[71] Presumably more than enough foreign women were now available for Oyo.[72]

Perhaps the clinching evidence that the amazons already existed as a fighting force in Kpengla's time is a bit of information Forbes picked up at Abomey in 1850. He was told that Gezo's grandfather, meaning Kpengla, "first raised the amazon army, but not to its present extent".[73] If Kpengla's amazons, unlike Gezo's, were *not* active-duty troops, Forbes most likely would have been told so since it would have reflected credit on the informant's sovereign.

Norris's 860 paraders and Dalzel's 800 troops may represent the high point of the amazons in the eighteenth century. Pires, who spent half a year in Dahomey in 1797, seemed to confirm their reports: he said that a "household squadron" of more than 800 women accompanied the king everywhere.[74] The female army corps would indeed be greatly enlarged by Gezo some time after his seizure of power in 1818, and come to Western Europe's much closer attention in the 1840s.

4

WHY DAHOMEY?

The foregoing discussion of historical origins begs the fundamental question of why the amazons arose in Dahomey and nowhere else. Eminent Victorian Richard Burton, who wrote one of the most important books on the kingdom, thought that the answer lay in the build of the local women.

On a diplomatic mission to Glele in 1863-4, Burton first encountered amazons at a village on the way to Abomey. Four female musketeers danced for the British delegation. Two, Burton wrote, "were of abnormal size, nearly six feet tall, and of proportional breadth", while some men who performed were "smooth, full-breasted, round-limbed, and effeminate-looking". He went on to generalize about Dahomean women:

Such...was the size of the female skeleton, and the muscular development of the frame, that in many cases feminity could be detected only by the bosom. I have no doubt that this physical superiority of the 'working sex' led in the...Dahoman race to the employment of women as fighters. They are the domestic servants, the ploughboys [hoers would have been more accurate], and the porters,...the field hands, and market cattle [transporters of wares] of the nation – why should they not also be soldiers?[1]

Later in his book Burton again traced "the somewhat exceptional organization" of the amazons to "the masculine *physique* of the women, enabling them to compete with men in enduring toil, hardships, and privations".[2] He also thought that women in the Niger Delta were the physical equals of men but did not try to explain why they did *not* become warrioresses. In fact, West African women in general are a sturdy lot. Their unique experience in Dahomey could be explained by demography.

More perhaps than any other African state, Dahomey was dedicated to warfare and slave-raiding. It may also have been the most totalitarian, with the king controlling and regimenting practically every aspect of social life. With good reason Burton called Dahomey "this small black Sparta". But this did not prevent it from having to pay tribute to a neighboring realm, Oyo, for three-quarters of a century. One need look no further than population figures for the answer.

The Fon language is spoken today by less than 2 million people, Yoruba by about 20 million, and the ratio was probably similar in the eighteenth and nineteenth centuries. While Oyo never embraced all Yoruba-speakers, it was by far the most populous kingdom in Yoruba history. Its manpower advantage over Dahomey was overwhelming. (Oyo had the added advantage of cavalry, an option unavailable to Dahomey because of the presence of the tsetse fly, which killed off horses by injecting sleeping sickness.)

To compensate for its narrow population-base, and for a higher male attrition rate due to warfare and a preference for young men in the slave export trade, Dahomey was almost compelled to turn to its women if it was to maintain its martial vocation.

A British naval officer, Commodore Arthur Parry Eardley Wilmot, who visited Abomey in 1862-3, noticed a heavy imbalance in the Dahomean population in favor of females. "As war is made one of the necessities of the State", he reasoned, "a constant drain upon the male population is required, and it naturally follows that the supply is never equal to the demand; hence the remarkable circumstance of nearly '5,000' women being found in the Dahomian army."[3]

5

RECRUITMENT

Every unmarried female in Dahomey was potentially the king's wife. In practice he sometimes expropriated married women too. But thousands who did become his wives became so only in name, although they lived in his palace at his beck and call, like the third-class royal wives of Whydah. Among these were the armed guards who metamorphosed into warrioresses.

Royal wives in general – all known as *ahosi* – were chosen in various ways. In the late nineteenth century at least, a male court official called the *Kpakpa* was in charge of recruiting women for the palace.[1] He toured the kingdom with his assistants, reportedly visiting each village every three years. A national census system that theoretically kept count of every individual by use of pebbles is said to have given the Kpakpa a good idea of how many young girls he might find in each household.[2] The king's representatives looked the girls over and picked those they judged suitable for royal service. A fleshy beauty, for example, would be intended for the king's bed, a particularly robust girl for the king's guard. Daughters of slaves were earmarked as palace slaves.

The institution of the royal recruiter may have grown out of earlier, automatic provision of girls to the palace as a form of tribute. Pruneau wrote that "each private person" was obliged to give the king one of his daughters.[3] French voyager Pierre Labarthe, who visited Whydah in 1788, heard that all daughters (and sons) of "ministers" were at the king's disposal. "He keeps the girls in his seraglio", said Labarthe, "both for his pleasure and for the service and guard of his palace."[4] Répin (1856) was told that amazon recruits "were chosen from among the young virgin girls of the best families of the kingdom".[5]

Wealthy kin groups, or lineages, who could best afford the loss of daughters, voluntarily offered one or more to the king to increase their clout within the palace. Bouët asserted that nearly all the amazons were "daughters of chiefs or of rich inhabitants who are only too honored to make a gift of them to the king from the age of 8 or 10 years".[6]

Misbehavior could also land a woman in the palace. Methodist missionary Thomas Birch Freeman (English-born son of a white woman and a black) visited Dahomey in 1843 and noted that young wives who were "incorrigibly incontinent", badly behaved and unmanageable were turned over to the king. So were young daughters so disobedient to their parents that they were considered "irreclaimable", and rambunctious slave girls.[7] Another 1843 visitor, Frenchman Blaise Brue, heard that when an influential man complained of a wife's adultery, the king would confine her to "a house of discipline" at Allada and profit from her labor for the rest of her days.[8] Burton said that adulteresses who might otherwise have been executed were sent to the palace and enrolled in the amazon corps. Even intolerable shrews –"Xantippes who make men's hours bitter", in Burton's erudite prose – were donated to the king by their husbands and "very properly put into the army".[9] Ellis, perhaps embroidering Burton, called them "termagants and scolds".[10]

A personally blameless wife or daughter might wind up in the palace if the head of her household ran afoul of the king. Powerful men, for example, might be accused of disloyalty, their households destroyed and their womenfolk confiscated.[11]

One large pool of womanpower for the palace consisted of war and slave-raid captives. Indeed, some sources claim that King Gezo enrolled only young foreign prisoners as amazons because he could count on their loyalty. They owed him their lives, their livelihood, their legal freedom and their privileged social position, and were unlikely to side with any disgruntled Dahomean faction. "He created an élite corps out of these girls", the historian Edouard Foà writes, "devoted to his body and soul."[12] A one-time slave village named Sinwé-Jaloukou dating from Gezo's reign is said to have been the site of "a veritable school of amazons".[13] Burton noted some women soldiers chanting Yoruba songs, which suggests they were foreign-born.[14]

But even Gezo's amazons seem to have included native-born Dahomeans. The French historian Edouard Dunglas says that one female "regiment", which took part in that king's attack on the Yoruba city of Abeokuta in 1851 (chapter 17), was called Ahouâ-Na-Tô, meaning "Our Warrior Princesses". It was recruited from among the numerous female descendants of the kings of Dahomey, a group known for their loose ways. As Dunglas explains it, "young Dahomean blood, always hot, equally inclined to war as to love affairs, drove a good many young princesses into the profession of arms."[15] (Besides "regiment", incidentally, such European designations as corps, division, brigade, battalion, company and platoon frequently appear in the literature and are always inaccurate in terms of numbers of troops when applied to Dahomean military units.)

Some amazons were daughters of amazons, which proves that not all soldieresses were virgins, as is sometimes claimed. Burton estimated that about one-third had been married.[16] But as sacrosanct wives of a divine king, the amazons were sworn to celibacy under pain of death.

6

CELIBACY

Celibacy may not have been a particularly severe hardship for foreign-born amazons from ethnic groups that practised excision, euphemistically called female circumcision, in which the labia and sometimes the clitoris too are sliced off. Such operations, performed from infancy to adolescence, deprive women of the possibility of sexual pleasure. There is an oral tradition that Gezo had all the amazons excised for just that purpose, but it is credited to a single village source and therefore seems dubious.[1] The Fon in fact had a custom that produced the opposite effect: artificial elongation of the vagina lips, which heightened the joy of sex.

In the late eighteenth century both Dalzel and English ship captain John Adams reported that unusual custom among the women of Dahomey.[2] Three-quarters of a century later Burton wrote that labial elongation was so common that "a woman in the natural state is derided by others".[3] He also suggested that the clitoris too was artificially enlarged;[4] Ellis was sure of it, and linked the practice to worship of a priapic Dahomean god named *Legba*, distinguished by an outsized phallus.[5] Ellis's claim is indirectly supported by an observation made nearly a century earlier by Médéric-Louis-Elie Moreau de Saint-Méry in a description of slaves in Haiti. Some "Arada" women from the Slave Coast, he wrote, besides having nymphae distended "to astonishing proportions", also had "another part" enlarged, "to the point that one sex could in a way fill the role of the other".[6] (He also remarked that "Arada" females could be recognized by the "amplitude" of their hips and buttocks.)[7]

In the 1930s Herskovits looked into and clarified the

matter. He found that when Fon girls began to develop breasts, groups of up to a dozen were taught genital enlargement by a young married woman (and not operated on by "some ancient *sage femme*", as reported by Burton):

With a shaped piece of wood, [she] manipulates the lips of the vagina of each girl, pulling at them, stretching them, and lightly puncturing the vaginal tissues in several places. This she does eight or nine times for each of her charges during the first year of instruction, and during the next year the girls do this for each other. Freshly charged soot is injected into the vagina after each manipulation [and] rubbed into the irritated tissues to avoid infection. For two years at the very least this is continued and in addition there is the outer massaging of these 'lips' to cause thickening and muscular development, for 'thin-lipped' women are considered lacking in comeliness.

Such manipulation, Herskovits added, went on "more or less intermittently until marriage". Besides wooden instruments, he said, certain plant substances and stinging ants were inserted in the vagina to induce "irritation which encourages tugging and handling". The purpose of all this, the anthropologist determined, was to make sex play and coitus more pleasurable.[8]

Fon girls were programmed for sexual enjoyment in another way: cicatrization. Herskovits investigated this custom too and found that female scarring was viewed as "an enhancement of the erotic zones". Artificially raised skin surfaces, called keloids in anthropology and medicine, were intended to make sex more exciting.

A knife-wielding specialist performed the operation on groups of girls soon after their menarche. First food was sacrificed to Legba, then to *Gu*, god of iron and hence of the knife. Twelve sets of cuts were made in as many different parts of the body and in a specific order. A girl who could stand the pain of all twelve at a single sitting earned considerable prestige, but usually six or eight sets of cuts were administered first and the rest a year later. Scars on the sides of the neck and over the base of the spine were especially important in foreplay, but the ones "most immediately concerned with sex excitation" were on the inside of each thigh. The latter operation involved eighty-one small cuts on each leg. A mixture of a certain crushed leaf with soot and palm oil was repeatedly rubbed into the cuts to form the keloids. A girl was considered ready for marriage if she had been cicatrized and had menstruated for four years.[9]

A teenaged Fon girl was psychologically as well as physically conditioned for sex and marriage. Motherhood was the female norm, children were the ultimate blessing. Female bachelorhood was a weird notion, barrenness a tragedy if not a disgrace, and a childless wife an object of pity if not scorn. If a woman did not have offspring, who would care for her in sickness and old age and perform all-important memorial ceremonies periodically after her death? The closest emotional ties in Fon society were not between husband and wife but between a mother and her children; it was they who formed the elemental family unit. (And the closest generational loyalties were among siblings of the same mother.) If a wife did not become pregnant, a diviner was consulted to see whether a malevolent spirit was responsible. If that was found to be the case, either the spirit was appeased or another was asked to intervene favorably. Women also wore special charms to induce pregnancy.

Celibacy was so rare among early-twentieth-century Fon, according to one commentator, that it was observed only by those incapable of marriage, namely idiots, insane people, epileptics and lepers.[10] This was doubtless an exaggeration because in a society where upper-class men have multiple wives, as was true everywhere in West Africa, many lower-class men are bound to have none simply because there are not enough females to go round.

A partial solution to this problem is prostitution; in Dahomey it was institutionalized, like almost everything else.[11] The royal court appointed public women, assigned them living quarters – according to Burton, Abomey had two red-light districts[12] – fixed their (modest) fees, required them to accept any paying customer, and taxed them annually. They

took part in public festivities as a song-and-dance troupe –
Norris saw some 250 of them parade in 1772;[13] Forbes and
John Beecroft, a British consul who accompanied him to
Abomey in 1850, watched *"demoiselles du pavé"* or "votaries
of Venus" march;[14] Burton heard *"filles de joie"* sing in 1864
– and play a special drum.[15] In one of the more bizarre
manifestations of Dahomean dualism, "prostitutes" within the
royal palace matched the real ones on the outside. This
may have encouraged Burton to suggest that most amazons
were lesbians – preferring, as he put it, "the peculiarities of
the Tenth Muse [Sappho]"[16] – but he offered no firm evidence,
nor did anyone else. If many amazons were lesbians, there
would have been little need to resort to prostitutes. In fact,
homosexuality of either sex is almost unrecorded in the
European literature on precolonial West Africa.

Clearly, therefore, the vow of celibacy demanded of native-born amazons almost had to be a shattering experience,
breaking them loose from their cultural moorings. It was
not enough to call the amazons *ahosi*, the king's wives,
when everyone knew that the great majority would never
sleep with the monarch. (A few amazons did reportedly
become royal sexual partners.)[17] Nor was it enough to call
them, in addition, *mino*, meaning "our mothers", as male
officers and soldiers did in referring to their female counterparts. That was obviously no substitute for real motherhood.
No, new ideals and goals were needed, a new focus for the
energies of these young women, and in meeting these needs
the Dahomean regime was remarkably successful.

Amazon libidos were not, as one might guess, completely
sublimated, even though the penalty for breaking the vow
of celibacy could be death. A deity represented at certain
palace gates was thought to watch over the chastity of the
soldieresses; if an amazon committed adultery, the spirit made
her pregnant – or, in one version, gave her a bowel disease
– thus exposing her crime. Dread of such exposure alone
might force her to confess, even knowing that she and her
paramour might be executed.[18]

Dalzel heard of some royal "ladies of the seraglio" during Kpengla's reign (1774-89) who, bearing "evident marks of gallantry", named more than 150 men as their lovers. The latter were sold into slavery, "although most of them were afterwards found to have been innocent".[19] We do not know if the women were punished. Mention of the seraglio suggests that authentic royal wives and not amazons were involved.

Burton and Skertchly relate cases where female soldiers were explicitly the guilty parties and the supreme penalty was imposed on a few. The first involved "not less than 150" amazons who were found to be pregnant and were judged, along with their lovers, by King Glele himself in 1863. Eight men were executed, some were pardoned, and the rest were imprisoned or banished to remote villages. The amazons were "similarly treated", says Burton, who notes that female criminals were executed by female officers inside the palace with no men watching. In this regard, he commented, Dahomey was more civilized than Britain, where women were still hanged in public.[20]

Eight years later seventy-two of Glele's amazons and eighty men were tried for adultery. According to Skertchly, the king, addressing a court during a three-hour "palaver", waived his right to the lives of all the defendants but said that justice must be satisfied. Four men and four women were singled out for capital punishment; the former were immediately beheaded – the usual method of execution in Dahomey – and the amazons were sent into the palace, where they quickly met the same fate. The rest of the miscreants, according to Skertchly, "were drafted into the gate-opening company of the army, a corps exposed to the hottest fire and the brunt of the battle".[21] (Since no Dahomean army units were mixed, separate paired companies may have been involved.) Skertchly also reports seeing the heads of an amazon and her lover atop two poles flanking an Allada palace gate.[22] But it would seem that it was rare for violating the vow of celibacy to cost an amazon her life, and then primarily as an object lesson to deter the others. At stake was not

the king's *amour-propre* but the viability of the amazons as
a fighting force, unimpeded by pregnancy and motherhood
(abortion being unheard of).

The monarch may at times have released some amazons
temporarily from their vow to recruit male soldiers to fill gaps
in the ranks. At least that is what a French trader, Edmond
Chaudoin, heard in 1890 and subsequent authors repeated.
The "youngest and most artful" women soldiers were sent
out to the villages. One would remove ornaments identifying
her as an *ahosi*, and walk into the market with a calabash
on her head like any other girl, "simpering, chattering prettily,
while provoking young men with her glance". In the evening
she strolled along roads where young blades hung out, and
enticed one into the nearby woods. Next day she would
denounce him to the authorities for messing with a royal
wife. He was then given a choice between the death penalty
and army service. Sometimes, Chaudoin was told, the amazon
fell for her lover and to save him named another youth. It
was her word against his, and off he went to the wars.[23]

Forbes asserts that particularly brave amazons were "given
in marriage by the king to his favoured subjects".[24] Burton
disputes it,[25] but Skertchly specifies that such awards were
made at the annual customs.[26] Pierre-Eugène Chautard, a
French missionary, reported in 1890 that the king exceptionally married off amazons "to his most deserving soldiers".[27]
Amazons disabled in combat, chronically ill or too old to
fight may also have been allowed to marry.[28] Guillevin, a
French naval officer who visited Abomey around 1857, heard
that after seven or eight years of service amazons, "depending
on their age and beauty, are destined for the [royal] harem
or as wives to various state officials".[29] Wilmot heard that
the king alone had the privilege of marrying amazons but
rarely did.[30] Skertchly says that Glele had several amazon
concubines,[31] Foà that he authorized amazon marriages to
chiefs.[32]

Herskovits quipped that "the rule of chastity was observed
at least as much in the breach as otherwise," probably sacrificing

accuracy for *double entendre*.[33] Of the thousands of women who served as amazons, relatively few may have dallied with men. For if they left behind a life of marriage and motherhood to embrace what Burton called "that utterly gratuitous virtue, celibacy", they also left behind a life of ceaseless toil and second-class citizenship, and instantly acquired semi-sacred status.

7

A PRIVILEGED LIFE

In Dahomey as elsewhere in West Africa the average woman's lot was difficult. She did all the housekeeping and cooking, reared the children, raised, harvested and marketed crops, engaged in petty trade, tended livestock, collected firewood, gathered wild plants, fetched water, carried headloads, processed palm oil, made pottery and baskets, spun cotton, dyed cloth.

In 1803 M'Leod remarked:

The state of woman is, upon the whole, very abject here. Wives approach their husbands with every mark of the humblest submission. In presenting him even with the calabash containing his food, after she has cooked it, she kneels and offers it with an averted look, it being deemed too bold to stare him full in the face.[1]

M'Leod's experience of Dahomey was limited to Whydah. So, too, was that of the British naval officer Henry Veel Huntley, who visited the port in 1831. Describing Whydah at dawn, he mused: "A woman is here and there getting something ready to satisfy the early appetites of those for whom she is a drudge."[2] But later Répin, who traveled in the interior, noticed that a Dahomean wife presented food to her husband on her knees and was not allowed to eat with him. A family head, he asserted, had such authority over his wives and children that he could sell them into slavery, but he acknowledged that that was "very rare" and that a man generally treated his family "with great kindness". Nevertheless, Répin added, women did "all the housework...while their lord drinks, sleeps or smokes", and (with considerable exaggeration) he termed hunting, fishing and war "the sole occupations of men".[3] (He was, however, more perceptive than Huntley, who had the impression that "in Africa women alone do the work".)[4]

According to Chaudoin, the women of Dahomey, like those "throughout Africa", were "ordinarily...regarded as an inferior being". He explains their "passion for motherhood" as "one of the consolations of their miserable life", a child being "the sole being who will return a little of their love".[5]

Chautard noted that in a country without a beast of burden, women and slaves shared that role.[6] And another French observer, Victor-Louis Maire, characterized the women of Dahomey as "*bêtes à reproduction*".[7] Edna Grace Bay, a modern American historian of Dahomey, notes that "in popular thought, women as women were the objects of scorn and contempt", regarded by men as disposed to "perfidy and treachery".[8] Even now, she relates from personal experience, a man in Abomey who wants to describe another's job performance as worthless will say "He is less than a woman."[9]

The Dahomean woman was, in short, a classic victim of male supremacy. But when she became an amazon, however humble her origins, she joined the female élite of the nation. "The amazons are lodged in the palaces of the king", said Répin, "who supports them sumptuously, and they pass their time there drinking, smoking and dancing."[10] Although their life was not easy, it was usually a great deal better than what they were used to.

Every inhabitant of Dahomey had to defer to a wife of the king, even if she was only a nominal one. When amazons, like all *ahosi*, walked out of the palace, they were preceded by a slave girl ringing a bell.[11] The sound told every male to get out of their path, retire a certain distance and look the other way. Even women, it is said, had to back away and avert their gaze. Violation of this rule invited severe punishment. A man who touched someone in an amazon procession risked death; the taboo shielded women slaves of the palace as well as their mistresses. Since palace women numbered thousands and groups of them were forever leaving the palace on one errand or another, the ban could be bothersome. While sightseeing in the Fon capital from a hammock, Skertchly "continually met gangs of the Amazons with their bells, causing our progress to be a succession of tacks from side to side, instead of making a straight course".[12] Burton called the interdiction one of the country's "greatest nuisances".[13]

The amazons' separateness and implicit superiority were also evident at state ceremonies and royal audiences. The soldieresses and other *ahosi* were set apart from the male world by a line of raffia palm midribs – called in the literature "bamboos" – laid end-to-end on the ground. In the midst of his women sat the king. The only other man who could cross the boundary at will was the chief eunuch of the palace, although ministers and other males expressly summoned by the monarch were allowed over. According to Skertchly, any other man who stepped across faced death.[14]

In Dahomey's dualistic system, royal protocol gave precedence to women officials over their male opposite numbers, and likewise to amazons over men soldiers (even the king being technically outranked by a "queen-mother"). According to Joseph Dawson, a long-time resident of Whydah in the 1850s and '60s, a man with a grievance could bring it to the king's attention through his amazon "mother", bypassing his own chief.[15]

Leaving a life with a large component of drudgery, the amazon recruit suddenly acquired her own female slave.[16] (According to Burton, amazons had up to fifty slaves each;[17] presumably he was referring to the highest-ranking officers.) Sometimes described as "servants" or "attendants" or "camp followers", these women may have been mainly war or slave-raid captives assigned by the king to work for the soldieresses. Others may have been hereditary Dahomean slaves. They seem to have spared the amazons most of the menial tasks that were the common woman's fate. They farmed royal lands, carried produce to the palace on their heads in big calabashes, cooked and served meals. They gathered wood for cooking fires. They headloaded huge pots of water from springs outside Abomey. The slave women also accompanied the amazons on military campaigns, forming their baggage train. They carried provisions – British traveler John Duncan reckoned a headload of provisions to weigh about 60 pounds,[18] Foà nearly 90[19] – and ammunition. For officers they carried muskets and such accessories as umbrellas of rank, and sleeping mats.

Burton says slaves of amazons also acted as spies.[20] Indeed, Dahomey had a well-developed intelligence system, but evidence suggests that only men were employed in this capacity. The one exception we have encountered is an oral-historical anecdote about two disguised amazons who seduced the military chief of a Yoruba town and stripped him of the occult powers that had guaranteed his success in the past, thus paving the way for a Dahomean conquest.[21] However, spies doubled as scouts in wartime, and it may be that the amazons used their women slaves in this way.

Among European visitors particularly impressed with the amazons' prestige and position was Commodore Wilmot. "The Amazons are everything in this country," he wrote, "...the mainstay of the kingdom. [...]They are first in honour and importance."[22] Foà credited Gezo with investing the warrioresses with "a sacred character" and obliging his subjects "to accord them the same honors as chiefs".[23]

An amazon's apartness and exalted status were reflected in her uniform – or uniforms, for each unit had its own – her armory, her bands, songs and dances, her special symbols and guardian spirits, and her carefully cultivated, swaggering *esprit de corps*.

8

WHAT THEY WORE

If Dahomey's women soldiers were unique in precolonial Africa, having a permanent military organization was rare in itself and wearing uniforms even rarer. The typical army in neighboring lands was mobilized when needed and disbanded when the fighting ended. Unexpectedly in ostensibly traditional, conformist societies, soldiers strove not to look alike but as different as possible. Identical dress was a European convention, and it is possible that Dahomey got the idea for military uniforms from watching behavior in the European forts at Whydah over a period of a century. Few European soldiers were stationed there, but African slaves of the forts did garrison duty.

Alternatively, liberated Brazilian slaves who began settling on the coast as early as the 1770s[1] and had contacts with the Dahomean government may have suggested the idea to Gezo. Or it could have been the celebrated Brazilian slave dealer Francisco Felix de Souza of Whydah, a longtime adviser to that monarch (and model for Bruce Chatwin's *Viceroy of Ouidah*). Exceptionally, Borghero speaks of 'officers from Brazil" who introduced "the European element" into the Dahomean army;[2] if true, that might have included dress.

One telling clue, however, suggests that the origins of Dahomean uniforms might be sought not in the southern port town but in the north. Some European visitors used the word *chokoto* for the knee-length shorts worn by both male and female soldiers in Dahomey.[3] The modern Yoruba word for trousers is *sokoto,* and the Fon word for shorts is *cokotò.* In 1900 Yoruba men (but not women) living in what had become the French protectorate of Dahomey wore

52

narrow knee-length trousers called *chocoto*.[4] The clear implication is that pants reached the region from Sokoto, capital of the Fulani (or Fulbe) caliphate that dominated much of northern Nigeria and part of Yorubaland during the nineteenth century, and converted many Yoruba to Islam. The garment may have arrived earlier since Dalzel tells us that Dahomean men wore locally-made cotton "drawers" in the late eighteenth century.[5]

(Dahomey's links to the Muslim world actually go back much further than the Sokoto caliphate. By the 1720s Muslim traders from the north called "Mallays" were familiar visitors to the country.[6] The designation would seem to derive from the Arabic word *mawlā* [mullah], meaning master or teacher, for these turbaned strangers carried Islam in their saddlebags. Conceivably they had some influence on Dahomey's military establishment.)

At any rate, there is no evidence for distinctive uniforms before Gezo. The four women musketeers that Snelgrave saw standing behind Agaja in 1727 "were finely dress'd from the middle downward, (the Custom of the Country being not to cover the Body upward, of either Sex)".[7] In Pruneau's time (1763-4), female soldiers wore only "a small silk pagne falling from the loins to the knees".[8] (If it was really silk, the material could only have been imported, from either European slave ships on the coast or Muslim traders from the north.) Male soldiers, he said, also wore only a pagne, either of silk or cotton.[9] In the first published illustrations of the amazons, Dalzel (1793) shows them uncovered above the waist.[10] And as late as 1830, i.e. twelve years into Gezo's reign, the slave-ship captain Augustin Lopez saw bare-breasted amazons at Abomey. (A hundred of them took part in the sort of mock attack that Father Borghero witnessed three decades later, except that live enemies, already tied to stakes, were captured and executed.)[11]

The tunic adopted in Gezo's time had nothing to do with modesty. Dahomean women routinely bared their breasts as a mark of deference, if indeed they were covered. Chaudoin, who took a lively interest in such details, noted that when women entered French commercial houses at Whydah, which legally belonged to the king of Dahomey, they stripped to the waist. They did likewise, he said, on presenting themselves to the Dahomean authorities or other dignitaries.[12]

Since male soldiers seem to have donned a tunic at the same time as the amazons, the covering-up may have been due simply to emulation of Fulani or European uniforms. Protection of sensitive bosoms from the rough and tumble of combat could have been a consideration. Or some value may have been seen in concealing feminine attributes from enemy warriors.

A modern historian of the amazons, Amélie Degbelo of the Republic of Benin, thinks "the major concern"in dressing them "was to hide their feminine nature". Their breasts, she says, were meant to be flattened, and their headgear had pointed side flaps to conceal the holes in their earlobes.[13]

Wearing similar uniforms, bearing the same weapons and accessories, draped with ornaments and amulets, and covered with the grime of a long campaign, men and women soldiers were sometimes hard to tell apart. At a critical moment in one of Dahomey's great battles, the attack on the Yoruba city of Abeokuta in 1851 (chapter 17), the defenders were said to be unaware that women soldiers had been pushing them back until one was captured. Customarily the first prisoner was emasculated. When her sex was revealed, the Yoruba soldiers, feeling their manhood challenged, staged a furious and successful counterattack.

The first eyewitness account of amazon uniforms dates to 1843. Prefiguring the surprise discovery at Abeokuta, Freeman saw a "brigade" of several hundred warrioresses who "were dressed so much like men, that a stranger would not have supposed that they were women". They wore "a loose shirt without sleeves, which comes nearly down to their knees, and is fastened round the waist by their car-touch-belt". Either the uniform did not yet include pants, or more likely the missionary forgot to mention them.[14]

Two years later Duncan noted the basic uniform that would serve the female soldiers during their last half-century:

[T]hese amazons...wear a blue and white striped cotton surtout [tunic or shirt], the stripes about one and a half inch wide, of stout native manufacture, without sleeves, leaving freedom for the arms... [It] reaches as low as the kilt of the Highlanders. A pair of short trowsers is worn underneath, reaching two inches below the knee. The cartouche-box...forms a girdle, and keeps all their dress snug and close.[15]

One amazon "regiment" wore white cotton skullcaps bearing the image of a crocodile. Gezo told Duncan that some of his warrioresses had killed one in the bush during a campaign a few months earlier, and that "he had ordered the figure to be worn on the cap as a mark of distinction"[16] – anticipating the Lacoste logo by more than a century. Forbes (1849-50) specified that the emblem was blue, and that each amazon "regiment" had its own, one a crocodile, another a cross, a third a crown.[17] Burton (1863-4) saw silver sharks on red caps,[18] Foà dark tortoises on gray-white caps.[19] William Winniett, a British naval captain who visited Abomey in 1847, tells us Gezo "requested that Her Majesty [the young Queen Victoria]...kindly make him a present of 2,000 war-caps for his female troops, and She very kindly sent them to him".[20]

Sometimes the amazons wore headbands instead of caps, with the same devices sewn on; it was a simple example of appliqué, a decorative technique the Fon developed into an art.

Several authors mention sashes round the waist: red, blue or white, with or without the cartridge belt.

Duncan did not say what the amazons wore under their uniform. Burton, who missed very little, mentioned "a zone of beads, supporting a bandage" as the basic female garment.[21] Chaudoin researched the question toward 1890. Little girls in Dahomey, where temperatures rarely dipped below 20° C. (68° F.), wore only a string of beads round the waist day and night, and kept it on when they grew up. Daughters of the more affluent families added strings; Chaudoin says some wore up to ten rows of beads, made either of thick glass or coral. When the time came – which Herskovits determined much later was between the ages of nine and eleven[22] – they put a small piece of cloth between their legs, attached front and back to the beads. This remained the only female underwear.[23] (Herskovits describes the first female garment as a small cloth that reached from the waist to just above the knees;[24] either he is inaccurate or it was an alternative fashion.)

Amazons actually had two uniforms, one to fight in, the other to parade in. Battledress tended toward somber colors: Bouët saw dark blue or "wood-colored" tunics and dark-colored headbands;[25] Borghero rust-colored tunics;[26] Burton "tunics of grey baft, stained brown with blood and barks", but white hair fillets and waist sashes;[27] Skertchly "a war-dress of grey, brown, or dark blue...[with] a white sash over the left shoulder";[28] Foà blue or "dingy white" war costumes with caps "originally white, but generally dark gray".[29] The blue-and-white-striped tunics that Duncan described seem also to have been meant for war. Répin noticed shorts with the same pattern.[30] Bouët saw "companies" of amazon scouts covered with "freshly cut long grass",[31] Burton "soldieresses in grass-cloth skirts".[32]

Parade dress was something else: brighter colors, finer fabrics, the addition of pagnes, a variety of headgear, each amazon unit striving to outdazzle the next. Tunics were red, or scarlet, or crimson, or green, or pale blue, or half-blue, half-red. Shorts were sometimes red or blue or multicolored. Materials included silks, velvets, chintzes and other Indian cottons. Knee-length or ankle-length pagnes covered or replaced the shorts, a jacket or vest replaced the long tunic. Burton saw amazons wearing "a sleeveless waistcoat of various colours,...buttoning in front like that affected by Hausa Moslems. [A] loin wrapper [pagne], of dyed stuff, mostly blue, pink, and yellow, extended to the ankles."[33] (The reference to the Hausa, the most numerous people of the Fulani empire,

Amazons as represented by three different artists. *Above left*, musicians
with a gourd rattle, a drum and a trumpet in the background; *right*,
two officers with long muskets and horns of rank on their heads. (A.
Bouët, "Le royaume du Dahomey", *L'Illustration*, X, 492, July 31, 1852,
p. 72) *Below Left*, an amazon in shorts and camouflage headdress with
a crocodile symbol on her chest. She holds a machete and a short rifle,
which may be a carbine. (A.L. d'Albéca, *La France au Dahomey*, Paris,
1895, p. 81) *Right*, an amazon in less formal attire balances a gun on
her head and grasps a machete. (*L'Illustration*, XLVIII, 2475, Aug. 2,
1890, p. 101)

An example of "insensitivity training": amazon musketeers, right foreground, attend human sacrifices at the royal customs. The victims are being thrown down from a platform to a mob. A crocodile will also be sacrificed. (A. Répin, "Voyage au Dahomey", p. 112)

Two romanticized amazon archers, one holding aloft two freshly cut enemy heads. (A. Répin, "Voyage au Dahomey", p. 96)

is another hint of northern antecedents for amazon garb.) Skertchly spotted gray knee-length petticoats, "brown waistcoats, with pink underskirts", "Prussian blue gowns" and crimson or yellow or white crossbelts.[34] Foà describes a sort of bodice above a skirt reaching mid-thigh.[35] Vallon, echoed by Burton, says the youngest amazons, equipped with bows and arrows instead of guns, wore the scantiest attire, exposing thighs "tattooed" (elsewhere the Frenchman says "painted") to the knees.[36]

Besides skullcaps, Burton noted "scarlet woollen nightcaps" and, on officers, red "Liberty Caps". He saw "privates" parading with hats dangling on their backs: "scarecrow felts, 'extinguishers' [shaped like candle snuffers?] of white cotton ...and low-crowned, broad-brimmed, home-made straws" covered with blue material.[37] Bouët thought he saw red berets.[38] In 1851 he gave Gezo fifty brass firemen's helmets with red plumes on behalf of the French government, and soon saw them polished to perfection and gleaming magnificently in the sun on fifty amazon heads.[39] Two decades later Skertchly observed amazons wearing what may have been the same helmets.[40] In a rare eighteenth-century reference to amazon headgear, Norris watched a "troop of forty women, with silver helmets".[41] Vallon saw elephant huntresses wearing blue turbans adorned with the long herbivore horns that fooled their prey.[42]

Officers' parade dress was more opulent and at least as varied as that of the rank and file. Forbes saw gold embroidery on their tunics.[43] In what seems to have been a reference to officers, Vallon wrote of "costumes resplendent with gold, silver, the richest silk materials".[44] Burton depicts one officer "in a man's straw hat, a green waistcoat, a white shirt, put on...à l'envers [backwards]...a blue waistcloth, and a sash of white calico".[45] Another wore "a vest, pink before and white behind, with a drooping slovenly collar: a black leather cartridge-belt kept in position her long blue striped waistcloth."[46] Skertchly describes an officer in a violet-and-white-checked toga.[47]

Small silver horns were among officers' headgear in Bouët's time.[48] Chaudoin noted a "chiefess" with gold horns.[49] Burton saw "captainesses" parading with a "cook's bonnet...steeple-crowned broad-brims...shaggy skull-caps, like pepper-corn hair, stained a deep indigo...big fool's caps of stuffs striped white, blue, and red, and hanging over their shoulders". One officer had "a broad-brimmed and gold-laced hat, apparently beaver, upon a head swathed in calico".[50]

Hairstyles varied among amazon units and between the warrioresses and their officers. Many women soldiers, and men as well, shaved their heads completely, which doubtless made them look even more alike. Some left just a crest or cock's comb, some a big circular patch at the top, combed out like a brush, some one or two tufts. Others shaved only "a breadth of two inches from the forehead to the poll".[51] And some had full heads of hair. Burton saw a "coloneless" with "her scalp...clean shaven and shining, a single little lock [holding] a silver knob like the finial of a tea-pot." Two "captainesses" were "silver half-heads", meaning that half their scalp was shaved, while the other half was covered with a silver half-helmet, a distinction that marked them as royal messengers. Some officers had dyed their hair a deep indigo, "which contrasted well with the silver ornaments". An amazon choral group had silver hair.[52]

ORNAMENTS AND CHARMS

Amazons seem to have been allowed even freer rein in their choice of ornaments and charms. The rank and file wore necklaces of imported glass beads or indigenous beads (of glass or stone) or coral; armlets of silver, brass or iron; bracelets of silver, copper, iron or tin; little iron bells. The amazons Lopez saw in 1830 were "naked to the waist but richly ornamented with beads and rings at every joint".[53] Archeresses had a wide ivory bracelet on their left arm, perhaps less an ornament than a wrist guard against bowstring backlash. (Répin says the arrow slid along the bracelet when it left the bow, but that seems wrong.)[54] Elephant huntresses wore pieces of pachyderm hide adorned with cowries. Monkey skins were another ornament.

Officers favored silver embellishments, some serving as insignia of rank: necklaces, pendants, armlets, bracelets, bells, round plates on the sides of the head, crowns or coronets for the highest-ranking. Beecroft mentions silver crosses.[55] Gold and ivory pendants were also used as insignia. Officers were more likely than common soldieresses to wear coral since it was a relatively costly import from Europe. Burton saw "captainesses...decorated with a human skull, or with a lower jaw, fixed to a thin brass plate dangling from the waist".[56]

Charms, referred to in the literature as amulets, talismans, fetishes, gris-gris or magic relics, came in many forms, often unspecified and apparently confused sometimes with simple ornaments or insignia. Foà says the king rewarded amazons for heroism with amulets intended to make them invulnerable in battle. He lists rings, beads, cords and jackal-skin bullet bags, all soaked in human blood.[57] There is no doubt charms were worn to protect amazons from the enemy, if not guarantee them immunity.

Ornaments and charms decorated weapons and equipment as well as persons. Cowries were glued to gun stocks with blood. Duncan heard that each seashell was a royal reward for one killed or captured enemy, and that the blood was human.[58] (Cowries were, in fact, the money of the kingdom, brought by Europeans from the Indian Ocean.) Skertchly was told the cowries were "private fetiche charms of the owner" and the blood came from fowls.[59] Cowries also appeared on sword straps and copper ornaments on scabbards. Pink streamers were seen on knife handles. Copper eagles with wings outspread decorated war-club heads. Unspecified amulets adorned musket muzzles and bullet bags. Tassels dangled from gun barrels. More than likely some talismans were small, square leather sachets containing bits of paper with Arabic quotations from the Koran. Muslim traders from the northern savanna brought these down to the coastal regions of West Africa and sold them to nonbelievers.

One of the most prized ornaments in Dahomey and elsewhere in West Africa was the horsetail. In Répin's day, the amazons' commanding general was recognized by the horsetails hanging from her belt.[60] Foà also noted that amazon generals had one in their hand or at their waist,[61] but another French observer, Henri Morienval, said rank and file too affected horsetails (or cow or goat tails).[62] The tails also had a function: they were used as conductors' batons by amazon song and dance leaders.

Besides ornaments and charms, amazons wore various military accoutrements more suitably discussed in a chapter on their weapons.

9

THEIR WEAPONS

From their obscure beginnings in the eighteenth century to the final year or two of their existence in the 1890s, the basic weapon of the amazons was the smooth-bore, muzzle-loaded flintlock musket. It was also the firearm of choice of the American Revolution and of all European wars through the eighteenth century to the mid-nineteenth.

Flintlocks consisted of the proverbial lock, stock and barrel. The metal barrel, from 38 to 47 inches long, was closed at the stock end by a screwed, and possibly welded, plug. It was secured to the wooden stock by pins or bands. Stock and barrel together were from 4 feet 6 to 5 feet 2 inches long. The complex metal lock mechanism was on the right side of the stock at the rear end, or breech, of the barrel, It was composed of the following: (a) a jawlike cock (now called hammer) that gripped a piece of flint, was under pressure from a mainspring and was controlled by a trigger; (b) a pan covered by a piece of metal called a frizzen that curved upward at the front end; (c) a vent or touch-hole, being a narrow passage connecting the pan to the interior of the barrel; (d) a metal or wooden ramrod attached to the underside of the gun barrel.

Powder, shot or ball and wadding were introduced into the barrel via the muzzle and tamped down with the ramrod. A small amount of powder was also put in the pan. The musketeer pulled back the cock with her/his thumb against the pressure of the mainspring, and the cock was held there by the trigger. When the trigger was pulled, the cock flew forward and the tip of the flint hit the frizzen, striking sparks. The sparks ignited the priming powder in the pan, which flashed through the vent to fire the powder in the breech and send the shot on its way.

All flintlocks were imported from Europe but their exact provenance was not often stated. Many came from Denmark, which had trading posts on the nearby Gold Coast, and were called "Dane guns" or "long Danes" (some Dane guns were actually made in Germany; they are still used by hunters in West Africa). Others were English-made, including a variety called "buccaneer gun" made in Birmingham and "Tower muskets" tested at the Tower of London arsenal. Still others were called simply "trade guns", meaning they were made expressly for the Atlantic slave trade. The French missionary Emile Courdioux, stationed at Whydah from the early 1860s, reported seeing "long Arab guns from Antwerp, known by the name of 'retreat guns'".[1]

Besides the standard flintlock musket, amazons used carbines and blunderbusses that functioned in the same way. Carbines were shorter and lighter than muskets, having been designed originally for cavalrymen. Carbine barrels measured 28 to 37 inches and the overall length ranged from 3 feet 8 inches to 4 feet 6. Whereas a musket might weigh as much as 15 pounds, a carbine might weigh as little as six and a half. A small variety of carbine was known as a musketoon. The blunderbuss was even shorter, from 2 feet 7 to 3 feet 4 inches long, with a larger barrel bore and a flaring muzzle.

As previously noted, amazons were seen with musketoons by 1763-4 (Pruneau) and with blunderbusses by 1772 (Norris). The earliest specific mention of carbines dates to 1856; Répin credits them to the elephant huntresses, but curiously describes the weapons as long and heavy.[2] However, the very first armed Dahomean women to be reported, the four who stood behind King Agaja in 1727 (Snelgrave), held "fusils", light flintlocks that closely resembled carbines (and were the original weapon of Britain's Royal Fusiliers).[3]

The flintlock musket, as one might imagine, took a long time to load. The eighteenth-century European and American soldier could fire it three or four times a minute. Exceptionally, Frederick the Great of Prussia had his men trained to fire off five rounds a minute. According to Foà, the average Dahomean male soldier needed 50 seconds to reload his weapon (which may generally have been of poorer quality than those used in Europe and America) while the amazon required "barely" 30 seconds.[4]

The flintock musket also had a very limited range. Military historians differ widely on the subject. One expert puts the accuracy of American Revolutionary War muskets at "up to about fifty feet",[5] but the standard "Long Land Service Musket" of the British Army was said to have an effective range of 200 yards. The consensus seems to be that a musketeer could expect to hit a target at 80 yards.[6] The main reason a flintlock was not more accurate was that the projectile, or rather projectiles since several bullets were fired at once, oscillated down the smooth barrel, and this initial motion capriciously affected their flight. The problem was solved by spiral grooving, or rifling, that made a bullet spin out of the barrel, dynamically stabilized.

As early as 1862 a Dutch trader named Euschart saw "a few select corps" parade with rifles at Abomey, but did not say whether women were among them.[7] By 1880 at least a few amazons had rifles, according to Ellis.[8] But it was not till 1891 that modern, rapid-firing, breech-loaded rifles started replacing flintlock muskets in the hands of the majority of Dahomey's male and female soldiers. They were sold to the king by German merchants established in Whydah and only too happy to discomfit the French (five years earlier Germany had occupied neighboring Togo). By the time of the French invasion in the fall of 1892, the Dahomean army had some 4,000 to 6,000 rifles: American Remingtons, Spencers and Winchesters, Belgian-made American Peabodys, Austrian Mannlichers, Werndls and Wänzls, German Mausers and Dreyses, British Sniders and Martinis, British or Italian Albinis, even French *tabatières* and *chassepots* (captured by the Germans in the Franco-Prussian war of 1870-1).

Blunderbusses and musketoons, heavy, often overloaded, and with a recoil like a mule's kick, were commonly used as artillery, i.e. they were fired with their butts on the ground (from a kneeling position). But a few amazons were real artillerywomen. In 1850 Forbes saw thirty-two female warriors parading with "wall-pieces", small cannons that were usually mounted on walls and could be loaded with musket balls. Another group carried "small brass guns". Forbes also mentions a "seven-barrelled arquebuse" but does not say who used it.[9] The following year Bouët saw an amazon "company" carrying "copper swivel guns on little wheels".[10] He presented to Gezo a French government gift of two bronze field howitzers and showed how they worked. The king, impressed, said that "such precious weapons could only be entrusted to safe hands, and that, consequently, he would name from among his amazons a company of cannoneers who would be exclusively assigned to their use."[11] Gezo did as he said: later visitors saw the howitzers and their female crew.[12] It was a rare, perhaps unique glimpse of the formation of an amazon unit.

Amazons would handle a bewildering variety of cannons: 6-cm., 8-cm. and 12-cm. pieces, carronades, small mortars, wall-pieces on pivots, swivel "duck-guns", cannons only about a foot long, guns made of iron or brass or bronze. Bouët reported cannons "of all calibers and all epochs",[13] and Répin added "of all shapes".[14] At the end, modern Krupp cannons and even machine-guns were added to the arsenal. Sometimes the guns were mounted on crude carriages (which may have been the first locally made wheeled vehicles in the country). Vallon saw some "infernal machines" (booby traps) mounted on stands.[15] But all these weapons were used much more for salutes and general noisemaking than for combat. Dahomey and environs had few roads wider than single-file bush paths. The country had no draft animals, the few available horses being merely status symbols for chiefs. Usually the cannons lacked proper ammunition. And they were too cumbersome for Dahomey's wars of stealthy, encircling advances and swift surprise attacks.

A few observers suggest the flintlock musket was not the key Dahomean weapon because of its slow reloading time and inaccuracy. It has been said of the American Revolution that after two or three exchanges of musket volleys, the issue typically was decided in hand-to-hand bayonet fighting. Similarly, the decisive weapon in Dahomey's wars may have been a broad, slightly curved, single-edged blade with a hilt that usually lacked a guard and which was called variously a short sword, a cutlass, a saber, a falchion, a billhook, a cleaver, a bush knife or a machete. The blade was about 16 to 20 inches long, and up to four inches wide. Burton describes a related weapon about twice as long that he terms a chopper, and that Skertchly says was stained blue.[16] Unlike firearms, these weapons were usually made by local smiths (although they figured among European trade goods too); like firearms, they were a royal monopoly distributed to warriors (and apparently sold to civilians) by the king.

Machetes, as we shall call them, may have been amazon weapons as early as muskets. Pruneau and Norris saw female palace guards carrying them, along with guns.[17] Freeman saw both weapons in the hands of Gezo's female bodyguards,[18] and almost every subsequent account of the amazons mentions the machete as well as the musket. Chaudoin, dismissing the Dahomean musket as ineffective at 30 meters, calls the machete "the real weapon, the national weapon", that both male and female warriors "wield with much skill and with which they lop off a limb or a head with a single blow as if it were an ordinary cane of bamboo". He notes that the cutting arm doubled as a work tool in peacetime, used to clear land and open up roads, even to till the soil and build houses.[19]

Another weapon made locally for royal distribution was the dagger or poniard. It was not remarked in amazon hands until 1843 (Freeman).[20] In 1856 (Répin and Vallon) each elephant huntress sported a dagger at her waist "with a very

strong and curved blade".[21] Vallon also noted that archeresses
wore "a little dagger fixed to the hand by a thong",[22] and
Burton made a similar observation, placing the thong round
the wrist.[23]

Bayonets appear in the record in 1850: Beecroft noticed
two on poles carried by male soldiers in a procession.[24]
Next year Bouët watched about 500 amazons parade at
Abomey with the thrusting blades attached to their guns.[25]
Vallon saw a unit of about 200 men who had adopted the
bayonet.[26] Burton, a compulsive wordsmith who got carried
away appending the suffix "-ess" to describe amazons and
Dahomean women officials, watched "bayoneteeresses"
parade, fire and perform "a single very *gauche* thrust".[27] Skertchly,
who transparently competed with Burton nearly a decade
later in relating Dahomean detail, looked for but did not
see bayonets on any guns, and it may be that the weapon
had been abandoned.[28]

One of Dahomey's *armes blanches* was unique: a gigantic
razor. Invented by one of Gezo's brothers, it simply copied
the standard European straightedge but was several times
bigger, and is said to have weighed more than 20 pounds.
A blade about 24 to 30 inches long folded into a black
wooden handle. (Burton put the blade length at about 18
inches; Skertchly corrected him.)[29] When extended and held
open by a strong spring, the razor measured four to five
feet. It was carried over the shoulder. Vallon, who first
reported the weapon, said it was made specifically for the
amazons who wore Bouët's firemen's helmets (which somehow had doubled from 50 to 100). He dubbed them "the
Reapers".[30] The razor was wielded with both hands, and,
according to Borghero (who raised the total to 200 or 300),
could slice a man in half.[31] Skertchly heard they were intended
to decapitate enemy kings.[32]

Maire claims the razors were not only for heads but for
enemy genitals, and that the amazons "had to triumphantly
bring these bloody and ignoble trophies back to the palace".[33]
He may have made this up to shock or titillate readers since

emasculation would not have demanded such monstrous weapons. (Degbelo also says the female soldiers brought male genitals back to their king as war trophies, but does not suggest that other than ordinary knives were used.)[34] Burton termed the razors "portable guillotines" and thought that if nothing else, "the terror which they inspire may render them useful".[35]

Battle-axes show up in the record in 1847: Archibald R. Ridgway, a doctor who accompanied an English mission to Abomey, said women of the royal bodyguard were armed with them. He also saw female war chiefs shaking battle-axes with their right hands while making speeches.[36] Vallon includes axes among weapons made locally for kingly distribution.[37] Skertchly mentions an amazon "troop" equipped with skull-decorated axes and assigned to smash open the gates of Abeokuta next time that city was assaulted (a project never consummated).[38] He also describes an axe with an oblong iron blade a few inches long that formed an acute angle with the handle, "something like a hoe" and "made more for show than use". It was carried in this instance by slaves of male soldiers.[39] Foà says amazons often used axes but at the same time calls the weapon "the emblem of the caboceer", a West African term for chief that included women officers.[40] He and other authors sometimes mistook authority symbols called récades (see chapter 13) for small axes. But a post-conquest study of Dahomey asserts that axe-headed emblems of rank, with sculpted handles and richly incised blades, slung by chiefs over the shoulder, did indeed double as percussive weapons of war.[41] If so, they would have been arms of last resort.

After firearms and blade weapons, clubs seem to have been of next importance in the amazon armory. Duncan reports "a sort of club" carried by each member of a 600-woman "regiment", along with musket and sword.[42] Bouët saw amazon "companies" equipped with "war clubs".[43] Skertchly listened to amazon singers who carried "short truncheons".[44] He saw elderly warrioresses with iron-bound sticks similar to the lathi wielded by police in India.[45] Courdioux mentions iron bars.[46] Jean Bayol, who headed a French mission to Abomey in 1889, reports "a curved stick of very hard wood", but it is not clear if female as well as male soldiers used it.[47] Though Maire reached Abomey after the French conquest, his reference to an amazon "war club with round head"("*casse-tête à masse ronde*") seems authentic.[48] Borghero says women reservists, called up from the provinces in wartime (and not to be confused with amazons), carried small clubs to strike enemies in the legs.[49]

Bows and arrows were amazon weapons by 1776, when Labarthe's informant remarked that the more nimble of the king's guardswomen carried them.[50] Doubtless the arrows were from the start tipped with poison, standard procedure along the whole coast of West Africa. "The more nimble" amazons were the young recruits, the scantily dressed girls with ivory bracelets on their left arm. Répin thought them "charming".[51] Brue put the Dahomean bow at a meter long;[52] Burton found it peculiar: "It is not straight nor a segment of a circle, but partly both, the lower end being much less bulged than the upper horn, which, to protect the strain, is armed with iron rings."[53] And he did not think much of the arrows the girls carried: "a quiver of poisoned light cane shafts – mere birdbolts, with hooked heads, spiny as sticklebacks".[54] The archeresses had indeed become more of a show troop than a fighting unit as their weapon was eclipsed by others. Burton said that in the field they were used as scouts, porters and to carry the wounded to the rear.[55]

Dahomeans were familiar with the crossbow but apparently it was never used by amazons, perhaps because it was too hard to tense, even for those sturdy females. Brue saw male soldiers armed with the weapon.[56] In the waning years of the kingdom, only hunters seem to have had them.[57]

From time to time in the nineteenth century, beginning in 1830 (Lopez),[58] amazons were seen carrying spears or lances or more precisely assegais, light wooden javelins tipped with iron. Répin gauges the weapon's length at 8 to 10 feet, and says that throwers "almost invariably hit the trunk of a palm tree at forty or fifty paces".[59] This seems to refer to both male and female warriors. Skertchly saw amazons with "long red-handled brass spears".[60]

In an illustration of Dahomean arms, Courdioux includes a slingshot.[61] This doubtless was an indigenous weapon,[62] but we do not know if amazons ever used it.

ACCOUTREMENTS

The assortment of weapons meant that amazons were draped with military accoutrements as well as ornaments and charms. Machetes (or "swords" or "falchions") usually hung from waistbands in scabbards. Pruneau describes scabbards of crimson velvet,[63] but by Burton's time they were made of black leather.[64] Répin saw swords suspended from amazon shoulders by leather straps; he says their hilts were covered with sharkskin.[65] Burton reports hilts sheathed in shagreen (untanned granulated leather).[66] An early-twentieth-century French historian of Dahomey, Auguste Le Hérissé, mentions swords hung from rope or cloth shoulder-belts.[67] Arrows demanded quivers; Bouët noted some "covered with beautiful fur skins",[68] Skertchly others made of black leather.[69]

Muskets, carried behind the back on a leather or linen sling, required a number of accessories. Cartridges, containing the gunpowder, and bullets were separate. In Europe and America, the cartridge case was usually made of paper; Répin informs us that in Dahomey it was made of dry banana leaf.[70] Eight to twenty cartridges carrying individual powder charges were kept in wooden or leather cups, tubes or boxes fixed to a leather waist-belt or sometimes to a cloth waistband. Foà noted that amazon dancers and paraders had a modified cartridge-belt with only six to eight boxes.[71] Belts worn during the mock attack witnessed by Borghero were covered by a leather strip to protect charges from the rain.[72]

A few observers speak of powder gourds or flasks or of pouches containing cartridges or priming powder. All the powder had to be imported.[73] A leather bullet-bag or pouch hung by a shoulder-strap to the right side. It usually contained not the lead balls of European or American muskets, which had to be imported, but iron balls or slugs, which could be made locally. Herskovits was told there were twelve forges in the realm and that each ironworker had to furnish the king with a certain number of bullets.[74] Duncan says that Dahomeans did not use wads to compact their powder and ball,[75] but Burton saw wadding of "bamboo fibre",[76] which may have been more accurately described by Bayol as "very fine straw, called *mandine*, which comes from the fibers of oil-palm leaves". Bayol says that cornhusks were also used.[77] Wads were carried either in the bullet-bag or a separate bag. Ramrods are almost never mentioned, perhaps as too obvious to comment on in the musket era. Forbes says that off-duty warriors, male and female, kept their muskets in covers.[78] Burton saw amazon muskets "protected from damp by a case of black monkey-skin tightly clasping the breeching, and opening to the rear".[79] Skertchly reports leather covers for musket pans and muzzles, and rags attached to the butt for wiping the flint and cock.[80]

Duncan says each Dahomean soldier, implicitly including the amazons, carried "a piece of small grass rope" for tying captives round the neck, and a piece of chalk to put his or her personal mark on the captive's back.[81] Nearly half a century later Foà confirmed that both male and female warriors carried, "wound round their left wrist, a cord 60 centimeters long" for binding prisoners.[82]

Shields are mentioned so rarely that it is clear they were not standard equipment, at least not after the early eighteenth century, when Snelgrave reported that (male) warriors were all equipped with them. Even then, a soldier already had his hands full with musket and sword, his shield being borne by a boy apprentice.[83] By Norris's time (1772), some shields were just for show. He noted that the commander of 420 marching women, apparently a royal favorite, was screened from spectators by "long targets of leather, covered with red and blue taffata", held round her as she advanced.[84] Forbes says that both the male and female army corps had shields ornamented with human skulls, and he and Beecroft watched women perform shield dances.[85] Two amazon bucklers of the same kind were displayed for Skertchly.[86] Burton saw two crimson leather ones held up by warrioresses in a royal entourage. He explained shields as "a remnant of the old days...now looked upon as a kind of aegis".[87]

Burton paints the most complete verbal picture of amazons setting off on a campaign:

The privates carried packs on cradles...containing their bed-mats, clothes, and food for a week or a fortnight. [...] Cartridge-pouches of two different shapes were girt round their waists, and slung to their sides were water-gourds, fetish sacks, bullet-wallets, powder calabashes, fans, little cutlasses, wooden pipe-cases enveloped in leather tobacco-bags, flint, steel, and tinder, and Lilliputian stools, with three or four legs, cut out of single blocks. Their weapons were slung, and behind their backs dangled their hats, scarecrow felts, 'extinguishers' of white cotton useful as *sacs de nuit*, umbrellas of plaited palm leaf, and low-crowned, broad-brimmed, home-made straws, covered with baft more or less blue.[88]

10

HOW MANY AMAZONS?

As with any army, the number of amazon troops fluctuated radically over time. Pruneau was the first to count them (though not very precisely), in the 1760s, as they paraded past him at Abomey. He saw five or six contingents of eighty to 100 teenaged girls each, all armed with musketoons and swords, making a total of 400 to 600 warrioresses.[1] A few years later Norris counted fourteen units totaling 860 women marching in a procession. It is not clear whether they were all amazons – he describes only the first ninety as armed guards – but the total corresponds with Dalzel's figure of 800 women for the military campaign of 1781[2] and Pires's of more than 800 for the king's "household squadron" in 1797.[3] A half-century later, in 1843, Brue estimated the number of women soldiers at exactly the same 800.[4] The same year Freeman saw only a "little brigade" of 'several hundred".[5]

Suddenly, in the space of two years, the amazon corps grew enormously; we do not know why, but can make an educated guess. Gezo, mounting the throne in 1818, had apparently been content for a quarter-century with the same modest female contingent as his predecessors, but 100 miles to the east of Abomey a new power had arisen. A Yoruba group known as the Egba had founded Abeokuta in 1830 and soon built it into a walled city. According to oral traditions, Dahomey destroyed some Yoruba towns in the early 1840s. Possibly fearing Fon encroachment, the Egba mounted a successful surprise attack on a Dahomean force near the village of Imojolu in 1844. Gezo barely escaped capture and lost some of his regalia to the enemy, including his stool and a particularly valued umbrella. The next year European visitors to Abomey started seeing thousands rather than hundreds of amazons. The implication is that Gezo had determined to avenge his humiliation and, in the face of superior Yoruba numbers, urgently needed to expand his army. It has been said that only two amazon "companies" existed before Gezo and that he created six new ones.[6] If so, it probably happened at this time.

At a royal review in 1845, Duncan reckoned that he watched about 6,000 amazons march past, at another about 8,000.[7] In 1847 Winniett thought he saw 8,000 in a review.[8] Ridgway, who accompanied him, more cautiously estimated the female guard at 4,000 or 5,000.[9] Forbes counted 2,408 amazons in a parade in 1850, and guessed that an equal number were on frontier duty, thus putting the total at about 5,000.[10] Beecroft counted a round 3,000 in the same parade.[11] Burton later dismissed such totals, alleging that Duncan, Forbes and Beecroft were hoodwinked by "the heroines [being] marched out of one gate and in through another" so that they were counted more than once.[12] But the evidence tends to support them: the Dahomean army that stormed Abeokuta in 1851 may have included as many as 6,000 amazons but probably no fewer than 4,000. Even Burton accepted the latter figure.[13]

The amazons suffered terrible losses in that battle – at least 1,000 and possibly 2,000 dead – but somehow the gaps in their ranks were quickly filled. Arriving in Abomey less than four months after the catastrophe, Bouët gauged amazon strength at 4,000 to 6,000.[14] Five years later Répin and Vallon agreed that about 4,000 warrioresses paraded past them; Vallon put their overall total at 5,000.[15] Guillevin, one of the last Europeans to see Gezo alive, made a more conservative estimate of 3,000.[16]

Glele's reign saw no immediate change. In 1861 Father Borghero saw 3,000 amazons rush thorny barriers. He thought a reported total of 4,000 or 5,000 for the women's "legion" included only those residing permanently at Abomey.[17] In that year a smallpox epidemic is said to have ravaged the Dahomean army.[18] If so, the women soldiers' losses were swiftly made up. Euschart was so bedazzled by a military review at Abomey in mid-1862 that he estimated total troop strength at "scarcely...less than 50,000 including 10,000 Amazons all apparently well disciplined".[19] The same year Dawson thought the female warriors numbered about 4,000.[20] Wilmot was certain he saw 4,000 amazons in the Dahomean capital in 1862-3 and figured that a further 1,000 were garrisoned in royal palaces elsewhere in the country.[21]

Now we come to Richard Burton and his prodigious gift for detail. The world traveler was not about to take anyone else's word, and relished debunking his predecessors. Before he even saw an amazon, he wrote: "They cannot be estimated at more than 2000."[22] On a day in 1863 he counted 2,038 amazons in Abomey and, "allowing for omissions", put the grand total at no more than 2,500. But of those he saw, "one-third were unarmed, or half-armed", leaving effective strength at 1,700. "The fact is", he wrote, "these 'most illustrious viragos' are now a mere handful. King Gezo lost the flower of his force under the walls of Abeokuta, and the loss has never been made good."[23]

Burton's figures may have been on the low side, but two disparate events in the next two years conspired to reduce amazon numbers. In 1864 Glele hurled his army against Abeokuta and was no more successful than his father. Skertchly, updating Burton, heard that "the flower of the [amazon] corps perished" in that engagement too,[24] and much later Foà advanced a figure of more than 2,000 female dead,[25] but these seem to have been overstatements.

The following year, 1865, saw the extinction of Dahomey's Atlantic slave trade. The death-blows were dealt by the British Navy, which intensified its antislavery patrol of the Slave Coast, and by the Spanish government, which closed Cuban ports to slavers.[26] (It has been calculated that over a period of more than two centuries, nearly 2,000,000 human beings were exported from the Slave Coast to the New

World.)[27] The annual slave raids did not end – there were still markets to be served in Muslim regions to the north, and as late as May 1892 Dahomey was said to be supplying virtual slaves (camouflaged as voluntary contract labor) to Portuguese São Tomé, German Cameroon or Belgian King Leopold II's "Congo Free State".[28] But the drop in demand must have led to a downsizing of the Dahomean army. Médard Béraud, French consul at Whydah in 1866, seems to confirm this. He reported that the amazons now numbered "no more than 1,000 to 1,500".[29]

From then till the French conquest, estimates of amazon strength varied between 600 and 5,000,[30] but the actual range would appear to have been from about 1,000 to 3,000. One of the most widely accepted figures was 2,000, an official French calculation of Dahomean women soldiers who took part in the Battle of Atchoupa, near the coastal town of Porto-Novo, on April 20, 1890. After the final campaign in September-November 1892, Frédéric Schelameur, a veterinarian with French cavalry forces, asked the chief Dahomean peace delegate how many amazons remained. About fifty or sixty, he replied, out of 1,200 in the field at the start of the forty-seven-day struggle.[31]

11

WHERE THEY LIVED

When the amazons were not in the field, they lived in royal palaces, with the possible exception of a tiny minority composed of those married off by the king to his favorites.[1] There were a number of these palaces: in Abomey and its outskirts, in the town of Cana 8 miles to the southeast (the royal country residence, facetiously termed by Bouët "the Versailles of Dahomey"),[2] and in Zagnanado some 30 miles to the east. Allada, ancestral home of the Dahomean dynasty, also had one. However, the bulk of the women's corps resided in the principal palace of the capital, known since the French conquest (but not before) by the name of Singboji (or Simbodji) – from the Fon word for a two-story building (we shall call it by that name here for convenience). Certain features were common to all the royal residences, going back to at least the last half of the eighteenth century.

The palaces were large, roughly square compounds surrounded by high walls made of red laterite mud – the ubiquitous soil of the country – rock-hardened by the sun. The walls were 2 to 8 feet thick, wider at the bottom than the top, and anywhere from 10 to 33 feet high (the consensus on the Singboji wall was 20-26 feet). Estimates of their length ranged from about half a mile to more than two and a half miles, and of the space enclosed by the walls up to a square mile and more. Norris paced off one side of a palace wall at Cana and counted 1,700 steps, or between 4,000 and 5,000 feet; he guessed it encompassed "almost as much ground as St. James's Park" in London (meaning 85 acres).[3] In his previously cited letter of 1726, Agaja puts the circumference of his main palace at about 3 miles.[4] A French trader, Jules Lartigue, measured the Singboji palace's front wall at 431 meters (1,414 feet) in 1860.[5] Burton describes the palace as "a rude circle, measuring, if we cut off the various angles, 2,560 paces in circumference".[6] A. Angot, a French official, says that it took more than an hour to walk around it in 1889.[7] Another French official, Emmanuel G. Waterlot, who made casts of royal bas-reliefs in 1911, thought the palace covered 35 or 40 hectares (86 to 99 acres).[8] A 1970 guide to Singboji gives the area within the walls as 37 hectares, or 91 acres.[9]

The walls were pierced with multiple gates, each protected by a guardhouse. Some accounts speak of four gates;[10] Burton says that there were usually eight to ten;[11] the 1970 Singboji guide has a map showing twelve.[12] According to Waterlot, the gates were about 4 meters wide.[13] From at least the early eighteenth century, the tops of outer palace walls were adorned with the heads of slain enemy soldiers. Agaja says he had been "so fortunate in warr" that he had been able to decorate in that manner all 3 miles of the main palace walls plus more than a mile of wall round the palace in which he lived before becoming king.[14] Dalzel was told that Kpengla had 127 war prisoners decapitated just to fill a gap in the décor.[15] The trophies were stuck originally on wooden stakes and later on iron spikes, hooks or forks. Agaja claimed his enemies' heads were aligned "as close as they can lye one by another".[16] But Freeman estimated the distance between skulls along the outer wall of Singboji at 20 to 30 feet,[17] and Duncan used the latter figure.[18] Répin, examining the same wall, saw some heads "already bleached by time, others still covered with a few shreds of flesh, and a few freshly cut".[19] Freeman describes a Singboji gate flanked by vertical rows of skulls embedded in the clay.[20]

The space within the compound walls was divided into many courtyards, each defined by its own, lower walls and connected by doors. Some were quite large: Freeman saw two in the Cana palace each 80 to 90 yards square,[21] and Guillevin wrote of one interior court of the Singboji palace that was "spacious enough to allow the royal guard, composed of amazons, to maneuver".[22]

The courts contained a variety of structures, all made of the same red earth and thatched. There were separate living quarters for the king, his true wives and small children, his mother and the "mothers" of past kings, his sisters, grown princesses, female doctors, and female bards who memorized Dahomey's history and the glories of its kings; barracks for the amazons and the women servants and slaves; audience and council rooms, sheds, kitchens, storehouses, temples and altars, royal tombs (in both Abomey and Cana) and stables (for status-symbol horses). A twentieth-century Dahomean historian, Maximilien Quénum, would add prisons to the list of structures,[23] though the palace ban on male residents makes this questionable.

Dalzel and Guillevin say that eunuchs dwelt in the Singboji palace but Burton has them living in town.[24] Brue said that Singboji contained a "house of castration" where, he thought, the operation was "a punishment habitually inflicted on chiefs of vanquished enemies".[25] More likely it was where, as Burton reported, young men were turned into eunuchs for royal purposes.[26] (Pruneau saw a "company" of eunuchs and said the king had twelve men castrated yearly.[27] But the only figure we seem to have for the total number of eunuchs was reported by Louis Fraser, a British vice-consul who visited Abomey in 1851: "The King has about one hundred of them," he was told.)[28]

The typical large building was an elongated, one-story rectangle of red clay with a thatched roof. A wall along its main axis divided it in two, one side enclosed, the other an open porch or loggia with the roof supported by sturdy earthen or wooden pillars along the outer edge. The historical clay bas-reliefs mentioned earlier were set both in the pillars and in the median wall at the back of the veranda. One such structure in the palace today is close to 130 feet long. Presumably the amazon barracks were buildings of this kind.

Smaller palace buildings were square or round. One of

the latter was the king's bedchamber at Singboji, known only through eyewitness accounts by Norris and Dalzel of visits to an ailing Tegbesu.[29] The circular room was about 18 feet in diameter, and had a thatched conical roof. Its wall was whitewashed on the inside (doubtless with a "milk" of kaolin clay, a local resource). Furnishings included a bedstead, mattress and carpet of European origin. A 3-foot wall outside the chamber was lined along the top with human jawbones, and the small area within it paved with the skulls of prominent foes that the king "might enjoy the savage gratification of trampling on the *heads* of his enemies, when he pleased" (according to Norris, who related such details with too much relish to be wholly credible).[30] (The Englishman also neglected to remind us that his sixteenth-century compatriot, Sir Humphrey Gilbert, lined the path to his tent in Ireland with the heads of everyone his troops had killed that day.) A modern visitor to the palace is shown similar round buildings, their eaves reaching almost to the ground (though corrugated metal has replaced the thatch). One is described as Gezo's tomb, another as the tomb of forty-one wives of Glele chosen to accompany him to the other world.

The two-story houses that gave the Singboji palace its name were a perquisite of the king; no one else could build or live in one. They seem to have been inspired by European models at Whydah. They were 30 to 65 feet high, rising above the outer palace walls, and had windows that were sometimes shuttered but apparently never fitted with glass.

The Singboji palace contained at least two two-story buildings, one attributed to Agaja, the other built by Gezo. The first was known to Europeans as "the house of shells" or "the cowrie palace" because during the annual customs, at least, it was festooned from top to bottom and on every side with strings of the money mollusk to display the king's wealth. Bouët put the number of shells in the millions.[31] Skertchly asserts the building was also draped with silver dollars "in the good old times".[32] Borghero makes the startling statement that the cowrie house was 100 meters long.[33] Since no other observer remarked on its length, his claim is dubious. The building does not seem to have been lived in after Agaja's time and may have been used only to store and flaunt the king's treasures.

Gezo lived in his own two-storey house. It stood about 40 feet high, the top floor boasting eight window-holes with green wooden shutters. Burton says the red clay walls blushed through a thin coat of whitewash.[34] Skertchly spotted a ladder used to reach the second floor.[35] Borghero saw four banners bearing Gezo's name in Portuguese flying from the roof.[36] When the French entered Abomey on November 17, 1892, they raised the tricolor on the same roof.

(Tegbesu's round bedroom and Gezo's two-storey dwelling contradict a statement by Répin that the king did not have "private apartments" but literally slept around, living in his wives' huts, "one by one".[37] Burton seems to second Répin on one page [the king "is ever changing his sleeping apartment"] but speaks of the two-storey house as Gezo's "favourite place of residence" on another.)[38]

For major festivals, conical tents were hoisted in palace courtyards. One, at least, was king-size, as befitted the man who sat in an armchair or reclined on a sofa within, surrounded by his women. Norris, the first to describe it, made it about 50 feet high and 40 feet wide. It was open round the bottom and fixed to a circle of "small iron rails".[39]

Seventy-eight years later Gezo invited Forbes and Beecroft into *his* big tent. He said it was very old, pointed out its dilapidated condition, and asked for an identical replacement from Queen Victoria. The tent measured 35 feet in height and 45 in diameter. It had a wooden frame wrapped in local cloth and over that a red baize cover ornamented with designs including human and bovine heads. On top was a figure holding a flag.[40] Burton actually brought Glele "one forty feet circular crimson silk Damask Tent with Pole complete" (as Her Majesty's Government's gift list read). It "was found to be too small", and its wooden pegs unsuitable "in

a land of white ants".[41] At Glele's request, a member of
Burton's party measured the king's biggest tent: it was 54
feet in diameter at the base, and about the same height.
Besides the central pole, it was supported by an inner circle
of twenty-four wooden posts, and had an outer flap or
valance fixed to eighty-five iron rods planted in the ground.
Burton thought the structure homemade. It was of coarse,
faded red, yellow and check cloth, covered with multicolored
appliqué "heraldic" designs and surmounted by a "fetish figure".[42] In its stead, Skertchly found a "gorgeous" silk pavilion
with a scalloped valance of figured damask, mainly crimson
and yellow. The statue at the top was now a six-foot woman
carrying a powder-keg.[43]

One other noteworthy architectural feature of Dahomey's
palaces was their sheds, also called piazzas, verandas or galleries
in the literature. "Bamboo" rafters (probably raffia palm
midribs) sloping from freestanding or building walls supported
a thatched roof and rested on posts about 4 to 7 feet high,
and set 12 to 15 feet from the wall. The top of the roof
might be as high as the highest wall; Burton reported a
steep-thatched shed 60 to 70 feet tall.[44] Some sheds had
foot-high clay floors and clay benches, and some clay parts
were whitewashed. Some were just outside palaces, flanking
the gates, while others looked out on interior courts. It was
in the shade of such sheds that kings, surrounded by wives
and amazons, received visitors or presided over public events,
when the occasion did not call for a tent.

Palaces were villages within villages or, as in the case
of Abomey, a town within a town. Estimates of the capital's
population ranged from 20,000 to 50,000; Burton allowed
that the lower figure might have been reached "at times".[45]
Lamb thought at least 2,000 wives inhabited Agaja's "own
House, or Palace, which is as big as a small Town".[46] In
his 1726 letter, Agaja boasts of having at least 7,000 wives
plus household slaves dispersed among his seven "great
houses".[47] But we must wait until Angot (1889) for a ballpark
estimate of Singboji's population: "The king's palace alone",

he wrote, "forms a city of 7 to 8000."[48] Le Hérissé came
after the French conquest had all but emptied the palace,
but he was able to interview Dahomean personages who
had lived through the final years of the kingdom. "We've
been assured", he said, that the palace housed more than
8,000 individuals under the last two independent monarchs,
Glele and Béhanzin, "and that figure does not seem at all
exaggerated to us."[49] Dunglas, who also depended on Dahomean informants but did not reach the country till 1927
and so might be less reliable, made a more conservative
estimate of "three or four thousand women (Amazons included)".[50]

Singboji and the other palaces were indeed a woman's
world, and the soldieresses were probably in the minority.
Edna Bay thinks amazons comprised roughly a quarter of
the total female palace population.[51] They were housed with
their slaves and servants in a distinct wing of each palace.
Degbelo, who collected and transcribed a remarkable number
of oral traditions about the amazons in the 1970s, was told
that contrary to Dahomean (and indeed West African) custom,
the barracks were built by the amazons themselves, not by
men. They divided the long buildings into several rooms,
each occupied by from one to ten warrioresses, depending
on the strength of the garrison. Degbelo says the walls of
their compound were also fortified by the women themselves,
to keep them isolated from the outside world.[52]

Beginning with Lamb in the 1720s, it was clear to foreign
visitors that the Dahomean palace was a female domain.
Apropos the king's seven "great houses", Agaja told him,
"no man sleeps within the walls of any of them after sun-sett
but myselfe."[53] Pruneau noted the royal compound at Abomey
was "guarded within only by his wives".[54] Two other Frenchmen, de Chenevert and Father Charles-Pierre-Joseph Bullet,
reported in 1776 that "no male penetrates the interior".[55]
Dalzel wrote, with more exactness, that "its recesses are scarce
ever entered by any human being of the male gender, and
the female apartments are guarded from intrusion, with more

than eastern [Oriental] jealousy."[56] In fact, the ban was waived during public fêtes: male soldiers, for instance, could then enter a palace courtyard as long as they stayed on their side of the "bamboos".

TONONU AND KANGBODÉ

Among the few exceptions to the ordinary ban on men were two officials titled the *Tononu* and the *Kangbodé*. We seem to meet the Tononu first in de Chenevert and Bullet's manuscript, though not by that name. He was the chief, they said, of a group of eunuchs who guarded the palace exterior, and was a eunuch himself.[57] (Norris had already seen twenty eunuchs as well as about forty armed amazons in a palace guardhouse. The eunuchs held "bright iron rods", presumably a kind of billy club.)[58] The Tononu was, in fact, majordomo of the palace and one of the most powerful men in the kingdom, but three-quarters of a century would pass before other European visitors, co-travelers Forbes and Beecroft, would take notice of the head eunuch.

Forbes watched the "too-noo-noo" and a female counterpart pass objects and messages back and forth across the "bamboo" line that marked off the female preserve. But he also saw him seated at the foot of the throne during a military review, and disbursing royal largess to army officers at the king's side on another occasion.[59] Beecroft heard the "Too-no-noo" rebuke the king's second-ranking minister for allowing his stool-bearers to come before the monarch "in a dirty state".[60] The Britons' testimony also suggested a special relationship between the head eunuch and the amazons. At a public ceremony the Tononu "play[ed] upon his Silvery Tongue" to extol the women's singing and tell them how much the king enjoyed it. A little later he enjoined them to sing out against the people of Abeokuta.[61]

A few years later Vallon and Répin recognized the full dimensions of the Tononu's role. He was, they reported, "minister of the royal residences, feared and absolute chief of the king's household". As such he was "responsible for watching over the conduct of the amazons and the women of the seraglio". Under his surveillance the warrioresses were "subject...to severe discipline". The Tononu was helped in this police job by a squad of eunuchs who, as insignia, wore "two little horns of polished silver held on their forehead by a thong circling their head".[62]

The head eunuch was also the king's chief body attendant and mouthpiece. While, as we have seen, wives catered to the monarch's every whim, a non-female intimate was apparently deemed necessary. A modern British commentator, W.J. Argyle, plausibly (if somewhat cryptically) explains it as an answer to "the ritual impurities to which [women] were subject in Dahomey, as in most primitive societies".[63] What he means is that menstruating women were considered an abomination, their presence exposing the king to spiritual danger, and one could never be positive that a female dabbing the monarch's brow was "clean". In the enforced absence of virile menservants, a neutered male would fill the bill.

Vallon and Répin saw the Tononu serving drinks to Gezo after tasting them first to ensure they were not poisoned. He also held up a silk foulard veil as the monarch drank because divine-kingship protocol decreed that no one should witness him engaged in such a common activity. The Tononu was also seen bearing Gezo's silver spittoon and feathered fan or fly whisk.[64]

More significantly, the Tononu bore royal messages. He was, Répin noted, the king's intimate, "the only one His Majesty deigns to speak to directly when he has some order to give".[65] Vallon specified that when Gezo wanted to say something to the public or to foreign visitors, he spoke to the chief eunuch who relayed the statement to the Meu (the king's second-ranking minister) who passed it on to the audience. Replies returned to the sovereign by the same route in reverse .[66]

All in all, Vallon ranked the Tononu as "third personality of the court", although his authority did not extend beyond the palace walls except when he accompanied the king out-side.[67] Burton rated the official "fourth personage in the realm – royalty not included", and said he commanded the eunuchs' quarter in town. He heard that Tononus customarily accompanied their masters to the great beyond but Gezo had ordered his highly experienced Tononu to be spared this so he could perpetuate court ceremonial. The old sur-vivor, like his palace police, sported silver horns.[68]

The Kangbodé, called the "grand chamberlain" by Vallon[69] and "inspector of the night guards" by Skertchly,[70] was the Tononu's immediate subordinate. A French merchant named Blanchély who visited Abomey three times in 1848-50 said "Cambodé" commanded the army's rear guard and was in charge of provisions.[71] Forbes called him "camboodee", and Beecroft "Cam-baa-dee"; both thought that he was the royal treasurer.[72] At one point Burton referred to him as the king's storekeeper.[73] The Kangbodé does not seem to have been a eunuch but had special reponsibility for those who guarded the palace exterior (as distinct from those who kept watch on the women inside). When the king left the palace, the Kangbodé and his deputies led the way, clearing sticks and stones from the royal path, and alerting the monarch to uneven ground. He and his men wore silver bells round their necks which they rang to obtain silence before public pronouncements.[74] The Kangbodé also served as intermediary between foreign visitors and the king, which led Jules-René Poirier, a chronicler of the French conquest, to refer (ap-parently) to him as "a kind of chief of protocol".[75]

Like all other officials and officers, the Tononu and Kangbodé had their female doubles. "By the custom of this strange kingdom," as Burton put it, there was thus a chief "eunuchess", and, Skertchly added, a corps of "female eunuchs" under her.[76] There is no evidence, however, that any of these women were anything but heterosexual. Their duties included transmission of messages across the sexual divide. According to oral tradition, they were the only persons (besides the

king himself) empowered to speak to the sovereign's highest-
ranking spouses, known as the *kposi* (literally "leopard wives").[77]

In a kingdom awash with symbolism, Singboji palace was
the most imposing symbol of all. It was the handiwork of
ten reigns: each monarch added his own residence, his own
cellular complex, on its western side. This relived a seminal
event in Dahomean history, when the second king, Wegbaja,
moved westward from one conquest to seize the land of
the chief of Abomey. It also symbolized a dynastic injunction
to make Dahomey ever larger.

The aura of mystical apartness and secretiveness cultivated
by Dahomey's kings came to envelop the whole palace. As
Burton remarked, "the boldest speak in whispers when a
stranger begins to question concerning what takes place
'within'."[78] A permanent state of dynamic tension seems to
have been cultivated between the feminine interior and the
masculine world without. The palace was not simply the
monarch's private residence but, in Argyle's words, "a distinct
sphere enclosing all that was most mysterious and impressive
about the kingship".[79]

12

MILITARY TRAINING

One of the palace mysteries was the kind and amount of training the amazons received behind those high red walls. All contemporary written testimony concerns their participation in public events connected either with national celebrations or with the presence of important foreign visitors. This has led some historians to emphasize the ritual and ceremonial nature of their performances and to question whether there was any real training, apart from those appearances and the on-the-job experience of the military campaigns themselves.

According to David Ross, a modern student of Dahomey's resistance to the French, "the Fon seem to have had no concept of rigorous battle training" and "There appears...to have been no attempt either to drill or to train in the best use of weapons."[1] He and other commentators, it would seem, have been unduly influenced by an assessment of Dahomey's military forces made by Bayol. There was no formal shooting instruction ("*école de tir*"), the French official reported, and besides, firearms were "not held in high honor by them on expeditions", and were usually fired without aiming. "In principle they use only their cutlass and...club."[2] Bayol was echoed by Foà, who claimed the amazons "shoot badly, without aiming, but...excel at hand-to-hand combat with sword or club" and "handle [knives] admirably".[3] A French armchair expert, G. de Wailly, opined that the warrioresses lacked "the least notions of military instruction" and did not even know how to load, much less aim, their muskets.[4]

Scoffing remarks by Burton and Skertchly also helped distort the historical picture. Duncan likened an amazon

87

attack to the swift rush of a pack of hounds,[5] Vallon to a whirlwind,[6] whereas Burton saw the women "manoeuvre with the precision of a flock of sheep".[7] Skertchly admired the amazons' skill in loading their muskets and their speed in firing, and said they kept the weapons "in splendid order", yet he could not resist a gratuitous quip: "Of their qualities as marksmen, I never had any experience, but I should think the hitting of a haystack would be about the sum total of their accomplishments."[8]

Fortunately we have more than enough evidence to set the picture straight. Agaja's 1726 letter contains a hint that Dahomean troops already practised for war. He often went out in the country, he said, installed himself "under some great shadey tree", and reviewed his "armed people". When he had smoked his pipe, and his "people" had "pretty well exercised themselves in activety of body, by running, leaping, and firing thare arms, *as if engaged* [emphasis added]", he distributed brandy, then returned home "with the acclamations of my people, with my drums beating, and hornes of different sortes sounding".[9] It is hard not to see in this custom the genesis of sham amazon attacks such as the one Borghero witnessed 135 years later and similar ones by male soldiers reported over the years by other visitors. Agaja does not specify that the participants were in fact all men; elsewhere in the letter he says "all" his subjects were bred to battle but adds, perhaps too hastily, that "the women stay at home to plant and manure the earth".[10]

Palace women were almost certainly receiving some sort of military training by the 1760s, when Pruneau described wives who guarded the king as appearing *"enregimentées"*.[11] In the next decade a Labarthe informant related that they "perform shooting exercises with much skill"[12] and, as mentioned earlier, de Montaguère saw the amazons form two parallel lines that "kept up a general fire which was very well executed".[13] Dalzel confirmed their reports: "Several hundreds of these [palace women] are trained to the use of arms...These warriors are regularly exercised, and go through their evolutions [drills] with as much expertness as the male soldiers."[14]

Mock attacks on thorny redoubts were obviously designed not only to rehearse amazons for real assaults on enemy targets but to foster stoical acceptance of pain. They were first described by Lopez (to a fellow slaving skipper, Théophilus Conneau) in 1830. He saw 100 warrioresses take off at a signal from Gezo to storm a 9-foot-high mud make-believe fort "surrounded on all sides with a pile of briars of astonishing growth". They raced toward it, "brandishing their weapons and yelling their war cry,...and mindless of the thorny barricade, sprung to the top of the walls, tearing their flesh as they crossed the prickly impediment." Inside, according to Lopez, were fifty captives tied to stakes who were to be immolated that day. The fifty women who got to them first brought them before the king, who opened the sacrificial ceremonies by beheading one with the cutlass of the bravest soldieress. Lopez says the whole performance was repeated daily for five more days.[15] If so, his figure of fifty victims at a time is suspect since 300 would far exceed the number normally executed at the annual customs.

The next testimony is from Duncan, who was told it had taken fourteen days to erect "three immense prickly piles of green bush...of a sort of strong briar or thorn". They were about 70 feet wide and 8 high, in a single row about 400 yards long with two narrow gaps "to distinguish each clump appointed to each regiment". On examining the barrier, the British traveler wrote, "I could not persuade myself that any human being, without boots or shoes, would, under any circumstances, attempt to pass over so dangerous a collection of the most efficiently armed plants I had ever seen." Three hundred yards behind the barricade were "large pens...fenced with piles seven feet high, thickly matted together with strong reeds". In them were several hundred royal slaves representing inhabitants of a town.

A female "regiment" assembled about 200 yards from its segment of the thorn row and shouldered arms. "In a few seconds the word for attack was given, and a rush was made towards the pile with a speed beyond conception, and in less than one minute the whole body had passed across this immense pile, and had taken the supposed town." Two other amazon regiments followed at twenty-minute intervals, crossing their thorn piles "with equal rapidity".

If Duncan's distances are correct, the assaults could hardly have taken less than a minute, but completing them in even two or three minutes would have been an extraordinary feat. Gezo asked him if he thought like numbers of English-women could have done as well. Duncan admitted they could not and, that England had no women soldiers but did have "females who had individually and voluntarily distinguished themselves".[16]

Winniett said that Gezo showed him "models of the different forts that his female troops have captured", and that he was "amazed at the fortifications that they...regularly carried by storm".[17]

Forbes and Beecroft watched 2,000 amazons pantomime a slaving expedition from beginning to end. In this case the targeted "town" was a 100-foot-long stockade of palm branches, unprotected by thorns, containing three large enclosures filled with royal slaves. The stockade was at the south end of a long market square. The women soldiers massed at the north end, "under their different regimental colours".

First an advance guard moved in single file along an imaginary path, reconnoitering and posting sentinels along the way. The main amazon army followed, divided into two "battalions". They marched with muskets over their shoulders, muzzles in front. "Next came the Fetish gear, the war-stools, and equipage [carriage] of the monarch, guarded by a reserve, and in the rear the commissariat (all females)." (Gezo himself was sitting with his court under a canopy of umbrellas on the east side of the square, watching the drama with Forbes and Beecroft.) Twice the female army repeated its march-past, with variations; the last, in close column order, was said to represent a night advance.

Then scouts were sent ahead. They soon returned with a Dahomean "spy", played by a man swathed from head to heel in native cloth. He was debriefed by a council of amazon chiefs. Aides-de-camp kept running between the council and the troops, carrying orders. Scouts were sent out again, and this time returned with six "prisoners", who also were questioned by the council. Female officers then reported "the state of the country and the position of the enemy" to the king, who decided that young warrioresses should take the lead as heavy fighting was not expected.

A musket shot signaled an attack on the stockade. A first wave forced its way in, and quickly re-emerged, some amazons with prisoners, others with small bundles of grass representing severed heads. (Beecroft counted about 250 such bundles; as he saw it, they were carried by prisoners.) More units rushed in. Slaves broke out of one enclosure and "a slave-hunt followed with much spirit, until all were caught." The rest of the army, except for reserves who guarded the prisoners, now massed in front, and at a signal dashed against the stockade, throwing it down. More slaves escaped, and another hunt ensued.

The amazon army then divided into its component regiments and "surrounded" the enemy country. As a grand finale, all the slaves, who Forbes thought numbered about 2,000, were let loose "and again hunted until all were recaptured, tied, and dragged before the royal canopy". The mass of amazons moved so fast, says Beecroft, that the earth shook amid a cloud of dust.[18]

The most colossal mock attack ever witnessed by European visitors may have been the one seen by Bouët a year later (1851). It was completely orchestrated by Gezo on an "immense plain" outside Abomey. He and his whole army, male and female, were dressed for war. A palisaded village had been erected "as if by magic" for the occasion. Inside were women and slaves posing as the enemy. While waiting for the attack they uttered "loud yells of defiance and threat".

Gezo had his troops deploy in battle array. Male musketeers

formed two giant wings in a sort of crescent, flanked by many scouts. In back were a large corps of male reserves and rear guards. "The king had placed himself in the center, surrounded by his five or six thousand amazons forming his guard, and which he launched forward or toward the wings, according to circumstances." They alone were to carry out the attack.

At a signal from the king, a "company of amazons, covered with long grass, lay down on the plain and crawled toward the...palisade, firing from a prone position and responding to very heavy fire from the besieged." (Bouët does not make clear whether this was real gunfire.) At a second royal signal, the amazon company "rose, and ran forward screaming toward the...palisade which it crossed and from which it dislodged the enemy". Several more such attacks were made on other parts of the stockade, then the amazons poured into the "village" and set it on fire. They came back, "pushing ahead of them, bound or loaded with booty, the poor devils who had served as the enemy, and carrying at the end of their guns men's heads made of wood crudely painted and carved".[19]

Bouët was genuinely impressed. He congratulated Gezo because the whole affair

....had really been executed with cohesion and vigor, and his orders had always been carried with surprising celerity by messengers leaving his tent. [...] I was really struck by the marvelous promptitude with which his orders were executed, without him making a fuss, and above all by the kind of tactics that governed [the amazons'] movements. [...][20] I was very surprised to see such a perfect analogy between the movements of this army and those of a European army: scouts, advance guard, rear guard, reserve, music, bugles, drums, etc. ...everything was there.[21]

Bouët's tribute may be unequaled in the literature, but five years later Répin and Vallon were hardly less impressed. They watched two successive and identical simulations, the first by the male army, the second by the female. Except for the noise it was pure mime, without the usual props: no barriers to scale, no visible enemies.

The male warriors formed themselves "rather smoothly" into several lines five or six men deep by about fifty across and spaced some distance from each other. They were armed with muskets and blunderbusses. The men in the first rank of each line opened fire, then passed "smartly" through the ranks behind them to the rear to reload while the second rank fired in its turn and then moved to the back, and so on.

Soon a few soldiers broke ranks and, guns on safety and knives in hand, crawled a certain distance "with astonishing speed" to surprise the enemy. Then "they rose up as one man, discharging their guns and uttering dreadful yells". Some, wielding cutlasses, pretended to decapitate fallen enemies and bring the heads back in triumph. Others fled "as if to invite pursuit" and led their imaginary foes to certain doom. Suddenly the whole army broke ranks and, "brandishing its guns, surged forward in a furious charge, with cries, shouts and...almost terrifying grimaces". Surviving enemies were routed and chased to the end of the square, then the army returned "intoning...a song of victory", and massed motionless opposite the king.[22]

At a signal from the female commanding general, known by horsetails dangling from her belt, some 4,000 amazons repeated the same scenario, "but with more animation and *furia*", according to Répin.

It's difficult to describe, even to imagine, the picture they presented, under a fiery sky, amid the swirl of dust and smoke, the crackling of musketry and the roar of cannons, these four thousand panting women, intoxicated by powder and smoke, moving convulsively with the contorted faces of the damned and uttering the most savage cries. Finally, when all was exhausted, the ammunition and the energies, order and silence were restored.[23]

Vallon, too, thought the warrioresses had upstaged the warriors. Spurred on by the gestures and yells of female generals and

....more impassioned than the men, they soon merged into a

whirlwind headed toward the point of attack; their fantastic banners, on which the strangest figures of animals grimaced, floated here and there, giving this spectacle the most bizarre character. One would have said [it was] an army of demons spewed up by a volcano and covering the ground with its black battalions: nothing in these intrepid creatures recalled the most beautiful and most timid half of the human species.[24]

After the mock attack watched by Borghero in 1861, we have no further eyewitness accounts, but an obviously second-hand description by Foà[25] suggests this form of military training may have lasted till the final years of the kingdom. Every detail indicates that these were real rehearsals for battle, the fruit of careful preparation, and not simply staged *ad hoc* for the entertainment of foreign visitors or as mere ceremonial.

The same might be said of shooting demonstrations. An occasional refrain in the literature is that the Dahomeans did not know how to shoot because they often fired from the hip or at arm's length instead of from the shoulder. It is said that they were afraid of the recoil, or of the musket — frequently a cheap "trade" gun — blowing up in their face. And that they did not even take aim but fired in the general direction of the enemy, usually too high. "It is a miracle", de Wailly asserted, "when the projectile...hits the closest target."[26]

Critics overlook the fact that off-the-shoulder shooting was observed during maneuvers, not combat. Despite his jibe about haystacks, Skertchly saw amazons shooting from the hip with their musket barrels pointed upward and explained plausibly that this was done "to prevent accidents".[27] With hundreds or thousands of comrades on the field, it made little sense to aim straight from the shoulder. And yet, even during maneuvers the amazons sometimes did just that. Fraser watched men drill, then women. The latter, he observed, "were very dexterous, with their muskets, generally firing from the shoulder, which the men do not."[28]

Bayol considered the lack of formal shooting instruction a serious flaw, a judgment echoed by other writers. He said

that soldiers instead had to learn how to load and shoot
from their companions.[29] This squares with an earlier statement by Wilmot that girls of 13 or 14 were attached to
amazon "companies" and learned their duties from them:
"They dance with them, sing with them, and live with
them, but do not go to war with them until they have
arrived at a certain age, and can handle a musket."[30] To
someone schooled in French military traditions like Bayol,
this informal kind of instruction might have appeared in-
adequate, but for an American with Minutemen, frontiers-
men, cowboys and assorted untutored gunslingers in his
heritage, the criticism carries little weight.

The idea that guns were not a decisive Dahomean weapon,
also traceable largely to Bayol and embraced by others, is
also not very convincing. European muskets were reaching
Dahomey through coastal middlemen even before the kingdom entered written history. According to a folk memory,
firearms became important during Wegbaja's reign in the
seventeenth century.[31] "Boath I and my predecessors", said
Agaja in 1726, "ware and are, gret admirers of fire armes,
and have allmost intirely left of [off] the use of bows and
arrows...[W]e think [no weapon] better than the gunn, and
a...cutlass, which wee make ourselves."[32] A year later Snelgrave
saw hundreds of Dahomean male soldiers armed only with
muskets, swords and shields.[33] And nearly all the earliest
references to female palace guards or soldiers mention muskets
or musketoons.

A long series of European visitors, spanning more than
a century, vouch for the shooting know-how of the black
warrioresses. Labarthe's 1776 source notes that the king's
armed female guards "perform shooting exercises with much
skill".[34] His 1777 source, as already mentioned, saw the women
form two lines and keep up "a general fire that was very
well executed".[35] Dalzel got the impression that palace women
were "trained to the use of arms".[36] Freeman thought that
"the brigade of women fired their muskets and blunderbusses
remarkably well."[37]

Duncan may have been the first European to attend a demonstration of marksmanship at Abomey. Gezo invited him to watch how his soldiers, male and female, "procured their food when in the bush". Sheep, goats, ducks, guinea fowl and chickens, all representing wild game, were tethered in front of a high clay wall. Warriors and warrioresses were lined up parallel to the wall at 70 yards' distance. Each was armed with a long musket, Danish or English, loaded with iron bullets. The women fired first. "I was certainly much surprised", said Duncan, "to see the certainty of their deadly aim...[V]ery few missed their object; and I did not observe one who fired wide of a man's body." The men's fire was even more accurate. "I believe that the whole of them", the Briton concluded, "were picked shots; but even if that were the case, the feat was astonishing, and would have done credit to our best riflemen."[38] Elsewhere he remarks that the amazons in general "seem to use the long Danish musket with as much ease as one of our grenadiers does his firelock".[39]

Wilmot, too, saw a shooting drill including both sexes, but in this case the women seem to have had the edge over the men. He had asked Glele "whether he ever practised his people in this way". The king said yes, and invited him to a demonstration outside Cana. Goats were staked out on mats under a mud wall about 10 feet high. Wilmot neglects to give the distance involved, but says the amazons "distinguished themselves by their good shots", every one of which "would have struck a man". Considering the quality of the flintlock guns, he comments, and of the iron ball, "which is jagged and fits loosely in the barrel", the performance of both sexes was "really astonishing".[40] Borghero saw a young amazon general who seemed to be "so well trained in the handling of arms that one would think they were an extension of her limbs".[41] A tradition recorded by Degbelo says that the women soldiers had several of their own shooting ranges on which to practice.[42]

One of the question marks about Dahomean military efficacy is how fast they could fire their flintlocks. As mentioned above, European and American soldiers were trained to get off three or four rounds a minute, with Frederick's Prussians managing five. And Foà claimed the Dahomean warrior needed fifty seconds to reload, the warrioress barely thirty, meaning only two rounds a minute. The evidence suggests he was underrating them.

Duncan says only that the amazons handled muskets with the ease of grenadiers "but not, of course, with the same quickness, as they are not trained to any particular exercise".[43] But Wilmot was so impressed with the shooting speed of the women soldiers he mentions it three times in his report. "They fully understand the use of the musket", he concludes, "and load and fire with remarkable rapidity."[44] Skertchly also saw amazons shooting "with considerable rapidity".[45] Neither would have made such comments if the women had fired only twice a minute.

Foà himself heard that the king personally saw to the amazons' military education, keeping them busy in the palace, "from morning to evening,...handling weapons and doing the most tiring drills".[46] A French contemporary, Adolphe Burdo, writes (1890) of "quite frequent...shooting exercises" that enabled Dahomey's regular army, including the women, "to acquire a really formidable precision".[47] After a firefight with women soldiers in 1892 (by which time, it is true, rapid-fire rifles had largely replaced flintlocks), a French lieutenant exclaimed to a Foreign Legionnaire: "I don't know who taught them military tactics, the handling of arms and shooting, but that one certainly didn't steal his money."[48]

Like the good career soldiers they were, the amazons took care of their guns – "great care" according to Forbes. Both male and female warriors, he said, polished the barrels of their flintlocks and, when not on duty, kept them in covers.[49] Skertchly made similar observations. The warrioresses, he wrote, kept all their guns and accessories "in splendid order", their muskets and blunderbusses "scrupulously clean". In court they were "constantly polishing their weapons".[50]

So much for Bayol's contention that Dahomeans did not "honor"firearms.

About training in the use of other weapons we know next to nothing. If Répin was including amazons when he said assegai throwers almost invariably hit a palm trunk at forty or fifty paces, they obviously would have had to practise. As already noted, Foà says they excelled at hand-to-hand with sword or club, and wielded knives "admirably", also implying practice.[51] He does assert that such combat was "the object of continual exercises", but offers no evidence.[52] Degbelo informants say training included fencing and archery.[53] It may also be that the miming of close-quarters action seen in some dances was a standard training technique.

Besides assault tactics and the use of weapons, the amazons were schooled by some means in parade-ground maneuvers. A good number of witnesses, beginning with Dalzel and his comment on their expert "evolutions", were struck by the discipline of their drills – and discipline clearly is a virtue instilled, not inborn. Reporting on a review of both male and female soldiers, Forbes writes: "Order and discipline were observable throughout,...no review could have gone off better. There was no delay, no awkwardness, no accident...; it was noble and extremely interesting." During the review, Gezo kept turning to Forbes's party "with an enquiring eye as the amazons went through their evolutions: he is justly proud of these female guards".[54]

Vallon watched female "evolutions of surprising regularity".[55] For Chaudoin, the women soldiers were "marvelous to contemplate", their bearing "as disciplined and as correct" as that of the men as they "lined up straight as a bowstring".[56] Foà conceded that for such a "barbarous" country the amazons had "marvelous discipline" and were "admirable at maneuvers. They form very straight lines; squads execute turns skillfully from a standing position, less so while on the march."[57]

PHYSICAL EDUCATION

The warrioresses seem to have received physical as well as military training. We have seen how observers were astounded by their speed in mock attacks; litheness, agility, dexterity and endurance were other qualities attributed to them. Duncan once watched as 600 amazons, after a ceremony, ran off at full speed with their flintlocks shouldered in a sort of race. It would surprise a European, he said, to see how fast they can go carrying not only a long Danish musket but also a short sword and a club.[58] Beecroft saw fifty women soldiers salute Gezo, and "display their strength of arm and agility of body", by running up to his tent with a musketoon held in one hand above their heads.[59] The amazons, Wilmot wagers, "would run with some of our best performers in England",[60] and he almost surely means men. Foà says "footracing" was part of their training but does not claim to have witnessed it.[61] Bayol says the same about "gymnastic exercises", again without actually seeing them.[62]

According to oral traditions collected by Degbelo, the amazons "practised almost all the sports current in Dahomey", including wrestling. Moonlit nights are said to have been favored for the one-on-one wrestling matches. A circle was marked off on the ground; a woman placed one foot forward and the other on the circumference, and defied her opponent to dislodge her.[63]

If we can believe traditions gathered eight decades after the French conquest, the amazons underwent an almost endless round of physical training. Awakened before dawn, they donned combat dress, hefted their arms and walked briskly or ran a long distance. They were accompanied by their officers who, it is said, selected the fastest women in these workouts as musketeers and the slower ones as archeresses.[64] The latter could join the first group if they increased their speed. Later in the day they might repair to a thorny obstacle course where they alternately crawled and sprinted, and learned to endure pain. Royal doctors bound up their wounds.

Glele is said to have been so impressed by one amazon's tolerance of acute pain that he genuinely married her.

Occasionally the women were sent into "thick forests" for periods of five to nine days "almost without provisions" to learn how "to support hunger, thirst, wounds and the presence of wild animals with equanimity". Trainers taught them how to avoid ambushes, and also to imitate certain bird calls that they would use as signals in combat.[65]

If contemporary European visitors never actually witnessed athletic training, what they all saw was the amazons dancing, and Bayol rightly surmised that it developed their strength.[66] Borghero thought this was the deliberate aim of military dances.[67] Ridgway watched the warrioresses dance strenuously with "much gesticulation" involving musket, sword and battle-axe, and "violent leaps".[68] Skertchly saw dancing male soldiers "performing every gymnastic exercise that could be imagined", and doubtless the females tried to outdo them.[69] Writing four decades after the demise of the women's army corps, Quénum transcribed a song "whose beat", he says "was accentuated by the amazons' somersaults and feats of strength and balance".[70] (Dancing was, to be sure, a morale builder as well as a body builder, and as such will be taken up in the next chapter.)

Incontestably the training regimen of the warrioresses produced sturdy physiques. Lopez professed to be revolted by "the Medusas" but admitted they were "generally well-built women".[71] Duncan found the amazons "generally fine strong healthy women".[72] Winniett called them "remarkably fine women, standing five feet eight, nine and ten" and none over the age of thirty-five.[73] According to Ridgway, "the greater number...were exceedingly finely formed".[74] Wilmot called them "a very fine body of women...very active in their movements, being remarkably well limbed and strong".[75]

As we have seen, Burton theorized that the amazons owed their organizational origins to their "masculine" build and even maintained that they were physically "superior" to the men. Freeman thought them the equal of men "in muscular strength". He cited their constant training but also observed that women "of the lower classes" in the region were unusually sturdy.[76] Jean Laffitte, a French missionary stationed at Whydah in 1861-4, was persuaded that "the heroines of Dahomey [have] broken completely with the delicacy of their sex". He credited this to an "education in keeping with the kind of life that awaits them". The amazons' bodies, he wrote, "used to the most violent exercises, acquire extraordinary litheness and strength; accustomed from a young age to the hardest privations, they endure hunger and thirst with admirable steadfastness."[77] A French ship's captain and gunpowder merchant named Buzon who visited Abomey in 1874 found almost all amazon faces "bestial", which spoiled their "generally well proportioned bodies".[78] A few years later Ellis illegally peeked at a party of fifteen or twenty women soldiers on a road and thought "all...looked wiry and muscular".[79]

Testimony to amazon robustness piles up during the Franco-Dahomean wars. For Chaudoin, they were "as solidly muscled as the black male warriors";[80] for Foà, of "mannish" appearance and "superior muscular strength";[81] for Foreign Legionnaire J. Bern, "well formed and solidly built".[82] Four decades after the fighting, the French general Fénelon-François-Germain Passaga, a hero of Verdun, reminisced about the amazons he had fought as a young lieutenant with a Senegalese company. One day he and his men surprised three women soldiers and shot them dead. "[T]wo...seemed very young, 14 or 15 years old; they were very beautiful, strongly muscled, but finely too; the third was old, her face crossed with scars, she must have led a squad."[83] (Passaga also remembered stripping red shorts off the bodies, presumably as souvenirs.[84])

It should not be imagined, however, that all women soldiers had athletic silhouettes. Among participants in the mock attack that Bouët witnessed were some amazons of twenty-six or twenty-eight who "had lost their sylphlike waists [and] acquired...a rather voluminous corpulence. So when they wanted to leap across the palisade in a. single bound, the vigor of their spring did not make up for their weight, and they fell on one side or the other in unsoldierlike postures."[85] "As a rule", Burton writes with his presumptuous air of authority, "the warrioresses begin to fatten when their dancing days are passed, and some of them are prodigies of obesity."[86] It may be doubted, though, that their dancing days ever passed. Burton himself describes "a middle-aged officeress, stout as the most 'bulbous' Englishwoman, and round in every part where curves should be", who performed a knife dance.[87] He depicts another amazon officer as "a huge old porpoise", and a third as "vast in breadth".[88] When he saw the amazon army off on a campaign, he noted the officers "were mostly remarkable for a stupendous steatopyga [excessive fat on and around the buttocks], and for a development of adipose tissue which suggested anything but ancient virginity – man does not readily believe in fat 'old maids'."[89] In a procession of dancing amazons, Skertchly saw "fat officeresses cutting a ludicrous figure as they waddled along".[90]

Le Hérissé met several surviving amazons who had gone on to motherhood. Far from lacking a breast as in the classical myth, he reported, they "exposed charms that many a French wet-nurse might covet".[91]

INSENSITIVITY TRAINING

If, in their ordeals by thornbush, the amazons were taught to shrug off physical pain, they also seem to to have received training in what might be called psychic insensitivity. This would explain, for example, their occasional role as executioners.[92] At Abomey in 1779, Abson watched as King Kpengla handed cutlasses to five of "his women". They had to behead five other women who had been captured in war, taken into the palace and allegedly treated as royal wives, and had then committed the crime of escaping. The executioners were so inept that the king stepped in and showed them how to do it. There is no evidence, however, that they were amazons, and Abson's description of them as "fat and over-grown" suggests otherwise while not ruling out the possibility.[93]

In 1830 Conneau was told that amazons accused of adultery or cowardice were tried by their peers and if found guilty executed by them.[94] At the annual customs in 1850, Beecroft and Forbes saw four amazons take part in a traditional ceremony – described many times in the literature – in which sacrificial victims were executed by the Abomey mob. Trussed up and gagged, the prisoners were carried in baskets or wooden mini-canoes on to a platform 12 to 16 feet high and then thrown down alive to the people. In this case, four of the victims, all men, had been captured by the amazons in the second Atakpamé war (chapter 16) and the women were given the honor of sliding them to their doom by tilting the baskets.[95]

Burton heard that female criminals were executed out of men's sight, within the palace, by amazon officers, and that under Glele there were as many as forty such executions during the annual customs.[96] Skertchly saw a high amazon officer tell in public how she had decapitated three persons the night before. He also watched as amazons led two women prisoners to the place of execution, but both received last-minute reprieves.[97] Chaudoin glibly averred that the best training exercise for both male and female soldiers was lopping off the heads of sacrificial victims with one deft machete blow.[98]

A French delegation in Abomey in December 1889 saw an amazon recruit, a "ravishing" girl named Nansica, "who had not yet killed anyone", being put to the test. We have two accounts of her performance, with details varying. The victim was a trussed-up "vigorous" man seated in a basket, the usual mode for human sacrifices at the royal customs. Nansica reportedly walked jauntily up to the victim, swung her sword three times with both hands, then calmly cut the last flesh that attached the head to the trunk. One witness claims she then squeezed the blood off her weapon and swallowed it. The other says that "seized with a sort of delirium", she waved her bloody sword before the crowd, and her fellow amazons resumed their "furious" dancing.[99] Less than three months later, Nansica was killed fighting the French.

A bizarre amazon ritual seen by the same French delegation in 1889 and then by a group of French hostages the following year may also have been designed to desensitize the war-rioresses. Chaudoin dubbed it the "Fête of the Ox". A small native ox weighing about 200 kilograms (440 pounds) was led into the midst of an amazon unit. The women surrounded it, and closed ranks so that it could no longer be seen by spectators. Uttering wild cries, they then attacked it with their bare hands and presumably knives, disemboweling it, skinning it, tearing it to pieces and eating it raw, even the entrails, their faces smeared with blood. All this, said the French, took less time than it did to butcher a sheep in a European abattoir.[100]

A few observers were so impressed with the military and physical training of Dahomey's regular troops, men and women, that they rated them the best in tropical Africa. In the early nineteenth century a British traveler, George A. Robertson, saw a review of nearly 5,000 male warriors outside Whydah and judged "their system of military discipline...better than any which [he had] seen in Africa".[101] Duncan ranked the female soldiers above the male, then added: "From all I have seen of Africa, I believe the King of Dahomey possesses an army superior to any sovereign west [south?] of the Great Desert."[102] Forbes believed Dahomey's troops had made it the "most powerful monarchy in Western Africa".[103] Bouët thought that if French officers were ever brought in to train Gezo's army "in European fashion," one could, "with a people as warlike as that of Dahomey, conquer all of Africa, and repeat, I could almost guarantee it, the history of *Alexander the Great.*"[104]

Against the background of the ongoing partition of Africa by European powers, Bern suggested that the conflict with

Dahomey was the first in which France had met such resistance in its wars against the blacks.

The reason is that the army of the king of Dahomey, at least the permanent part..., has for a long time been trained to the roughest toil, familiarized with every suffering, made ready for every audacity. This special training is certainly an exception in Africa, where no other army of a black monarch that may have to fight Europeans is prepared for war in this way.[105]

13

BUILDING ESPRIT DE CORPS

DANCE, SONG AND MUSIC MAKING

Amazon morale was built in many ways, probably none as important as dancing, singing and playing music. To this day dancing is a ubiquitous pastime in Black Africa, the principal form of entertainment. In Dahomey it was a duty. Forbes observed that both male and female soldiers were required to be proficient dancers.[1] According to an amazon song fragment transcribed by Skertchly, the women felt that if they were not good dancers they would disgrace the king;[2] if so, they seem never to have failed him, although the same author heard that male soldiers were fined and imprisoned for throwing their guns in the air while dancing and not catching them.[3] Vallon remarked that "in every Dahomean military gathering, no move is made without singing and dancing, before, during and after the exercise."[4] And Borghero, who marveled that even marchers danced rather than walked, ventured that nothing important was done in the kingdom without military dances.[5]

The martial character of the dances was self-evident: the amazons (and male soldiers) used their weapons as props. Muskets were not only thrown in the air and caught but held aloft or waved like clubs or struck against each other. Forbes saw a circle of dancing amazons, each holding her musket muzzle to her neighbor's head.[6] Skertchly watched male soldiers "catch hold of their gun by the butt and muzzle and leap over it, bringing the weapon up behind the back, after which they would extend the gun vertically and pirouette on one foot".[7] Doubtless their female comrades could

106

do the same. Dancers sometimes paused to load and fire their muskets, singing all the while. Swords and daggers were drawn, clubs and battle-axes and super-razors brandished, bayonets thrust, shields wielded, bows and arrows and quivers flourished.

Amazon dancers simulated attacks on the enemy and hand-to-hand combat. One of their favorite routines mimicked beheadings. As Forbes describes it, "the right hand is working in a sawlike manner for some time, as if in the act of cutting round the neck, when both hands are used, and a twist is supposed to finish the bloody deed."[8]

The women sang as they danced, or between dances, and their songs spoke of war: their willingness to die for their king, their eagerness to do battle, their superiority over men fighters, their own prowess and valor, the sin of cowardice, past and future victories, and so on (we take a closer look at these songs later).

Dancers provided some music of their own with little iron bells attached to their persons – high officers are said to have worn silver ones – and sometimes rattles to shake, but every amazon unit had its own band. In a review of 2,408 women soldiers, Forbes counted 252 musicians.[9]

The basic musical instrument was the drum, which came in various sizes and shapes. Most were made of hollowed-out tree trunks, either cylindrical or conical. One or both ends were covered with animal skins, kept taut by thongs attached to pegs fixed down the sides. Sheep, doe and bullock skins are mentioned, but goatskins seem to have been preferred. Some of these instruments were giant, booming war-drums, up to 2 meters long by a meter in diameter (Bouët gauged the king's own war-drum at nearly 3 meters long).[10] They were adorned with enemy skulls; Duncan sighted one wreathed with twelve crania.[11] At least some of these big ones were sculpted: Burton saw bayonet women escorting a drum "rudely carved with native figures".[12] The larger amazon drums were carried crosswise on a woman's head

—a slavewoman's, presumably—and beaten by a musician walking closely behind.

Another type of drum was made of two calabashes attached back to back in the form of an eggcup. The skin drumhead was fastened by thongs to the open end. The drummer held it under his left arm and could vary the note by squeezing or relaxing the thongs with his arm. Both this so-called pressure drum and those made of tree trunks were beaten with either crooked sticks or bare hands.[13]

Forbes and Beecroft saw brass drums that the former identified as English-made.[14] Burton reported "kettledrums",[15] which may have been the same instruments. Despite Africans' virtuosity as drum makers and players, or perhaps because of it (i.e. professional appreciation of exotic versions), drums figured among European trade goods. Bouët saw some in Abomey of obviously French origin painted with the tricolor. He also saw French tambourines and two European barrel-organs.[16] Forbes and Beecroft spotted English tambourines.[17]

Horns, sometimes called trumpets, were another basic instrument. Often they were made of elephant tusks with a blowing hole near the small end. Ox and bullock horns were also used.[18] Forbes and Beecroft saw long brass trumpets[19] and Bouët 4-foot-long copper trumpets,[20] both of which may have been of European origin.

The flute, called variously reed or bamboo and perhaps more precisely a fife, was among the earliest musical instruments reported. Dalzel (1793) thought it the only one in Dahomey worthy of praise: "Though the most simple that can be imagined, being open at both extremities, with a little notch at the mouth end, where it is scraped thin, to divide the wind, [it] produces very agreeable notes."[21] Metal flutes may have been a late European contribution.[22] Forbes saw girls in a procession playing "long-mouthed instruments, like clarionets", but gave no further details.[23] Beecroft and Bouët mention whistles.[24]

Rattles were another common instrument. They consisted of long-necked calabashes covered with a net. Noise-makers were tied to the knots in the mesh. Cowries, human teeth and sheep vertebrae are mentioned in the literature, but the main noise maker was clearly snake vertebrae. Beecroft thought that the calabashes contained peas or small pebbles,[25] Skertchly stones or cowries;[26] other authors say they were empty. The rattles were both shaken and struck with a little wooden paddle.

The only other important instrument was the iron gong or gong-gong, sometimes compared to a cow or sheep bell and called by Burton a cymbal. Skertchly tells us it was composed of "two gauntlet-shaped bells of different sizes, the one being soldered to the other at an angle of about thirty-five degrees, and the whole fixed to a wooden or iron handle, often carved into the resemblance of a man's fist." [27] Some gong-gongs had only one bell, some more than two. They were struck with an iron rod about a foot long.

Dahomey also had stringed instruments – one likened to a mandolin, another to a lyre – but they were not used by military bands. Totally absent from the records is the balaphon, the xylophone with calabash resonators played in other parts of West Africa.

Besides instruments, the amazons used their hands to produce sound, rhythmically clapping or slapping their thighs and buttocks. They also used their mouths, punctuating dances with war-cries.

Dahomey's military music was, therefore, overwhelmingly percussion, with only the flute able to play a tune which, as Répin remarked, might be inaudible in the general din.[28] To European ears, the music was sheer cacophony. For Duncan, it was "barbarous", Bouët "dreadful", Borghero "a horrible racket". It "made up in noise", commented Ridgway, "what it wanted in melody." Répin thought the musicians all strove "to prove the strength of their breath or arm". Skertchly was "tortured" by the sound. Laffitte joked that the noise produced by a Dahomean band "could make the boilermakers of Auvergne swoon".[29]

Clearly the purpose of the bands was to provide tempo

not melody. "Rhythm is...the sole element of Dahomean orchestration", Quénum observed in the 1930s,[30] and that was no less true in the days of the kingdom. The amazons danced to music but did not generally sing to it since they risked being drowned out.

Both dancing and singing were often led by women specialists, who seem to have rehearsed the warrioresses beforehand. "After singing the opening phrase of the appropriate song", Vallon noted, "and giving an example of the step to be executed, [the] directors, horsetail in hand, set the measure and cadence."[31] Once he saw them move briskly along the front rank of some 4,000 amazons, "performing numerous contortions". Then, "little by little, a dance almost in place, three steps to the right, three to the left, accompanied by a monotonous song, set the whole female army in motion."[32] Burton watched as two "mistresses of the ceremonies, armed with horsetail chauris, chanted and sometimes pranced to give time" to an amazon troupe.[33] Skertchly, too, saw song-leaders waving their horsetails "in time to the tune".[34]

Frequently a solo singer or dancer would step out from amazon formations and perform. "Sometimes one woman only would dance," says Ridgway, "sometimes three or four, and occasionally more than a dozen would rush from their ranks."[35] Forbes heard one amazon sing to King Gezo in verse, "whilst the chorus was taken up by all".[36] Another performed "a *pas seul*, screeching wildly", followed by six who did a spear dance, twenty a sword dance and twelve a musket dance.[37] Burton watched "a grand *pas de deux*" that followed a mass amazon dance.[38] Describing military dances in general, Borghero wrote: "[N]ow it's a single actor on stage, now two, now a greater number; finally, it's a general swirl."[39]

On the quality of the singing and dancing, European observers were divided. Dalzel, the earliest commentator, apparently referring to the amazons, was impressed by the ability of "the King's women" to harmonize. They "understand and practise the combination of perfect concords, thirds and fifths", he wrote, "and their little airs are not inelegant."[40] Ridgway heard the amazons sing "with much energy".[41] Forbes believed all singing, male and female, was practised before public performances and was "well considered". He thought amazons practiced in the Kangbodé's compound. On an early-morning walk, he and Beecroft surprised a group of about forty of the Meu's entourage rehearsing songs in a secluded field. They were sure the songs would be performed before the king as supposedly extemporaneous pieces.[42] At a public event, one soldier-songstress made Beecroft think of Jenny Lind, the great contemporary Swedish soprano.[43] Burton, too, was certain that songs were diligently rehearsed. "I rarely passed a palace when the King was out", he remarked, "without hearing a loud singing lesson within."[44] He listened to amazon "dirges in the minor key" and songs "in chorus and in solo". Burton rated the women "indefatigable singers", and if he withheld praise his critical silence can almost be taken as a compliment.[45]

Dancing drew much more comment for and against. Ridgway perceived "much gesticulation...and violent leaps, but...could not trace any particular figure".[46] More acutely, Borghero said at first that the "contortions, stompings, caperings of all kinds" look like "complete disorder, but by the end you recognize an admirable plan, which develops successively in calculated stages, with a design understood by all, and executed seriously despite an appearance of great lightheartedness...[It] is always combined with songs, yells, even howls."[47]

Burton took pains to describe amazon dancing but judged it harshly:

The dancers stamped, wriggled, kicked the dust with one foot, sang, shuffled, and wrung their hands – there is ever a suspicion of beheading in these performances – bending almost double, ducking heads, moving sideways to right and left, fronting and facing everywhere, especially presenting the back, converting forefingers into *strigils* [scrapers], working the arms as in Mediterranean swimming, and ending in a prestissimo and very violent movement of the shoulders, hips, and loins...The whole merits of the ballet were time and unison: nothing could be less graceful or more deficient in the poetry of motion.[48]

Elsewhere the English traveler taxed the women soldiers with agitating their "shoulder-blades and posteriors...to excess".[49]

As he often did, Skertchly rivaled Burton in detail...and distaste. At the end of a song, he wrote, the amazons began their dance:

Standing in line, one behind the other, they performed a series of hops to the right and left; at every tenth movement jerking their bodies to the front and rear, and finishing the figure with a hop and a twist round, so as to bring themselves to the right about. A similar set was then performed with their faces pointing in the opposite direction, and the dance concluded with a march round and a kind of swimming motion of their hands, followed by a violent jerking of the shoulders to the rear, until the elbows met behind the back.[50]

Of another amazon dance, Skertchly wrote: "[B]allet-girl twirlings were attempted, with every possible antic that a party of escaped lunatics, who were afflicted with chronic St. Vitus' dance, could be expected to go through."[51] He *was* impressed with the women's stamina, describing one performance as "three hours of...violent exercise". However, there was, "very little to admire in the display, except the gymnastic and salutary influences induced by it; the whole idea seeming to be to keep perfect unison in the most corybantic [frenzied] actions."[52]

It would seem that in general French visitors were more appreciative than the British of the amazons' dancing skills, perhaps because they came with different aesthetic preconceptions. Their reaction was all the more remarkable in that they shared with the British a sense of cultural and racial superiority. Répin, for example, was rhapsodic about the youngest group of female soldiers, the teenaged archeresses:

The young amazons, armed with bows,...lined up in front of us, and, led by one of the youngest and prettiest of them, performed, singing, a martial dance, holding their bow in one hand and an arrow in the other. There is nothing more graceful than the slow and rhythmic movements of these pretty children guided by a sweet and monotonic song, which reminded us of old Breton airs. These were no longer the black children of Dahomey; they were the beautiful girls of ancient Greece, or of voluptuous Asia, who delighted our eyes: one must have danced like that at the fetes of Diana, or at the court of the Persian satraps. Many times I had seen the dances and heard the songs of various negro tribes..., but I had never encountered anything comparable, even remotely, to what we were seeing. We were...surprised and enchanted.[53]

Répin's fellow witness, Vallon, was charmed as well. The girls reminded him of the ballets of small French theaters. "In their light and bright costumes, with their painted legs and their confident air", they elicited applause at will. "We couldn't believe we were in Dahomey; even long study could not produce dancers more graceful or nimble."[54]

At times the king himself joined the amazons in dance or music making, to the delectation of all. Forbes and Beecroft saw the warrioresses sing Gezo's praises and then call on the elderly monarch "to come out and dance with them, and they did not call in vain".[55] Burton watched Glele do "a simple morris" – a strenuous English dance – "before a semi-circle of armed women, who were chanting and cheering him lustily."[56] On five different occasions Skertchly saw Glele take part in amazon performances. Once he took up a set of drumsticks and accompanied three female drummers. Another time he performed the first figure of each of twenty-seven different dances, "then calling upon one of the Amazonian captainesses to finish it for him". In the midst of one mass amazon choreography, he suddenly "stalked into the dancing throng, and began to follow their movements", which set off a spate of celebratory gunfire and shouting of his "strong names" (the nicknames kings were given for each great deed).[57]

WHAT THEY SANG

The special, almost symbiotic relationship between the

amazons and their king was a frequent theme of their songs (and speeches). A modern historian, Boniface I. Obichere, has aptly remarked that the sovereign was "the supreme force of their lives".[58] In a song recorded by Forbes, amazons credited Gezo with their rebirth as men instead of women, while at the same time inconsistently calling themselves his wives and daughters. They were also his sandals – an apparent allusion to a Dahomean rule that only the king could be shod – and, by implication, they were also the road he trod to victory.[59] Another song emphasized that Gezo clothed and fed them.[60] Forbes heard an amazon orator describe the women as the king's fingers.[61]

Amazon songs heaped praise on the monarch and pledged unshakable loyalty, absolute obedience and the defeat of his enemies. Duncan listened to a "regiment" sing a song of compliments to Gezo, then warrioresses stepped to the front one by one to declare their fidelity.[62] In a dance seen by Ridgway, the women begged the king to send them to war so that they could encrust their clean sword-blades with the blood of their foes and thus gain him honor.[63] Forbes watched the amazon army point to the sky and sing: "May thunder and lightning kill us if we break our oaths", which obviously included that of loyalty.[64] On another occasion he heard women soldiers sing:

> Gezo is the king of kings!
> While Gezo lives we have nothing to fear.
> Under him we are lions, not men.[65]

Beecroft heard them sing of themselves as slaves of the monarch, who was their sole leader and protector, their power, the only person they cared for, and who met their every need.[66] The adolescent girls who entranced Vallon and Répin ended their dance by shaking their quivers and arrows in front of the king and promising to be "faithful and devoted guards of his person".[67] An amazon "victory hymn", written down by Bayol, addressed the king as "master of the universe" and "our God".[68] After singing such songs, the amazons would sometimes kneel before their monarch, scoop up the red dust around them and cover themselves with it – an obligatory ritual of self-abasement for even the highest male officials when approaching the king of Dahomey.

Another favorite theme of amazon songs was the women's rivalry with and superiority over male warriors. It made good psychological sense for kings to encourage competition between the sexes in their armed forces. We do not know if it originated in a conscious decision, but there is no doubt that rulers came to appreciate the advantage in such rivalry, particularly in building female *esprit de corps*, and promoted it. Wittingly or not, they almost surely tapped a deep well of hitherto suppressed or unexpressed female resentment at male domination. And in vague references to amazon "jealousy" there is a suspicion that penis-envy may also have played a role.

It was clear to Forbes in 1849 that "what the males do, the amazons will endeavour to surpass".[69] The following year, after watching male and female troops perform identical moving-and-shooting exercises, Beecroft credited the amazons with "much more uniformity".[70] In 1861, to the intense delight of an amazon audience, Borghero exclaimed "that to possess an army of warrioresses whose valor was recognized as quite superior to that of the men, was a privilege exclusively reserved to the king of Dahomey."[71] And for Wilmot in 1862-3, the women were already "far superior to the men in everything – in appearance, in dress, in figure, in activity, in their performance as soldiers, and in bravery".[72] Other visitors found them more warlike, more disciplined, better marchers, better shooters, more fearless. "[I]f undertaking a campaign", said Duncan, "I should prefer the females to the male soldiers" of Dahomey.[73] And when a House of Lords committeeman asked Winniett: "Do they fight better than the men?", he replied "Very much".[74]

Since very few Europeans actually saw the amazons in combat before the Franco-Dahomean wars of 1890 and 1892, such assessments of their fighting abilities were necessarily based on their public performances on the parade ground and obstacle course, and on what European visitors were told by their (mostly male) informants, including the king himself. These judgments may also have been influenced by the amazons' own songs, speeches and swagger. In one song reproduced by several authors, they tell their male counterparts to stay home and grow maize and palm trees while they go off to war to plow the enemy's guts.[75] In another they tell them to harvest cassava roots while the amazons dig up their own hearts, an apparent metaphor for a fight to the death.[76] In still another they scold allegedly cowardly men: "If soldiers go to war, they should conquer or die."[77] In public discussions they taunted the male warriors. Skertchly heard amazons belittle the men as "sheep, vultures, and similar epithets".[78] On another occasion, as candidates for the post of male commander-in-chief (the Gau) were announcing their qualifications, the women broke in to say "they would have to come to them before they could learn the proper way to fight".[79]

Borghero watched a three-hour "epic poem" acted out by ten singers celebrating the exploits of Gezo and Glele. When the honor of a particular victory was attributed to the male part of the army, women spectators "got up furious to complain to the king", and vice versa. "Amid this uproar the singers stopped and the scene took on a stormy intensity, an indescribable animation, of thousands of persons arguing with loud cries, with the most expressive gestures." The king listened calmly, then when he "had amused himself enough with this verbal battle, he made a sign, and instantly, on a drumbeat, everything returned to order."[80]

One might expect that in thus belligerently asserting themselves and besting the men at their own game, the amazons would exalt their own womanhood. But when they sang praise of Gezo for their "rebirth" as men, or for turning them from men into lions, they were not joking. They in fact saw themselves as basically transformed.

In her book on warrior queens cited in the Introduction,

Antonia Fraser tells us that such women have commonly considered themselves "honorary males".[81] The amazons of Dahomey carried that much further. By equaling or surpassing men in the arts of war, they felt not that they had proved themselves as females but that they had qualified as males. Forbes was the first to report this extraordinary claim, which he heard several times from the amazons' own mouths. A woman officer proclaimed: "As the blacksmith takes an iron bar and by fire changes its fashion, so we have changed our nature. We are no longer women, we are men." Other amazons sang a similar refrain.[82] Forbes suggests they could not have gotten away with such statements unless they were "fundamentally true" in the sense that the women had successfully emulated "the most daring acts and achievements" of the men.[83]

An amazon song that has come down to us orally contains the lines

We are men, not women...
Whatever town we attack
We must conquer,
Or bury ourselves in its ruins.[84]

Another exhorts

Let us march in a virile manner,
Let us march boldly, like men.[85]

This masculine self-image may account for reports that when amazons were captured, they preferred to be killed rather than marry an enemy.

An early-twentieth-century Dahomean ethnologist, Paul Hazoumé, recorded the memoirs of an amazon named Tata Ajachê who had disemboweled an enemy farmer with his own hoe. She recalls that when she returned from the war a heroine, people praised her by shouting, "You are a man!", which meant that from then on she would be esteemed.[86]

Qualifying as males meant being strong, brave, resolute, fearless, disciplined, loyal, reliable – virtues that females were supposed to lack. In becoming men, the amazons adopted their stereotypical views of women. Forbes heard the female soldiers sing about a victory over the men of Atakpamé, in modern Togo northwest of Abomey:

> We march'd against Attahpahms as against men,
> We came and found them women.[87]

Burton says that to insult a male warrior who had disgraced himself, the amazons called him a woman.[88] Skertchly agrees that one way they taunted the men was to tell them they were women.[89] When they sang that the male soldiers should stay home and raise crops, they were looking down on farming as women's (or slaves') work.

For Burton, the amazons' insistence they were men betrayed the reality that while women were "officially superior" in Dahomey, they still suffered from "male arrogance". And while kings seem to have been loath to discourage the amazons' illusion of sex change, Burton says that Glele "repeatedly" told him "that a woman is still a woman".[90]

The amazons' songs and speeches were suffused with braggadocio, and they were commonly seen to strut like the élite troops they were. In 1850, a year before the first big Dahomean attack on Abeokuta, Forbes and Beecroft heard a long series of amazon orators, both officers and ordinary soldiers, vow to conquer the Yoruba city or die. Their themes were few, and often reiterated: war is good; let's go fight; send us against the strongest foes; we'll never retreat; anyone who does should be executed or die from smallpox or be destroyed by the thunder god; we have proved that we are great warriors; we will demolish Abeokuta and thrash the Yoruba.

One officer said that the Dahomean army without the amazons was as useless as a cask of rum with no one to roll it, or a table with nothing on it. A rank-and-file amazon vowed that the women would break any enemy as a dog breaks a bone. A group sang that if any country insulted their king by word or deed, he had only to issue orders and they would soon go and destroy the place. One flourished a knife newly issued by the king and said that she would perform a feat with it in the next war to please him. Another displayed a basket and pledged to fill it with enemy heads for him. One female orator admitted that "originally the amazons were not relied upon: now they are the most useful of troops." Some bragged that forty Dahomeans (apparently male or female) were equal to 1,000 other Africans. A female "colonel" pledged to pursue the Abeokutans even if they ran into water or fire, or up trees. Another amazon swore they would be cut down as grass was cleared from a road. Between speeches, the warrioresses sang

> *The amazons are ready to die in war:*
> *Now is the time to send them.*

And on another occasion, female officers chorused

> *With these guns in our hands*
> *And powder in our cartouch-boxes,*
> *What has the king to fear?*
> *When we go to war, let the king dance,*
> *While we bring him prisoners and heads.*[91]

Some thirteen years later, before the second major assault on Abeokuta in 1864, Wilmot and Burton heard similar boasts. In the former's presence amazons sang "they were ready for war, suiting the action to the word by going through the motions of cutting off heads."[92] "These women," Wilmot observed, "seem to be fully aware of the authority they possess, which is seen in their bold and free manner, as well as by a certain swagger in their walk."[93] Burton watched a "captainess" step forward "with the usual affected military swagger", make "a violent speech", cut off the head of an imaginary corpse, and declare: "Thus would they treat Abeokuta!"[94] Blunderbuss women then chanted

> *We like not to hear that Abeokuta lives;*
> *But soon we shall see it fall.*[95]

Another day he saw women, who were receiving rewards for bravery, "make short speeches with a pert air, and [strike] their bosoms as to say 'I am the woman to do it – I.' At times a dozen or so stood up, sang, and raised one or both arms, the forefinger as usual being extended, thus swearing to brave deeds before the King."[96]

Skertchly remarks that even the young archeresses, though "mostly used as a show corps", were "as boastful as any of the veterans".[97] Foà describes the amazon army as "proud and haughty from the favor it enjoyed" and "extravagantly fanatical".[98]

The four following amazon songs that survived the demise of the kingdom may give us the flavor of them all. The first was recorded by Le Hérissé, the next two by Maurice Ahanhanzo Glélé, a direct descendant of King Glele, and the last by a Dahomean scholar, Alexandre Adandé. They are translated here from the French.

> *If one day we meet*
> *An audacious army,*
> *We'll fear nothing;*
> *We'll be invincible;*
> *We'll resemble the buffalo*
> *Who knows his way*
> *In the midst of sheep!*
> *Yes! Yes! Yes!*
> *We'll take our guns to kill them!*
> *We'll take our swords to kill them!*
> *How loud our footsteps!*
> *You'll all die together!*
> *We'll take our guns to kill them!*
> *Blood flows in torrents,*
> *Your heads are cut off!*
> *How loud our footsteps!*
> *You'll all die together!*[99]

> ★ ★ ★ ★

> *Arise amazons,*
> *Arise soldiers of Glele,*
> *The powerful king of Abomey.*
> *The cold and dry north wind*
> *Has reached into the palace of Glele,*

The powerful king of Abomey.
Yes, the harmattan is cracking
The wood of our bows,
The tensed cord is ready to break.
The marshes and rivers have dried up,
Opening the way to combat and victory
For the fearless amazons.
Arise amazons.
We need slaves to turn the soil
Of Dahomey, victims to sacrifice
On the tomb of the kings of Abomey,
And blood, waves of blood
On which will sail
On the day of his triumph
The bark of our king,
Of our powerful Glele. [100]

(On a campaign by Glele against Dassa in a rocky region of northeastern Dahomey:)

Knife between teeth,
We'll scale the rocks.
We'll drive those warthogs
Out of their hole,
For our body is better armed
Than the porcupine's.
And if we no longer had ax,
Or arrow, or dagger to defend us,
Don't we have our filed teeth
Ready to bite and tear,
And our hard fingers stronger
Than iron claws? [101]

(The reference to filed teeth is the only one this author has seen for the Fon, although the amazons did bite enemies on occasion; conceivably it was a bluff to frighten the foe.)
And a final example:

We are created to defend Dahomey,
This pot of honey, object of desire.
Can the country where so much courage blooms
Surrender its riches to strangers?

As long as we live, any people would be mad
To try to impose its law on Dahomey.[102]

SYMBOLS AND REWARDS

As in all military organizations, amazon morale was boosted by symbols to rally around and rewards for achievement, categories that overlapped. From the very beginning, it would seem, the warrioresses had their own flags and banners which they carried on parade and into battle. Even the women who reportedly no more than padded Agaja's army in 1729 hoisted "Colours", apparently a different one for each "Company".[103] The armed female marchers seen by Pruneau carried silk flags.[104] By 1772 Dahomey was flying European flags obtained from white traders or officials: two Union Jacks preceded each of seven "troops" of women who paraded past Norris.[105] Over the years French, Portuguese, Spanish, German, Dutch, Italian and American flags, as well as English ones, were seen at Abomey. Some were homemade imitations. Half a century before the French conquest, Freeman saw Dahomean soldiers carrying the tricolor.[106] And in 1851 Gezo asked Bouët to relay a request to Louis Napoleon for many French flags "because he claims that it is the kind he has least of".[107]

The typical amazon flag, however, was of local manufacture and consisted of brightly colored images appliquéd on white cloth. Each unit had its own banner; as Burton remarked, "an armorist could tell the troops from the flag".[108] Skertchly describes half-a-dozen amazon standards, one emblazoned with a blue alligator, another with a scarlet shark, a third with scarlet zigzags "like a handful of Jupiter's lightning". Exceptionally a white tree with a blazing top was sewn on to blue cloth. Skertchly says blunderbuss women carried banners "of the most ferocious description", one showing "a man cutting an enemy to mincemeat" and another in which he blows the enemy "to fragments by a single discharge of his musket".[109] It may be supposed that the Englishman mistook depictions of female soldiers for males. Decapitation seems to have been a favorite theme of Dahomean flags, and flagstaffs were often topped with enemy skulls.

Certain amazons were designated as bannerwomen. Forbes counted twenty-seven in the review of 2,408 women soldiers; on another occasion he saw forty.[110] During an amazon parade that he watched, some flag-bearers stepped forward and declared: "These standards are in our charge: we swear to protect them or die."[111] Flags that had been through battle were especially cherished. Vallon saw several flying that were in tatters. These, he said, "attest to tough fighting in the bush and are preserved with religious care".[112]

Amazon detachments moved with umbrellas aloft as well as banners, but whereas the latter represented the unit, the former distinguished its officers. As a status symbol the umbrella goes back at least to 1200 BC in Egypt; it had crossed the Sahara to the royal court of old Mali by the fourteenth century, and reached Dahomey by the early eighteenth. The women officers of Agaja's crypto-amazons already had umbrellas;[113] doubtless they also had women servants or slaves to hold up the poles. French visitors to Abomey in 1776 observed that "One has to be at least an Army Captain to have the right to use a parasol."[114]

Dahomey's state umbrellas were giant affairs with multicolored canopies, some flat and quadrangular, often composed of costly fabrics obtained from Europeans. Figures were appliquéd on the lappets of scalloped valances. Burton said diameters varied from 6 to 10 feet, and that the poles were seven feet long.[115] Brue claims to have seen a royal umbrella with a radius of about 5 meters.[116] The umbrellas of amazon officers were more modest. Burton saw ragged white ones shading "chieftainesses of the she soldiers"; their condition suggests they had seen war duty.[117] A woman official he identified as the amazon "storekeeper" had a red parasol.[118] Skertchly saw a "captainess" striding under an umbrella bearing green squares on a white valance.[119] Burton says a newly-appointed chief received a "virgin-white" umbrella from the palace and was "expected to illustrate it by his actions". Often this took the form of cloth figures of knives and severed heads sewn to the lappets.[120] It seems likely that high amazon officers shared this privilege and obligation.

Rank-and-file amazons appear to have had ordinary umbrellas to protect them from the sun: recall Burton's observation that plaited palm-leaf models were taken on campaigns.[121] As we know, he also saw the warrioresses carrying tiny stools made from single blocks of wood,[122] and Skertchly confirms that male soldiers were similarly equipped.[123] But larger, carved stools were another perquisite of high status. Ridgway remarked that "no chief ever moves without his stool, by the height of which you may tell his rank, for these stools are the Dahoman order of the Bath, and are received from the king himself."[124] Female officers clearly had them: Forbes twice saw women parading with skull-adorned "war stools", three "covered with crimson and silver-velvet cloth".[125] A post-conquest French source describes the status-symbol stool as of yellow wood, decorated at times with "very bizarre designs", up to a meter high for the greatest chiefs, and made only at Abomey.[126]

Big drums were not only musical instruments but military icons. Courdioux wrote that on the Slave Coast generally, drums were "respected to the point of being worshiped".[127] In Dahomey, according to Forbes, drums, "ornamented with one or two dozen skulls, interlaced with jaw bones, [exemplified] the pride, pomp, and circumstance of glorious war."[128] Each army unit, including those of the amazons, seems to have had its own fetish drum.

Another distinctive emblem, both of high officers and individual military units, was the wooden baton known to specialists as a *récade*. Sometimes referred to in the literature as a club or an axe, it more closely resembled a tomahawk. The récade was less than two feet long with a bent head that was either sculpted or to which an ornamental iron, copper or even silver blade was attached. The carvings or metal castings represented the officer's coat of arms or the unit's outstanding exploits. Originally the *récade* seems to have been a royal monopoly: it was carried by the king's messengers and symbolized his authority. The word in fact derives from the Portuguese *recado*, meaning message. Later the baton became a perk of high rank.

Forbes and Beecroft inspected the wooden model of a hill fortress that had been successfully stormed by amazons. Their general's "club of office" – almost certainly a *récade* – had been planted on the model.[129] Gezo gave Bouët a silver-mounted "*bâton de commandement*" – again probably a *récade* – identical to the one carried by the amazon commander in chief.[130] As mentioned earlier, it has been said the baton was used in battle as a club or hatchet, but this is unlikely to have been the case with the more finely crafted specimens. Despite its European name, the *récade* seems to have been of indigenous origin, inspired probably by the hoe, the quintessential African farm tool, and possibly by the African axe too.

While shields were never standard amazon equipment, they seem to have figured among unit insignia.[131] Beecroft and Skertchly saw small numbers of amazonian brass shields, each ornamented with a human skull in the center.[132] Beecroft also noted three silver-plated shields being carried at the head of an amazon procession.[133]

All the foregoing symbols – flags, umbrellas, stools, drums, batons, shields – appear to have been among rewards the king conferred for distinguished service. There were many more, including silver-headed canes, ornamental swords, gold-laced hats and rich imported cloths. The highest personages, military and otherwise, received a horse or a mule which they rode in public ceremonies (but not in the field). These were listless, undersized beasts doomed to an early death by the tsetse fly but adequate as marks of prestige for the élite.

Another non-economic reward was the decoration. When Gezo was chatting with Répin and naval officer Vallon in 1856, he noted the latter's decorations, including the Legion of Honor, and asked about them. "They are", he was told, "the rewards that white monarchs confer on warriors who have shown valor in battles." "I too," he replied, "give my bravest chiefs marks of distinction." And he pointed out silver plaques on silver chains round the necks of several persons in his entourage. The plaques were embossed with the image of an elephant, Gezo's personal symbol.[134] Burton saw Glele awarding yellow and red bead necklaces to "the highest she-dignitaries", and a top amazon commander wearing a "score of coral and metal necklaces with which she had been decorated".[135]

Another type of royal decoration, and perhaps the most highly prized of all, was the amulet. If any talisman promised invulnerabilty to enemy weapons, it was one conferred by the king himself for acts of bravery. Degbelo reports a tradition that when the monarch awarded gris-gris to amazons, he also "baptized" them with a "strong name" that, in their minds at least, endowed them with "great power in the occult domain". According to another tradition, amazons consulted diviners before a campaign and sometimes obtained charms against enemy action from them too.[136]

The reader may wonder how the warrioresses could have had any faith in such objects after seeing comrades slain in combat. Such deaths could have been explained away as the result of a particular foe at a particular time having more potent gris-gris, or of a failure to carry out to the letter a diviner's prescription for rites and sacrifices, or as punishment for some misbehavior that had angered the spirits and deprived the victim of their protection. In 1891 a Dahomean official told a French delegation "very seriously" that amazons came back to life even after being beheaded. The same group watched amazons mime an attack on an invisible enemy. As reported by a naval artillery captain, Henri Decoeur, "one of them falls as if struck dead, her companions come to examine her body, then abandon her, after which she gets up all by herself; we're told this is the real image of what happens in war: the fetish restores life to those struck by enemy bullets."[137]

Hélène d'Almeida-Topor, who published a book on the amazons in 1984, suggests that what was really meant and understood by "invulnerability" was that the fallen heroine immediately joined her ancestors, presumably in preference to languishing in some purgatory.[138] This suggestion may be viewed skeptically, but in Dahomey, as elsewhere in West Africa, the line between the world of the living and the world of the dead was blurred at best, and certainly not the great divide it is for us Westerners.

Other royal rewards to amazons were goods such as cloth, pagnes, rum, tobacco. Skertchly adds guns to the list.[139] (Chaudoin says that successful male officers received broad-brimmed hats covered with black monkey skin.[140] Hazoumé records a tradition that swords attached to fringed velvet sashes were awarded to brave male soldiers.)[141] But by far the most common reward was cowrie shells, the national money.

In theory any person captured by his troops and every head of a slain foe belonged to the king on grounds that he financed and equipped the army, besides being the absolute master of his subjects. In practice the monarch paid for captives and heads at fixed rates, and he did it largely with cowries. The payments are sometimes called bounties or bonuses in the literature. The custom goes back at least to 1727, when Snelgrave saw more than 1,800 prisoners and "some thousands of dead Peoples Heads" being brought to Agaja's court after a highly successful campaign. Special officers paid the victorious soldiers 20 shillings' worth of cowries for each man and 10 shillings' worth for a woman, boy or girl. Each head brought 5 shillings of cowries; some soldiers carried as many as three or more on a string. The king's spokesman told the English visitors that the heads would be added to a monument of enemy skulls.[142]

In 1777, after a victory over Dahomey's northern neighbors, the Mahi, Kpengla paid 30 shillings' worth of cowries per head on top of the (unspecified) fee for a living captive, saying, according to Abson, "I want heads, not slaves". The

Mahi had previously repulsed a Dahomean invasion and the king was in a vengeful mood.[143] By then, presumably, amazons were earning bounties for prisoners and heads, but we have no evidence for it. By Duncan's day (1845) there is no longer any doubt. He saw an amazon "regiment" return from a mock attack leading young slaves representing prisoners. Curiously, the warrioresses also carried scalps representing slain foes – Duncan counted 700 such trophies.[144] The Briton was persuaded that Dahomean troops received bonuses for scalps;[145] more likely they were allowed to keep the scalps when they turned in the heads. In any case, we hear nothing more about scalps, except for a mention by de Wailly in 1890,[146] and he is not particularly reliable.

Dawson says that in 1862 Glele paid no more than 4 dollars' worth of cowries per war prisoner.[147] Burton saw heads being redeemed at 2 shillings' worth of cowries each. The minimum price for a captive was the same amount of shells plus 2 "fathoms" of cloth, while a male officer who had captured an enemy chief and brought back three heads to boot received 32 shillings in cowries and a long white cloth.[148] In the last years of the kingdom, prices for prisoners ranged from the equivalent of 2 to 10 French francs plus a pagne, while heads brought as little as half a franc.[149]

Among the most precious rewards at the king's disposal were human beings, either as slaves or as wives. The latter obviously were for male heroes. Heroic amazons did not receive husbands but did earn slaves, presumably in addition to the servants regularly assigned to the warrioresses. Duncan met a woman officer named Adadimo who had taken a male prisoner two years in succession and was recompensed by Gezo with two female slaves. She was, he reports, "a tall thin woman, about twenty-two years of age, and good-looking for a black, and mild and unassuming in appearance".[150] Tata Ajachê, the amazon who eviscerated an enemy with his own hoe, eventually received two female slaves from Glele. (She appears to have been a special case. Hazoumé says that she had a child by the king and kept its paternity secret

at his request and at great hardship to herself, being liberally
rewarded by him for that.)[151]

   An amazon who distinguished herself in battle could also
hope for a promotion. Courage and seniority seem to have
been the only criteria for elevation to officer's rank.[152] Many
amazon officers were presented to Duncan, who was told
the "deeds of valour" for which each had been promoted.
"No promotion takes place", he was told, "unless merited
on account of some [distinguished] act." Adadimo, for example, was rewarded with officer's rank as well as slaves.[153]
Foà wrote that amazon chiefs "were chosen among the oldest
[of the women soldiers] and those who distinguished themselves by brilliant feats of arms" and "repeated acts of courage".[154]

   According to Edna Bay, the foremost modern student of
Dahomey's palace women, available evidence suggests that

....an individual *ahosi*'s rise to a position of prominence might be
made most quickly and most directly through outstanding service
in the ranks of the army. Perhaps the kings reasoned that warring
represented the ultimate test of a woman's loyalty to her monarch-
husband. [...][T]he soldier *ahosi* openly, even deliberately, risked
their lives for the king, and thus demonstrated a fidelity which
presumably might serve them well in higher positions of trust.
[...]Their elite status, along with the possibility for direct advance-
ment to some of the highest levels within the palace, must have gone
far towards providing the incentive for their extraordinary
courage.[155]

ALCOHOL AND TOBACCO

Not the least of the rewards of being amazons was access
to alcohol and tobacco; their masters seem to have kept
them well supplied with both. While West Africans doubtless
drank palm wine and millet beer long before Europeans
introduced their own alcoholic beverages, the women soldiers
had a decided preference for the latter. Brandy, rum and,
at the very end, gin are almost the only drinks specified in
the records (besides water).

   Back in 1726, Agaja said that after his "people" went

through their military drills, he distributed brandy which was "soone made away with".[156] Those warriors may not have included women, but we may suppose that later in the century female soldiers shared in the brandy, which came mainly from France. The first explicit mention of amazons in relation to alcohol was in 1830, when Lopez, after watching a mock attack followed by human sacrifices, said "the Medusas returned to their kingly barracks drunk with rum and blood".[157] New World rum had indeed overtaken brandy as West Africa's chief alcoholic import and, according to Father Laffitte, it was appreciated by the women warriors in quantity. "A little glass of this vile liquor", he claimed, "produces a pitiful smile, a half liter barely cheers them up; their face beams only with a full bottle."[158] But his contemporary Father Borghero could still say, hyperbolically, in 1861 that "the amount [of *brandy*] drunk in Dahomey is hardly believable: you would say that alcohol is the god of the blacks."[159]

Forbes saw Gezo, after a dance, hand around a large pewter basin of rum to amazon officers. He also reported the popularity at Abomey (though not specifically among the female soldiers) of "a compound known in the United States by the name of 'stone wall', consisting of rum, brandy, beer, lemonade, and various kinds of liquors and wine, – rather likely to be deleterious in an African climate."[160]

By the time of the final campaigns against the French, alcohol was being used to embolden both male and female troops before battle. The practice may have been adopted much earlier: Burton heard that "a fighting draught of rum and gunpowder was...served out" before the 1864 attack on Abeokuta.[161] The evidence from the 1890s is strong. The French found empty English gin bottles on at least one battlefield, and bottles that had held "trade alcohol" are said to have littered abandoned Dahomean camps and trenches. Some reports speak of a rum ration. Maire was told that *anisado* (Portuguese anisette) and maize brandy were among the drinks distributed before combat.[162] D'Almeida–Topor relates a Dahomean tradition that the king kept a demijohn of a certain liqueur that he doled out to the amazons before they went into action. One glass, it was said, sent them into a murderous rage.[163] The native historian Luc Garcia suggests that rum strengthened the belief of amulet-laden troops in their invulnerability.[164]

A French officer, E. Nuëlito, who commanded Senegalese cavalry (spahis) recounts in detail how in October 1892 one of his men captured two male soldiers and an amazon hidden in a hole, dead drunk (the woman was later killed trying to escape).[165] But other reports of alleged amazon drunkenness are less precise and sometimes seem based on a presumption that only alcohol consumption could explain the women's extraordinary audacity, ferocity and tolerance of pain.

Like West Africans in general, Dahomeans became addicted to tobacco after its arrival from the New World near the end of the sixteenth century. It was smoked in pipes by both sexes. Along with umbrellas, récades and stools, locally-made pipes with small clay bowls and long, straight wooden stems were marks of distinction. Skertchly puts the stem at about 18 inches, but there exists a photograph that shows King Béhanzin puffing on a pipe more than two feet long. While senior amazons probably possessed similar pipes, the rank and file smoked short clay varieties. The warrioresses Burton saw marching off to fight carried "wooden pipe cases enveloped in leather tobacco-bags, flint, steel, and tinder... made of scrapings of palm-trunk mixed with a charcoal."[166] Skertchly says the tobacco was 'generally American leaf',[167] probably imported Virginia. Earlier the tobacco favored in the region was a molasses-flavored strain from Brazil.

14

EARNING A LIVING

When, in times of peace, the amazons were not training for war or indulging themselves, they had work to do. Just how much and of what kind is unclear. The king supplied them with at least some of their food from the royal plantations. He also provided them with uniforms and weapons, and with often effective medical care of priestly herbalists. Their serving women fetched water from springs outside Abomey. But these perquisites apparently did not meet all their needs: they performed a number of tasks to earn money, as did other royal wives. "Every woman in the palace had an occupation," Bay was assured by Sagbaju Glele, a brother of Béhanzin who lived till the 1970s.[1]

Some amazons were potters. Forbes speaks of a pottery that was a royal monopoly worked by royal wives, but he does not specify whether amazons were involved.[2] On a plain west of Abomey Bouët saw buildings where "beautiful micaceous pottery" was manufactured by royal wives who also guarded the enterprise.[3] The guards, at least, had to be amazons. Louis Fraser noticed earthen jars marked with "English letters". This, he was told, was the name of the maker, "one of the King's wives".[4] Laffitte says flatly that pottery was an amazon monopoly.[5] According to Burton, pots were made exclusively within the palace and sold elsewhere in Abomey.[6] Skertchly located the clay pits in the capital that were used for the pottery, and said that manufacture was "chiefly in the hands of the Amazons".[7] Presumably the same women who made pots made the small clay bowls for tobacco pipes of the élite. Burton placed that industry too within the palace,[8] and Skertchly said that the pipe bowls were made by amazons, "who formerly enjoyed the monopoly".[9]

Forbes had a bird's-eye view of another royal monopoly, a dyehouse that was off-limits to most people because it was worked by royal wives.[10] Again, we do not know if any were amazons. More than 120 years later, Sagbaju Glele articulated a tradition that some palace women were indigo dyers.[11]

Laffitte says that calabashes as well as pottery were an amazon monopoly,[12] but no other contemporary writer mentions them. Paul Hazoumé, in a 1938 novel titled *Doguicimi* set in Gezo's reign and rich in Dahomean ethnography, credits a male artist with engraving or burning designs on royal calabashes.[13]

Mat weaving was another possible amazon activity. Burton claims that the palace manufactured and monopolized them.[14] Sagbaju Glele recalls that his mother, a Yoruba captive domiciled in the palace, earned money weaving and selling mats.[15]

Women soldiers almost certainly had a hand in palm oil production, traditionally a woman's job in the region. Skertchly writes of a ruined palace in the Abomey area "used as a palm-oil manufactory by the king, who kept a troop of Amazons constantly on guard within". He also reports that amazons regularly carried oil to Whydah for export[16] (it is more likely that slave women carried the oil under amazon escort). Maire offers stronger evidence: the plan of an amazon barracks in Agaja's old palace showing "kitchens and large furnaces for the preparation of palm oil".[17]

Weaving cloth from local cotton was men's work, but women seem to have done sewing and embroidery. Forbes says that some cloth was made in the palaces at Abomey;[18] he may have been referring to the needlework. Burton includes cloth or clothes among products manufactured and monopolized in Singboji,[19] but it is unlikely that the palace would have opened its gates to a bunch of male weavers. The cloth was probably made outside and brought in for *couture*. According to tradition, 130 embroideresses and apprentices toiled in a "tailors' workshop" during Glele's reign under a family that specialized in appliqué. It is not clear where the workshop was located, but for Bay the number of seamstresses "suggests the relatively vast scale of the palace clothing industry".[20] Whether amazons were involved is not known.

Palace women probably worked on an extraordinary patchwork that is first mentioned by Brue (1843) and was still being added to in Skertchly's day (1871-2). It was composed of pieces of cloth of varying size including samples of every kind of fabric imported into the kingdom or manufactured locally. Customs officials at Whydah subtracted a swatch of every textile landed by European ships and earmarked it for the project. Brue called this multicolored, multipatterned patchwork a pagne and said that it floated like a flag.[21] But within two years it had grown to enormous size, if not the 1,000 yards long by 8 yards wide that Gezo claimed in a conversation with Duncan.[22] Burton and Skertchly explain to us the significance of the long cloth, and offer more careful measurements.[23]

The patchwork was called Nunupweto, one of Gezo's titles meaning "He is able to do anything he likes" or, more succinctly, "Omnipotent". It would keep growing till the day the king returned from the conquest of Abeokuta and wrapped it round him. It was not explained, as Burton pointed out, how he could support such a weight. Glele continued his father's project, and in a speech heard by Skertchly scolded his army for making necessary the constant expense of adding to the cloth. Burton gauged the patchwork at c. 350 yards long by 12 to 13 feet wide, Skertchly at 400 yards by c. 10 feet. At ceremonies it was unrolled and raised on poles more than twice the height of a man. As hopes of ever defeating Abeokuta faded, the Nunupweto disappeared from history.

According to Burton, the pure white umbrella presented to a new chief was "of palace manufacture".[24] If so, it was made by palace women. According to Hazoumé, the giant royal umbrellas were the work of male tailors.[25]

There is disagreement on whether the amazons did any farming, a normal duty of Dahomean women. When urged by Beecroft and Forbes to abandon the slave trade and grow cotton or oil palms, Gezo is said to have replied: "I cannot send my Women to cultivate the Soil – it would kill them."[26] The two Britons also heard an amazon complain before the king that she had gone into debt buying provisions for the latest war and was anxious to recoup by earning money in another war.[27] Laffitte, echoed by Foà, asserts that the king provided none of the amazons' food and that they had to grow their own.[28] Degbelo reports that most of her informants in Abomey and vicinity were sure the monarch furnished *all* their food from his vast, slave-worked plantations.[29] The truth would appear to lie somewhere between.

Relying on oral traditions, Degbelo says political authorities assigned agricultural properties to each amazon barracks, and the women "exploited" the land in their "free time". This was usually in the rainy season (summer), when military activity was at a standstill. One such property was at Zassa, a few miles southwest of Abomey. Degbelo says that it was worked by the amazons themselves, although one would think they would have reserved the heavy labor for their slaves. The crops produced in their own fields supplemented rations received from the king. Degbelo concludes that royal food policy toward the amazons was never rigid, varying "according to the state of the royal treasury, climatic risks and seasons".[30]

Some of their own produce was used by amazons to make prepared foods – bean fritters, cassava dumplings, cornstarch paste, fried yam cakes – that were sold by their slaves in public markets.[31] (Sagbaju Glele says the sellers were little girls,[32] which may have meant the same thing.) Within the palace was a market where the amazons could do their own selling to other women.[33] This petty commerce doubtless included craft products such as pots and mats as well as food.

Amazons may also have engaged in long-distance trade. In 1727 Snelgrave saw more than 1,800 war prisoners brought into Agaja's camp. He was told their people, the *"Tuffoes"*, had attacked Dahomean troops escorting twelve royal wives who were taking "a large quantity of Goods and fine things, carried by Slaves", back to Dahomey. The guards had been routed, the women slain and the goods seized. Agaja had sent part of his army against the *Tuffoes* "to revenge him for their Villany", and a complete victory was obtained.[34] The amazon palm-oil caravans reported by Skertchly may thus have continued an old tradition.

Among amazon sidelines we must not forget the hunting of elephants. It is not clear whether the *gbeto* had to give all the ivory to the king; Forbes seems to imply that the huntresses sold tusks to merchants at Whydah.[35] In the equally autocratic monarchy of old Benin, the king had the right to one tusk from every elephant slain and an option to buy the other. Perhaps Dahomey had some such arrangement.

Women soldiers may have profited too from one of the common occupations in the palace: piercing and stringing the king's cowries. Courdioux and Skertchly say this was done by the amazons, Dalzel credits "the King's women", Forbes "the ladies of the harem", Degbelo female slaves.[36] The money shells of Dahomey were threaded on twisted grass or palm leaf, normally forty to a "string" although Skertchly speaks of up to fifty.[37] However, the king's strings had fewer cowries than normal but were worth just as much as the others. Dalzel says that the palace women routinely deducted one shell, or 2.5 per cent, for their labor, but that during Kpengla's reign royal strings were reduced by between four and seven cowries.[38] In the last years of that reign, the head of the French fort at Whydah counted thirty-eight, thirty-seven and sometimes thirty-six shells per regal string.[39] In Forbes's time the king's cowries were 14 per cent fewer than standard amounts; in Burton's and Skertchly's time it was 20 per cent fewer.[40] Forbes's contemporary Fraser could find no more than thirty-three shells on the monarch's strings.[41] Courdioux said that each contained from thirty to thirty-five.[42] We may confidently imagine that the royal treasury was the chief beneficiary of this legal short-changing, and that if the amazons or their servants were involved, the soldieresses also benefited.

Finally, an amazon could look forward to relatively comfortable retirement when so compelled by age or disability. Winniett told House of Lords committeemen that no woman soldier was older than thirty-five, that Gezo "pensioned them off, and took care of them; [which] he was bound [to do] after they were of no use".[43] Guillevin thought they spent only seven or eight years on active duty.[44] But Burton described some of them as "old women",[45] and among amazons who danced for French visitors in 1891 were a few with white hair.[46] It would seem women remained in the ranks as long as they were physically fit for combat.

Retirement took several forms. According to Bay, most ex-amazons "appear to have been integrated into the non-military palace structures, though some apparently were granted to common men as wives by the king".[47] Garcia says women who could no longer stand the rigors of the field "busied themselves with palace housekeeping".[48] Bouët saw elderly soldieresses who had been invalided out of service guarding royal tombs at Cana.[49] In effect the king was the head of an enormously extended family – the women of the palace – and in good West African fashion took responsibility for its older members.

15

MAKING WAR

Dahomey waged war annually. This began at least in Gezo's time and perhaps much earlier. Foà thought that yearly campaigns had continued for two centuries, and, given the prominence of armed conflict in Dahomean traditions and written history, he may have been right.[1] "A good case could be made", Argyle even suggests, "that the main function of the kingship was the conduct of war."[2] Duncan seems to have been the first writer to remark that wars were annual affairs. He called them "slave-hunts",[3] as did many subsequent observers; French commentators used the term "*razzias*". But the expeditions ranged from classic slave raids on isolated, near-defenseless villages to full-scale attacks against relatively powerful neighbors.

Most European visitors assumed that the purpose of all military activity was to take prisoners, mainly for the export slave trade but also for domestic slavery and to provide victims for human sacrifice at the royal customs. But the Dahomeans themselves never conceded the point; whether feigned or not, there was always, in their view, an irreproachable *casus belli*.

Kpengla (1774-89) made the case in a two-hour discourse after Abson, who spoke Fon, translated some British abolitionist and proslavery pamphlets for him. "Your countrymen", he is quoted as saying, "who alledge that we go to war for the purpose of supplying your ships with slaves are grossly mistaken." The king cited the "incursions" of hostile neighbors and Dahomey's need to punish their "depredations" that produced "incessant wars". Besides, war was a universal phenomenon, practised by every kingdom. Before Dahomey got involved in the slave trade, his ancestor Wegbaja took prisoners and killed them all. Even with the option of obtaining European trade goods for captives, Kpengla had himself killed thousands when "policy or justice" required it. Sacrificing prisoners gave "a grandeur" to his customs, made his enemies fear him and was an "indispensible duty" to his ancestors who, if he "sent nobody to serve them", might arrange for him to be killed.[4]

Kpengla's response to Abson reaches us through Dalzel, an apologist for the slave trade, which casts doubt on its accuracy. But a modern African historian who has examined the traditional rationales of the many wars waged by Gezo also downplays the slave trade as an explicit motive. Adrien Djivo, in fact, finds no mention at all of the need for captives to sell, employ or execute. Among *casus belli* he puts the avenging of insults first – those particularly directed at the king, the queen-mother or the memory of former sovereigns. (Revenge for military defeats was a *leitmotif* of Dahomean policy and rhetoric, but it was never stated directly in public for that would have been to admit the inadmissible, that Dahomey was not invincible.) Next on Djivo's list comes the king's duty "to answer any insolent challenge without delay". The monarch must also foil any secret plans for aggression against Dahomey revealed to him by his spies. And when the weak and helpless ask for his protection he must come to their aid. "The higher interest of the kingdom explains everything", concludes Djivo, "as a function of which every Dahomean is convinced that his country must remain the strongest."[5]

The above rationales may sound like pretexts masking motives of aggrandizement, greed and blood lust. "Some pretence is...made for making what they call war", said Duncan, "although it is nothing more than a slave-hunt."[6] But one should not underestimate the importance of what enlightened Western circles might now consider irrational. Recall, for instance, the mischief caused by notions of personal and national honor in European history. Or the havoc that extreme nationalism still causes in Europe and elsewhere. In the twentieth century national security has been evoked to justify behavior that makes the kings of Dahomey look like choirboys.

When Kpengla said human sacrifice was necessary to provide his defunct predecessors with servants, he was undoubtedly speaking the truth as he and everyone else in Dahomey saw it. (The victims also carried messages to the deceased monarchs bringing them up to date on Dahomey's fortunes.) Both Gezo and Glele told European visitors they would lose their thrones, or worse, by popular revolt if they abolished such a time-honored custom as human sacrifice.[7] A wise Dutch historian, Johan Huizinga, warns: "There is not a more dangerous tendency in history than that of representing the past as if it were a rational whole and dictated by clearly defined interests."[8] Usually, it is certain, Dahomey wanted captives to sell to slave ships, but that is not nearly the whole story.

One modern student of the question even argues that Dahomey was not a slave-trading state at all. Dov Ronen contends that only "surplus" war prisoners were sold to the whites, primarily to obtain guns to assure the continuous supply of sacrificial victims needed for ancestor worship. The ancestor cult "dominated" Dahomean society, and the annual customs served to renew all-important ties between the living and the dead. The king was the "earthly link" to the ancestors; his ritual role was crucial to the cult and demanded human sacrifice. Therefore, Ronen concludes, war was waged far more for socio-religious reasons than for economic ones.[9]

The annual military campaign normally took place between November and April, the main dry season when watercourses could easily be forded, and lasted two or three months. A few sources suggest that in Glele's time there were sometimes two expeditions a year. Burton states that Glele "prefer[red] two slave hunts to his father's one per annum";[10] Laffitte thought this happened only when the first expedition had not satisfied the king's desires.[11] Dawson claims to have seen three expeditions set out from Abomey in one season.[12] According to Garcia, rainy-season campaigning was not entirely ruled out because rivers were fordable in places even at the height of the rains.[13]

SPIES AND DIVINERS

The king himself decided on whom and when to make war, and gave the order to mobilize the army, but there were certain necessary preliminaries. Spies had to report on potential targets. The king's chief diviner had to consult the fates about the outlook for success or failure of the venture. And presumably the monarch sounded out his principal advisers and generals for their views.

Fon traditions credit Agaja with founding Dahomey's external spying system[14] (there was an internal one too), and written history confirms that it already existed during his reign. In the first literary reference, Snelgrave states that Agaja invaded Whydah in 1727 after "finding by his Spies, how much the great Men and People were divided, and that the King was only a Cypher in the Government".[15] (Sometimes traditional history borrows from written history; this particular correlation could be an example of such feedback, but it could just as well be coincidental.)

Spies were disguised as itinerant traders. While selling their goods, they reconnoitered villages or towns, studying the location of headmen's and high officials' residences, markets and other public places, paths, outer gates and water sources and the nature of the surrounding terrain. They assessed the potential enemy's defensive capabilities and looked for his weak points. There is a tradition that this information was put on a cloth map with the various features shown in appliqué.[16] Argyle thinks that the use of such a map may have been more mystical than tactical, in the presumed belief that "knowledge of a thing in some way gives power over it".[17]

The spy's mission indeed included a large element of the occult, which Hazoumé details. The "trader" carried palm oil to which Dahomean royal sorcerers had added harmful ingredients. As a pretended offering, he poured it over the idol representing the guardian spirit of the targeted community, thereby destroying the spirit's protective power. In various places in the town at night, the spy buried *gris-gris* designed to sow discord among the inhabitants and bring on numerous calamities that would weaken their resistance when invaded by Dahomey.[18] Beecroft and Forbes were told that Gezo had a "fetish" to send to Abeokuta that would split the people and make them easy prey.[19] Sometimes the spy even persuaded the local ruler to accept such charms. Spies were also used to spread false information about Dahomean military aims and movements. Le Hérissé says that another role was to overhear (or make up) offensive remarks against the Dahomean king and people that would give the monarch a valid excuse for going to war.[20] Woe, of course, to spies who got caught: a comment by Laffitte that they were "tortured in the cruelest way" can hardly be doubted.[21]

After the spy reported back to Abomey and briefed the king and his ministers, he was closely guarded until the campaign began. Then, according to Hazoumé, he was bound and put in front (other authors say he served as a scout). If the Dahomeans were ambushed he was immediately killed, but if his information proved correct he was handsomely rewarded.[22]

Degbelo claims that amazons were sometimes sent abroad to spy but offers only one example, a tradition cited earlier that two of the women seduced a Yoruba war chief, then divested him of the magic power that had made him invincible. This is said to have occurred in the town of Meko, conquered in Glele's time.[23] But at any rate, the warrioresses all benefited from the activities of male spies.

"The King never does anything", Wilmot observed, "without the diviner first consulting the 'fetish', to find out whether it will be favourable or unfavourable."[24] The fetish in this case was Fa, an oracle-deity that expressed itself in a highly complex system of geomancy believed to have been introduced into Dahomey in Agaja's time. It had been brought in by the Yoruba, who called it Ifa and who may in turn have got it from the Arab world. Fa was Destiny, and its message was read in palm nuts and deciphered by priests called *bokono*. The king's chief *bokono* would tell him what Fa had to say about a projected campaign. Presumably the oracle's message was ambiguous enough for bad advice to be explained away later. It is said that Béhanzin ignored Fa's disapproval when he took on the French.[25] Diviners accompanied the king in the field so that Fa could be consulted when necessary.[26] Degbelo says that before a campaign the amazons consulted *bokono* on how they would personally fare. The priests were the source of some of the charms aimed at protecting the women from enemy weapons.[27*]

Another preliminary to the annual war may have been the census mentioned earlier that kept track by means of pebbles of the number of girls in each Dahomean household. Herskovits says that a separate count was kept of all males over the age of thirteen; each village chief had to deliver a sack of a corresponding number of pebbles to the king's chief minister, the *Migan* (also the chief executioner). After a campaign, if the number of soldiers sent from each village had not equaled at least half the pebbles in its particular sack, the headman was strangled.[28]

MOBILIZATION

When the king decided on war, there was no formal declaration in the European sense because the enemy was not to be forewarned. A French naval officer, Lieutenaut Commander Jérôme Félix de Monléon, who visited Whydah in 1844 recorded an old anecdote on the subject. It seems that

---

[*] This faith in diviners should be seen in perspective. In France, homeland of rationalism, some 10 million people are said to consult clairvoyants annually and the number who believe in astrology is even higher.

a director of the French fort there (which closed in 1797) had urged the king of Dahomey "to act like the sovereigns of civilized nations" and declare war before he attacked a foe. The king deferred to this advice in his next war. Enemy resistance was so strong that it took a furious assault by amazons to turn the tide and win the day. Many combatants died and no prisoners were taken. The monarch had all the slain enemies beheaded and sent the heads to the fort director, complaining that he had lost that quantity of potential slaves because of the Frenchman's bad advice. He obliged the man to pay for the heads as if they were live slaves. And he reverted to his previous system of making war by stealth "as being less murderous and more lucrative".[29]

Norris heard that Tegbesu (1740-74) launched wars by telling his commanding general, the Gau, that "*his house wanted thatch*". This, he explained, alluded "to the custom of placing the heads of the enemy, killed in battle, or any of the prisoners of distinction, on the roof of the guard houses at the gates of his palaces".[30] Norris's report is not implausible: we know that palace walls were garnished with enemy skulls, and allegory is a favorite rhetorical device in West Africa. The quotation has been accepted by some nineteenth- and twentieth-century authors as a lasting tradition. But as far as we know, it was never corroborated for any other king. Burton couldn't find anyone who knew about the palace wanting thatch and suspected that the phrase was obsolete.[31] According to Foà, when the king made up his mind, "one word, one simple word...war" was spoken to the Gau.[32]

Burton actually attended a "ceremony of declaring war" heralding Glele's ill-fated 1864 expedition against Abeokuta. The king gave a leather case containing "war-rum" to the Migan, who pirouetted with it three or four times, then passed it to the Gau, who made a fighting speech. The monarch then performed two "decapitation dances" with "a crooked stick" (probably one of his *récades*). Burton says

Glele indicated the war would be against the Egba; if so, it was a breach of custom.[33]

If a major campaign was planned, word was sent to all parts of the kingdom to mobilize. A big war drum is said to have sounded in the Singboji palace, and been echoed by relays of small, highly resonant drums. Throughout the land, local war chiefs called *ahwangan* mustered their men. Burton defined the *ahwangan* as "all officers that can bring ten to a hundred dependants or slaves into the field"; Ellis put the minimum troop figure at twenty.[34] Each *ahwangan* had his own umbrella, stool and other appurtenances of rank. Their soldiers were everyman reservists; each brought his own weapon, and they were indifferently trained. Certain high officials contributed little private armies that they themselves equipped. Vallon says of these bodyguards that they comprised 200 men or more.[35] Duncan tells of similar units of female soldiers, including two belonging to royal princes and another to the Migan.[36] Forbes saw uniformed women belonging to the de Souza slaving family of Whydah joining an amazon "regiment".[37]

Female civilians were also called up to join the army's baggage train. They carried mainly provisions and munitions. Some commentators, beginning with Borghero, say that they also carried clubs which were used when necessity arose to fell and capture enemy soldiers.[38] Laffitte speaks of armed women who stayed behind to guard towns and villages when the men left for war;[39] this may have been a generalization from the case of Whydah, where he spent most of his time and which could have received special protection because of its commercial importance. But a modern French scholar, Jacques Lombard, says an amazon "reserve company" stayed behind in Abomey in wartime to guard the palace.[40]

Male and female levies gathered at provincial assembly points and then marched to Abomey or sometimes Cana. Reservists seem to have joined the ranks of standing units around cores of professional fighters.

On the eve of a campaign, the army massed around an

artificial knoll in Abomey called "the Mound of Oaths" or "the Tumulus of Courage". Gezo is said to have had it erected before one of his campaigns against the Yoruba and, according to Dunglas, Glele built another in a different spot before the 1864 march on Abeokuta.[41] The knoll served as a speaker's platform from which the king whipped up the fighting spirit of his minions. In response, military orators swore to outdo themselves against the foe and bring back many heads. "It was one of the occasions", Degbelo tells us, "when the rivalry between the male warriors and the amazons...broke out openly: [the latter's] declarations, supported by theatrical demonstrations, were almost always bolder and more radical than those of their male homologues."[42] (Quénum relates that on its return from combat the army held a victory celebration at the same mound, hoisting its best fighters in triumph.)[43]

ORDER OF BATTLE

Dahomey's "order of battle"–the formal organization and staffing pattern of the army – is fairly well known. The male warriors were divided into right and left wings, plus an élite unit that reinforced the female royal guards. In the Dahomean scheme of things, right was always superior to left, and right-wing officers stood a notch above their left-wing counterparts. In peacetime the right wing was commanded by the Migan and the left by the Meu, the second-ranking minister of the realm. Under the Migan was the Gau, and under the Meu the Kposu. In wartime the Gau became commander-in-chief and the Kposu the next in command, with the two civilian ministers subordinate to them.

By written evidence, all four top positions dated back at least to Agaja's reign (1708-40).[44] According to most oral traditions, the posts go back to the seventeenth century.[45] The attested presence in the mid-seventeenth century of a top official in the Allada kingdom with a title resembling the Migan's bears out the antiquity of that office.[46]

Originally, it would seem, the monarch himself was commander-in-chief and led his army into battle. But after Agaja, the consummate warrior king, was wounded, it was decided to keep rulers out of harm's way. Kings continued to go on campaigns but stayed well back from the fighting, surrounded by amazons.[47] The Migan and Meu too, though nominally generals, may eventually not have taken part in combat for the same reason: their civilian duties were too important to put their lives on the line every year.

Besides being the prime minister and chief executioner, the Migan was supreme judge in all cases that did not go before the king, chief law enforcement officer with his own prison, supervisor of village chiefs with special responsibility for the Allada area and, it is said, in charge of all Dahomeans outside the (very numerous) royal family. The Meu was not only the second-ranking minister but collected revenue, including receipts from the port of Whydah; supervised public ceremonies; acted as the king's "linguist" (meaning that he relayed royal pronouncements to the public); was in charge of visitors to the royal court, and had authority over members of the royal family, including the right to execute wayward princes. Forbes dubbed him the "grand vizier".[48] The Migan and Meu together announced the king's death and named his successor (an original rule of succession by primogeniture soon gave way to considerations of ability and power). According to Forbes, the monarch did not "dare" make a treaty unless both officials approved.[49]

In the field the sovereign not only let the Gau command, but deferred to him in other ways. The Gau could smoke his pipe in the royal presence and sit on a higher stool than the monarch's, both being acts normally taboo. He could, it is said, even summon the king, an otherwise unheard-of impertinence.[50] The Gau planned all strategy and logistics, placed the troops, gave officers their assignments and, according to one tradition, was the only person authorized to fire the first shot and order any demolition.[51] The only exception to the Gau's full control may have involved the royal guards: only the king, it seems, could order them into battle.[52]

The king's passive role naturally absolved him of blame if things went wrong, but there was more to it than that. Herskovits's informants explained that by replacing the monarch as commander the Gau exposed himself instead to potential retribution by vengeful enemy gods. The king, in effect, could not be held spiritually responsible for prosecuting the war.[53] If enemy gods could be fooled about who held ultimate power, Dahomean chiefs could not. Le Hérissé's informant concedes that in the field the king went to unusual lengths to avoid being recognized, including mingling with the chiefs without any protocol, "but they watch for his slightest gestures", he adds, "which are orders."[54]

The female counterparts of the Migan, Meu, Gau and Kposu were, respectively, the *Gundeme, Yewe, Khetungan* and *Akpadume*. All four are not reported in writing until the nineteenth century, the Gundeme first by Duncan (as "Godthimay"), the Yewe by Freeman (as "Yawa"), the Khetungan by Burton, and the Akpadume by Duncan (as "Apadomey").[55] The Dahomean rule of symmetry would require the Gundeme and Yewe to lead, respectively, the right and left wings in peacetime and the Khetungan and Akpadume to lead them on campaigns, but we do not know how closely the rule was adhered to. Djivo claims that the she-Gau and she-Kposu did no more in wartime than furnish provisions, while other female officers led the amazons into combat.[56] In any event it is clear that the Khetungan did not share overall command of the army with the Gau.

Two other amazon officers should be mentioned: the Khetungan's second in command, called the *Zokhenu*, and the Akpadume's second in command, the *Fosupo*. Strangely, both first appear in print in the eighteenth century – as men. A Dutch document of 1733 mentions the "Sockene" and "Possoepo" as high-ranking officers, presumably male ones.[57] Abson reports a Dahomean campaign in 1778 in which the "Zoheinoo" led one "division" and the "Phussupoh" another.

Later he refers to the "Phussupoh" specifically as male, and leaves the impression that the "Zoheinoo" was too.[58] But by Burton's time the two officers were plainly women.[59] Citing Pruneau's eighteenth-century observation that female officers held the same titles as their male counterparts, Law reasons that for men the two prestigious titles had become obsolete.[60]

Each component of the amazon corps — right wing, left wing and center — appears to have consisted of the five branches mentioned in our discussions of uniforms and weaponry. Vallon was the first to list them, in order, as blunderbuss or artillery women, elephant huntresses, musketeers, razor women and archeresses.[61] These categories were repeated by many authors, but with the razor women usually put ahead of the musketeers. Borghero, perhaps under the influence of Greek myth, spoke erroneously of amazon cavalry.[62] Foà thought, also wrongly, that the *gbeto* had been disbanded when elephants became extinct in the region.[63] It would appear from Burton and Skertchly that by Glele's reign the archeresses had become no more than a show troop because their weapon had fallen into disfavor.[64] By the 1870s they appear to have been attached only to the amazon center, the royal guard.[65]

Besides the basic triple and then fivefold division of the amazons, there are frequent references to units ranging down from "regiments" and "battalions" to "companies". The right and left wings, for example, were said to be subdivided into two battalions each. Burton counted forty-two "captainesses", each presumably with her own troops.[66] Maire was told of some twenty amazon companies, and named thirteen of them.[67] Each king, beginning at least with Gezo, created and named new amazon units; we do not know how they fit into the basic pattern, but Ellis heard that the number of companies varied constantly, with old ones being broken up as new ones were formed.[68] Duncan saw a "regiment" of 300 women who purportedly only killed, taking no prisoners.[69] Degbelo theorizes that queens and princesses preferred not to mix with commoners in the amazon ranks, and that this would account for reports of female units composed exclusively of royal women.[70] Le Hérissé uniquely mentions an amazon outfit consisting of 160 wives of princes, high dignitaries and private citizens.[71] On one point there is general agreement: the amazons of the center, who as the royal bodyguard were the élite of the élite, were called the Fanti.

The army's order of battle, as displayed in formal state ceremonies – where right-wing brass lined up on the king's right and left-wing leaders on his left – and in parade-ground deployment, seems to have had little to do with actual behavior in the field, apart from the chain of command. The warriors and warrioresses of Dahomey were not redcoats but redskins, slipping noiselessly through 10-foot-high grass or forest undergrowth and pouncing on unsuspecting foes.

SURPRISING THE ENEMY

The supreme strategy was surprise; to achieve it the Dahomeans went to any lengths. Potential enemies were lulled with friendly diplomatic gestures, even phony alliances. Spies spread misinformation about the expedition. Before it got under way, colorful parade uniforms were exchanged for somber battle dress. The troops assembled on the far side of Abomey and headed off in a direction opposite the intended one, just in case the enemy had *its* spies. Later the army would double back. Beaten paths were avoided. Cooking fires and talk were banned as the troops neared enemy country. Sometimes the army marched by night instead of by day, particularly in the hours just preceding its attack. Scouts seized, bound and gagged individuals met along the way, such as farmers working in outlying fields. Small groups hived off from the main body of troops to envelop peripheral hamlets, making sure that no one escaped to sound the alarm. The army would conspicuously bypass an intended target and then sneak back to catch it unawares. Chaudoin describes the building of a dummy camp to lure enemy troops out of their town.[72]

Some of these precautions may have been meant to deceive enemy tutelary spirits as well as the enemies themselves. Argyle sees the former as the real purpose of the indirect approach to the foe's territory. He suggests that by attacking before daybreak, the Dahomeans hoped to avoid the notice both of supernatural forces and sleeping victims. "The elaborate preliminaries to the waging of war", he contends, including royal consultation of Fa and magic countermeasures by spies, "were an acknowledgement by the kings of Dahomey that even the smallest enemy village had gods whose power had to be nullified before it was safe for the army to attack."[73]

The spirits of natural obstacles in the path of Dahomean forces also had to be appeased. Beecroft and Forbes were told of offerings made to the deity of the Mono River on the way to Atakpamé. Cowries, fowl, goats, bullocks and even human beings, it was said, had been sacrificed to ensure the river god's benevolence and cooperation.[74] The British pair also heard of a certain leaf that if used as a "fetish" before a campaign would make Gezo invincible.[75]

"It appears", Beecroft summed up, "that they depend in a great measure on Stratagem and Superstition for their success."[76]

FOOD AND SHELTER

Military campaigns also required attention to more mundane concerns such as food and shelter. There is disagreement on the extent to which the royal government furnished provisions. Laffitte and Skertchly reported that soldiers had to procure all their own food.[77] Degbelo's oral sources say the amazons prepared their own rations, and d'Almeida-Topor notes the absence of a quartermaster service.[78] But Dunglas, who also relies on oral history, talks about food reserves being distributed in Abomey before the start of a campaign.[79] Djivo, as we've seen, thinks the main wartime job of the female counterparts of the Gau and Kposu was to supply provisions. Herskovits's informants told him certain products, such as honey, were royal monopolies used to feed the army, and that a pepper crop grown for the palace also went mainly to the troops.[80] One has trouble reconciling reports of skimpy amounts of food carried by the troops themselves, and of instances of acute hunger in the field, with reports of female baggage trains loaded with provisions, unless victualing practices varied markedly over time.

Whatever the case, there is not much dispute about the principal ration: a round, hard, spicy cake or biscuit made of beans, maize flour, hot pepper, salt and palm oil. It was highly nutritious, compact, lightweight and long-lasting. Gezo made a gift of some to Forbes, who calls it "war-food", and Beecroft, who describes it as "part of the Chop they carry on their war-excursions". Both found it hard to chew.[81] Dunglas refers to the bean cakes as the army's reserve food, to be eaten when other nourishment was not available.[82]

Another common ration was *cankie*, a word used in West Africa to describe a maize preparation often carried by travelers.[83] The corn kernels were ground into a coarse powder, mixed with boiling water to remove the husks, then boiled further to the consistency of porridge. After cooling, the substance was formed into balls the size of fists or oranges, and wrapped in plantain or banana leaves. To the stranger, according to Skertchly, it at first tasted like "dumplings boiled in soap-suds" but in time would be relished.[84] Manioc, or cassava, was also ground or grated into flour and, mixed with water, eaten as a pudding. Maize, beans and rice were sometimes simply roasted, toasted or fried before being taken off to war. Roasted palm-nut kernels were another provision. So was smoked fish, imported from the coast. Burton lists powdered red pepper (carried in a snail shell) and pods of malaguetta pepper (West Africa's "grain of paradise") among royal rations. He also mentions onions and bananas.[85] Most of these foods were general fare, and are still eaten in rural West Africa.

Répin and Vallon say nothing about rations, and were told that the army lived off enemy land.[86] Very little attention has been paid in the literature on Dahomey to this aspect of military provisioning, although it appears to have been important.[87] Warriors and warrioresses surely helped themselves to whatever the enemy's country offered by way of food. This would have included crops that are not cited among their provisions but were also grown in the region: yams, sweet potatoes, taro (known as cocoyams in West Africa), sorghum (called Guinea corn), millet, peanuts, okra, pineapples. Crops would have been taken right from the field or from storage facilities. In addition, trees would have furnished a wide variety of fruits: bananas and plantains; oranges, lemons and limes; oil-palm nuts, shea nuts, coconuts and cashews; mangoes, papayas, guavas, custard apples, pomegranates. Moreover, there were domestic animals to confiscate and devour: chickens, guinea fowl, ducks, pigeons, turkeys, goats, sheep, pigs, dogs, cattle. (And when an enemy was defeated, livestock as well as people were herded off to Abomey.) Finally, the bush abounded in edible game, from rats and bats to elephants (before their extinction) and including lizards, crocodiles, monkeys, antelopes, porcupines, hares and partridges. Recall that Gezo showed Duncan how his troops, female and male, "procured their food when in the bush" by staging a shooting exercise in which livestock substituted for wild animals.

Foà paints a bleak picture of Dahomean troops sleeping on the ground without cover, waking soaked with dew, and never getting decent rest because of night marches.[88] He was clearly mistaken. Among the personal accessories taken on campaigns were rush mats to sleep on and pagnes to wrap around the body for protection against damp and chill. If a soldier was wounded, he was rolled up in the pagne and carried to safety; if he was killed it became his shroud.[89] In 1892 a French officer was struck by the "ingenious simplicity" and efficiency of the carrier-pagne compared to the French army's stretcher.[90] Degbelo was told that the king gave each amazon a pagne before a campaign to be used as a shroud if need be[91] (according to the same informant, slain amazons were buried by their comrades if possible to forestall mutilation).[92]

Furthermore, troops did not customarily sleep in the open. If they had the time, and they often did, they threw up shelters. Way back in 1727 Snelgrave visited a Dahomean military camp near Allada. The army, he reported, "lay in tents...made of small Boughs of Trees, and covered with Thatch, very much resembling Bee-hives, but each big enough to hold ten or twelve Soldiers, who crept in at a hole on one side."[93]

In May 1863 Wilmot visited the remains of a large Dahomean camp near Abeokuta. The Fon army had abandoned it a few weeks earlier without attacking the city. The commodore said it was "composed of sticks and Palm leaves, with some [shelters] of greater pretensions to comfort and appearance". The site had been "carefully chosen by the Dahomian Chiefs", he noted, beside a forest laced with several streams.[94]

Skertchly describes "bamboo" huts about 10 feet square with thatched roofs,[95] Chaudoin palm-leaf shelters.[96] Burton says that when the army camped, mat enclosures were made for the king and his amazons.[97]

Schelameur, the cavalry veterinarian who took part in the 1892 war, gives us a detailed picture of a Dahomean camp that had just been captured by the French. It was a vast congeries of huts made of poles and palm fronds, roofed with thatch descending very low. The shelters varied in shape and grouping. Toward the center of the camp was a large open-sided structure about 25 meters long and 10 wide for war council meetings. Another big construction enclosed by a cornstalk fence housed the king, and a similar fence, in the form of a square, surrounded the huts occupied by amazons. The male warriors and porters had their own shelters, varying in size and solidity according to the importance of the occupants. Schelameur was impressed. "In

general", he wrote, "these shelters are very carefully con-
structed and much more comfortable than the best tents.
The whole camp is irreproachably clean...without the least
garbage around the huts."[98]

An anonymous French diarist whom Garcia tentatively
identifies as Captain. Edouard Demartinécourt (and to whom
I so refer in the notes) inspected the same abandoned camp
(near the village of Poguessa) and was likewise impressed.
Two or three large structures, he said,

....especially held our attention owing to the delicacy and orginality
of their shapes and the graceful meticulousness of the tiniest details.
These gems of shelters must have been the Amazons' quarters. They
had built them with their own hands, because men would not have
achieved such perfection. We were like wolves in a sheepfold; we
were amazed at this resourcefulness.[99]

THE ATTACK

The night before Dahomean troops swooped down upon
a village or town, no thought was given to shelter. According
to Foà, who elicited the details of an attack on a village
near Porto-Novo in 1889 and generalized from them, the
Dahomeans camped briefly 8-10 kilometers from the target
the previous evening for a cold supper and a little rest, then
set out in total silence. He explains that by halting at that
distance, then covering a lot of ground during the night,
they increased the likelihood that the enemy would feel
safe, given the radius in which no danger had been signaled
the previous day.

The troops, as they marched, were careful not to clank
weapons or communicate even in whispers, and followed
guides familiar with the terrain. As they neared the target,
they crawled through the vegetation, trying to avoid the
least crackling sound. Little by little they encircled the sleeping
community.[100] Accounts of the final moments preceding the
classic Dahomean attack, and of the attack itself, differ in
detail. Foà says the troops waited till the first cock's crow,

when it was still almost pitch-black, then moved on a signal from the commander, "doubtless transmitted by touch".[101] Le Hérissé says the cock's crow itself was the signal;[102] others speak of a second cock's crow or a gunshot or a cry.[103*]

The timing of the assault oscillates in the literature between "about two hours before daybreak" (Duncan) and "at daybreak" (Bayol); the majority view would seem to be "before dawn".[104]

Again depending on our source, the Dahomeans attacked at the weakest point in the defenses, or from front and back, or from the front and the two sides, or from all sides at once. In Foà's model, the invaders slither on their stomachs up to the village wall, sword between their teeth, pushing their loaded gun ahead of them. They probe for entrances. If the gates are open or easy to force, the attackers enter there; if not, they choose a place in the wall that seems the least maintained and climb over.[105] Duncan remarks that towns in the interior were "generally surrounded by a broad close-growing fence of a very dangerous prickly bush, about fifteen feet high" but that this (however improbably) was "scarcely deemed an obstacle" by the amazons.[106]

Foà tells us that once through or over the wall, the troops silently fanned out among the dwellings, prolonging the element of surprise till the last possible moment, and usually avoiding the need to fire their guns.[107] Nearly everyone else says that the assailants rushed furiously into the hapless community, through its streets and into its huts, yelling and/or shooting. Quénum says that oliphant blasts added to the uproar.[108] It may well be that the guns were fired only once, to demoralize the inhabitants, and not reloaded, and that swords or machetes, and possibly clubs, then wrought the necessary mayhem.

At this point all accounts converge. Most of the brusquely awakened and terror-stricken natives surrendered and were

---

* The cock's-crow versions make for a better story but are suspect. African roosters this author has known did not follow any particular timetable: they would sound off at any hour of the night. And instead of a distinct second crow, the call of one would set off an echoing chorus from his fellows.

tied with the cords that each Dahomean soldier carried. Whoever resisted was killed and decapitated, his head dropped in a soldier's sack.

Who else was killed is less certain. It seems that when the Fon were avenging a defeat or a betrayal, or punishing a particularly defiant foe, the slaughter was general. After the conquest of Whydah in 1727 and its reconquest the following year, massacres of unsalable captives were reported.[109] Abson heard of a retributive victory over the Mahi in 1777 when "men, women, and children [were] put to the sword, without distinction, and without mercy".[110] Forbes asserts that when the Fon captured Okeadon in 1848 (chapter 16), "all the aged were decapitated on the spot, to the amount of thousands".[111] When lex talionis was involved, says Burton, "quarter [was] given only to those...reserved for slavery or...sacrifice".[112] Even in run-of-the-mill raids, he claims, "the old, the sick, and the 'unmerchantable'" were routinely beheaded.[113] Foà adds 'the very young children" to those massacred".[114] Chaudoin says the slain included all who were not "ablebodied".[115]

Yet Burton himself allows that the object of the attackers was, "as a rule...to capture, not to kill".[116] Skertchly stresses the point: "[E]very man, woman and child [is] captured if possible. None are killed save in self-defence, as the object is to capture, not to butcher."[117] A lot of other commentators tend to agree.[118]

Persons who tried to flee the Dahomean invaders were usually intercepted by troops blocking every path out of the town. Ellis heard that regular troops, male and female, carried out the assault while reserve levies cut off the fugitives, and also plundered the place.[119] Once everything of value had been removed, all the dwellings were torched. Quénum says the outer wall was demolished too;[120] that seems questionable if it was made of dried mud layers, as many were. Destroying that would take some time.

By sunrise the deed was done. The prisoners, already lined up for the march to Abomey with a troop escort, could see their homes going up in flames. According to Foà, the captives themselves carried the booty, i.e. their own looted wealth, and even the bagged heads of their own people.[121] This is where the piece of chalk mentioned by Duncan as standard equipment may have come in: a soldier who did not return to the capital just then could put his or her personal mark on the prisoner, or the bag.

Sometimes a targeted community was not caught unawares. Forewarned in some way, it was ready and waiting for the Fon attack, and repelled it. A few writers, beginning with Wilmot, assert that in such circumstances the invaders quickly lost heart and went away.[122] Laffitte specifies that the male warriors took flight first, and 'the amazons, in spite of their courage, [were] soon obliged to follow them".[123] To mask a defeat, says Chaudoin, the Dahomeans would scoop up defenseless villagers along their route back to Abomey so that the king could pretend to have won a victory.[124]

The evidence suggests, however, that the Fon army rarely cut and ran. Towns that stubbornly resisted were besieged for weeks and even months, as the example of Ketu in chapter 19 shows. When enemy troops ventured out in force, the Dahomeans took them head-on and, says Foà, usually came out on top because they feared "neither danger nor death".[125] This was substantiated even at Abeokuta, scene of two of their worst defeats. Above all it was their terminal performance against the French that confirmed the Dahomean army's valor and tenacity for all to see.

Epithets like brigand, bandit, pillager and looter abound in the literature, and it cannot be denied that Dahomey preyed on its neighbors. Indeed it did what many African polities were doing at the time, only more systematically and efficiently.

AMAZONS IN COMBAT

If there is one fact about the amazons that is indisputable, it is their consistently outstanding performance in combat.

Not unexpectedly, practically the only author to cast doubt on this was Burton, for whom the idea that black females (not to speak of males) might excel on the battlefield was hard to accept: "The 'Amazons' boast themselves invulnerable, but readily retreat: an equal number of British charwomen, armed with the British broomstick, would – I lay, to speak Yorkishly – clear them off in very few hours."[126] Elsewhere he damns them with faint praise: "The women are as brave as, if not braver than, their brethren in arms, who certainly do not shine in that department of manliness."[127]

The first inkling that the women soldiers of Dahomey might be first-class fighters comes from Labarthe's informant who, in 1776, watched them perform shooting drills at Abomey and found them "very resolute".[128] By 1830, as Conneau learned at Whydah, their "bravery [was] a noted fact and [was] proverbial with the natives."[129] By the next decade the amazons' reputation was established among Europeans too. At Cana in 1843 Freeman saw a "brigade" of them fire their guns. Not only did they shoot well, he says, but they "appeared totally void of fear".[130] The next year de Monléon remarked that the women had "often given striking proof of courage and audacity".[131] In 1845 Duncan saw amazon officers being rewarded for their "valour".[132]

By the end of the decade Forbes was crediting the "sable ladies" with "prodigies of valour".[133] He also introduced a theme that would reverberate in the literature. He said that the women had come to "scorn the softer allurements of their nature", and indeed believed that their nature had fundamentally changed from female to male, and had surpassed their male counterparts "in cruelty and all the stronger passions". He linked all this to their forced chastity, and ventured a bit of pre-Freudian psychoanalysis: "The extreme exercise of one passion will generally obliterate the very sense of the others. The amazons, while indulging in the excitement of the most fearful cruelties, forget the other desires of our fallen nature." And, with their relish for battle, they had become "the terror of the neighbouring tribes"–another theme that would resonate.[134]

Tracing the battlefield fury of "the gentle sex" to their repressed sexuality proved irresistible. "Unfortunately", said Répin, "their ferocity equals their courage: indomitable in combat, they are pitiless in victory. It seems that in ridding themselves of the gentle qualities that are the ornament of their sex, women, extreme in all things, lose their humanity."[135] Burton agreed that celibacy "doubtless increases [the amazons'] ferocity in fight"–or, as he put it elsewhere, "'horrors' are... their succedaneum for love"–but he took issue with Forbes's judgment that one passion obliterated another. He suggested instead that bloodshed "gratified" their sex drive. Burton in fact opined that African women in general had a smaller libido than their European sisters: "A scanty diet, a life of toil, and the petty cares of domestic duties, blunt, if they do not destroy, the *besoin d'amour*." He also found it natural for the amazons to be crueler than their male comrades, quoting from Tennyson's *Idylls of the King*:

> For men at most differ as Heaven and Earth;
> But women, worst and best, as Heaven and Hell.[136]

Not coincidentally, Skertchly quotes the same couplet, assuring us that "whenever a woman becomes unsexed, either by the force of circumstances or depravity, she invariably exhibits a superlativeness of evil." Ever determined to outdo Burton, he goes on:

What spectacle is more calculated to inspire horror than a savage and brutal woman in a passion? and when we imagine such to be besprinkled with the blood of the slain, and perhaps carrying the gory head of some decapitated victim, one may cease to wonder at the dread with which these female warriors were, and still are, looked upon by the surrounding nations.

Skertchly's own passion for contradicting Burton then leads him, inconsistently, to minimize the celibacy factor. "I believe", he avows, "that if an army of married soldieresses were possible, they would be found to be equally cruel with these spinster-warriors, if not to surpass them in their ferocity." And in a further mental *volte-face*, he suggests that if an amazon gratified anything in slaughter it may have been "a bitter spirit of animosity against all men" inspired by the knowledge that she has "lived without performing the functions for which her sex was intended".[137]

Such speculation continues to find a place in writings on Dahomey. But one modern student of the kingdom's military history, the American Thomas C. Maroukis, offers the commonsensical view that the daily regimen of the amazons, their highly disciplined, focused and self-contained life, had more to do with their fighting qualities than anything else.[138] And Degbelo cites other practical reasons for their behavior on the battlefield: the confidence imparted by "occult precautions", the king's insistence that the women keep their bold promises or face punishment, the knowledge that acts of prowess would be rewarded with gifts, especially more powerful *gris-gris*, and promotions.[139]

Regarding the terror the women aroused among neighboring peoples, Chautard relates an anecdote from the 1880s. A group of amazons traveled from Whydah to Agoué, a port town beyond the kingdom near what is now Togo, perhaps as an escort for traders. The whole population crowded the town square to see the legendary ladies up close. The female "general" confronted the local male warriors and challenged the very best of them to a duel with swords to determine which sex was stronger. "In less than two minutes", she boasted, "his head will adorn the tip of my sword!" To the shame of his sex, says Chautard, not one warrior volunteered.[140]

The adjectives applied to the amazons over the decades were brave, courageous, valorous, valiant, fearless, intrepid, cruel, pitiless, merciless, implacable, relentless, bloodthirsty, fierce, ferocious, furious, audacious, impetuous, ardent, fanatic, disciplined, devoted (to the king), indomitable, redoubtable, formidable, vigorous, resolute, tenacious, determined, persevering. Often they were said to surpass their male colleagues

– in valor, in intrepidity, in courage, in bravery, in cruelty, in discipline. "In this singular country", Vallon reported, "the women's army is accounted much more warlike than the men's."[141] According to Bouët, there was no memory of any of the amazons fleeing combat whereas men had often been punished for doing it.[142]

The first commentator explicitly to recognize the amazons as "the élite of the army" may have been a Frenchman, Paul Merruau, who had not been to Dahomey but had read the accounts coming in from both his countrymen and the British.[143] He made the observation in late 1851, i.e. soon after the women had led the charge in the first attack on Abeokuta. For the next four decades, no one would question it.

CASUALTIES AND CAPTIVES

Despite their fighting skills and amulets, the women soldiers were not immune to death, injury, disease or capture. As we have seen, shrouds prepared for a decent burial, preferably away from the battlefield and if possible back in Dahomean soil. If it was not feasible to bring a body home, hair and fingernail clippings may have sufficed.[144] Degbelo says that the king held "pompous" ceremonies with full honors for amazons who had died courageously in combat.[145]

He also seems to have taken pains to ensure that wounded amazons received care. Archeresses and female porters may have carried them to safety. Maire heard that during the final campaign, the Dahomeans dragged their wounded off the field with ropes, like cannon, which tended to raise the death toll.[146] But Demartinécourt, who took part, emphasized that the Fon kept firing after a battle was lost just to cover the removal of wounded and dead, and that they used pagnes for transport.[147] Fa diviners who accompanied the king on campaigns are said to have served as doctors for the wounded.[148] Garcia speaks of "a specialized corps of healers...men versed in profound knowledge of medicinal plants", who treated the wounded.[149] When, in 1892, French forces reached a "perfectly kept" village named Kossoupa, Nuëlito was told that it was where Béhanzin had sent amazons to convalesce.[150] Pogla K. Glélè, a great-grandson of King Glele, informs us incidentally that a warrior could not claim a reward for a battle wound if it was inflicted from behind, which was equated with cowardice.[151]

The amazons, along with the rest of the army, were prey to fatal or enervating diseases, particularly smallpox. Dysentery and scurvy are also mentioned, as are deaths from hunger. Without doubt, energy was often sapped by malaria.

The women soldiers' total dedication to king and country was illustrated by their behavior as prisoners. Both in 1851 and 1864, those captured at Abeokuta – who were treated as the private property of the Egba who caught them – were reported to have continued resisting in any way they could. The Yoruba historian Saburi O. Biobaku notes that in 1851 several amazon prisoners of war "proved exceedingly troublesome to their captors in their state of unabated ferocity".[152] Bouët heard soon after the battle that the women "get killed or take flight rather than remain housekeepers for the enemy, who often accepts them as such because the majority are very pretty."[153] "[E]ven when disarmed", said Ellis, "the Amazons...refused to surrender, fighting on, and biting their foes, and were consequently hacked to pieces."[154] The women did more than bite: two are said to have killed persons bringing them food.[155] In 1864, according to the Yoruba historian Samuel Johnson, among the prisoners were "Amazons so ferocious, that although chained, many found means of killing their captors, and were of course killed in turn."[156] Burton tells us that in both 1851 and 1864 many amazons "refused to become a wife till the captor, weary of opposition,...killed the [woman] as a useless animal."[157] Two months after the 1864 attack, Borghero toured the battlefield and was shown the unburied corpse of an amazon who, lying wounded, had hurled insults at approaching Egba soldiers and had, seemingly, been put to death.[158]

Getting captured by the enemy was apparently not considered

a disgrace, for Dahomey made efforts to ransom its people after both debacles at Abeokuta. The first American missionary in Yorubaland, Southern Baptist Thomas Jefferson Bowen, who witnessed the Dahomean attack in 1851, visited the Yoruba town of Ketu midway to Abomey about a month later. The Egba, he reports, were bringing many Dahomean prisoners to the market there "to be redeemed by their countrymen". One of them was a Ketu native who had been captured by the Fon as a girl and trained as an amazon. "Her parents found her out", he relates, "and were delighted with the opportunity of purchasing her freedom, but she said, 'No; I will go back to my master,' " meaning the king.[159] After the 1864 battle, a Brazilian merchant at Whydah complained that Glele had diverted palm oil from the export trade to ransom troops captured at Abeokuta.[160]

Two incidents from the Franco-Dahomean war of 1892 are also revealing. Nuëlito's story of a Senegalese spahi who captured an amazon and two male soldiers found dead drunk in a foxhole had a sequel. When they sobered up, the three Dahomeans were interrogated by a French major about enemy strength and deployment. They contemptuously refused to answer, even when threatened with slavery. The black cavalryman took them back to his quarters and pampered them to try to get them to cooperate, but during a break to care for his horse, the amazon and one of her comrades slipped away. They had almost reached the safety of a forest when two other spahis spotted them and gunned them down. The surviving prisoner, "no longer fearing reprisals from his compatriots", then talked freely to the major.[161]

General Passaga relates that returning to camp one day he saw a woman lashed to a tree and being guarded by a Foreign Legionnaire with fixed bayonet. "She was young and of admirable beauty," he recalls. He asked the soldier why he was being so cruel. "She's an ugly customer, *mon lieutenant.* We took her prisoner, we let her alone, but she tried to knife us while screaming curses. We had to tie her up."[162]

16

EARLY AMAZON BATTLES

While, as we have seen, women may have fought for Dahomey as early as the first decade of the eighteenth century, their only armed engagement in that century of which we can be reasonably sure was the attack on Agouna related by Dalzel. The amazons' regular use in combat may date to about 1830. It apparently came about in the following way.

After Gezo seized power from his brother Adandozan in 1818, his first priority was to end Dahomey's tributary status toward the Yoruba empire of Oyo. Between 1726 and 1748 Oyo, with its manpower advantage and cavalry, invaded Dahomey at least seven times. After the first invasion, Snelgrave reports, Agaja sent the king of Oyo "great Presents...to prevent his attacking him a second time".[1] An invasion in 1730 led to a settlement which apparently made Dahomey tributary to Oyo. In the last years of his reign, Agaja seems to have defaulted on payments of an annual tribute. Hostilities finally ended with a treaty in 1748 that confirmed Dahomey's subordinate position, reset the annual tribute and imposed other humiliating conditions, but did not restrict the Fon kingdom's freedom of action in areas considered outside Oyo's sphere of interest.[2]

The tribute is remembered variously in oral traditions; Dunglas gives us the most detailed rundown. There were forty-one of each of the following: young men, young women, muskets, barrels of gunpowder, bales of pagnes (forty-one in each), baskets each containing forty-one strands of beads or coral each, rams or billy goats, ewes or nanny goats, cocks and hens. Dunglas explains that forty-one was the Dahomean "noble number *par excellence*" and only the king could make a present of that number of objects.[3] He does not explain why Oyo agreed to the figure.

Beginning with Kpengla, Dahomean kings balked at paying the full tribute and sometimes any of it. They could usually get away with it because Oyo was distracted by other, more pressing problems, and starting about 1790 it entered a period of decline culminating in its total collapse about 1836.

Gezo resolved to restore Dahomey's complete independence. As the story goes, when he received Oyo's annual envoys for the first time after ascending the throne, he offered them "a tiny piece of cloth – enough for one man's underpants" and two bags of cowries. "Tell your king", he said, "that anything more would be disproportionate to Dahomey's wealth." Later, four more envoys arrived, and Gezo had them beheaded, a *casus belli* if ever there was one.[4] A Yoruba army was sent against Dahomey and decisively defeated; this was probably in the early 1820s.[5]

Gezo then turned against the Mahi people to the north, possibly because some had sided with Oyo. Two campaigns against the Mahi stronghold of Hounjroto, the first a severe defeat for Dahomey, the second a success, were the background for Hazoumé's novel *Doguicimi*. Hazoumé dates the victory to 1828, Djivo to 1829.[6]

Gezo later told Freeman that he began using the amazons as regular troops after the Hounjroto campaigns, apparently to make up for manpower losses. He called it "a most important and happy" initiative "as it had enabled him to make such valuable use of the female part of the population in strengthening the kingdom."[7] From this time on, Dahomean military annals were to be studded with amazon heroics.

Wars against the Mahi continued. The women soldiers distinguished themselves in at least two of them. Duncan relates that on one occasion a Dahomean trading party was robbed and murdered in Mahi country. Gezo was enraged and, assembling both male and female forces, dispatched them against the enemy. They returned emptyhanded. He sent them back with orders to destroy the Mahi "capital" within three days. Arriving after forced marches, the troops found the town "to be strongly fenced round with...prickly bush", but the same night or early next morning "the female soldiers took the place". The Dahomeans claimed to have gone on and overrun 126 Mahi "towns" in three days, making a great haul of prisoners.[8] Ellis dates this campaign to *c.* 1839.[9]

The wooden model of a hill fortress that was shown to Forbes and Beecroft in 1850 almost surely depicted a Mahi stronghold. They called it Kangaroo. A "large city" stood on a flat hilltop, protected on three sides by perpendicular cliffs. The fourth side, sloping downward, "was guarded by a high stone rampart." Amazons led by the Yewe scaled the rampart and captured the place. Forbes says that the female general's "club of office" projected from the model "out of all proportion".[10]

A bas-relief found by the French in Gezo's main palace probably refers to the same action. It shows a woman raising a flag, Iwo Jina-like, atop a big rock; her *récade* is also depicted, highly magnified. The relief is said to represent the seizure of the Mahi town of Kënglo (whence Kangaroo); the woman is identified as "Sôfignan, one of the wives of King Gezo", which could have been the Yewe's personal name.[11]

Répin and Vallon describe another battle also apparently involving the Mahi. In it the Dahomeans were said to have been led by Gezo himself. "Routed by his warlike adversaries", says Répin, "the king owed the salvation of his army and himself only to the heroism of his amazons, who covered the retreat while losing half their troops."[12]

Two bas-reliefs at one of Gezo's residences showed the women soldiers herding Mahi captives, but did not indicate the occasion. Maire says that in one "the amazons have attacked the Mahi and those they have not killed they lead in chains to King Gezo"; in the other "one amazon leads a powerful, recalcitrant Mahi, another comes up behind him and strikes him [with a club or stick] to make him move."[13]

In 1840 the Fon attacked the commercial center of Atakpamé 60 miles northwest of Abomey, which had a mixed population including Yoruba and Mahi. Forbes heard that all the inhabitants but about 400 soldiers fled at the enemy's approach. "Yet these 400 resolute men kept the Dahomans in check, killed many, put the males to the rout, and had it not been for a rally of the amazons, would have discomfited the Dahoman army."[14]

A decade later, in late 1849 or early 1850, Atakpamé was again attacked, and again the women soldiers outshone the men. Beecroft and Forbes witnessed extraordinarily frank and heated public rehashing of this expedition in the presence of Gezo, who had accompanied the army. It included, Beecroft remarks, "terrible Bickerings between the Amazons, and men Troops".[15] The campaign seems to have been badly mishandled although ultimately it was more or less successful. Many inhabitants of the town had escaped. Forbes was convinced the Gau himself had been killed.[16] A body of male soldiers had strayed from its positions to go foraging, leaving an amazon unit without support when the enemy attacked. Several women officers had been lost. Five male officers were found guilty of the blunder and officially disgraced: their heads were shaved and their muskets replaced with clubs (a telling illustration of the Fon esteem for guns). The public debate even included recriminations among amazons.

On the other hand, the Akpadume boasted how her women had regained lost ground and "saved the war" after male troops under the Gau had fled. The claim was backed up by one of Gezo's brothers, who went further, saying that "the amazons had saved the Dahoman army from destruction" at Atakpamé.[17] This was the battle about which the women soldiers sang that they marched against men and "found them women". The amazons were said to have taken at least 346 prisoners and brought back, in addition, thirty-two heads. Three women carriers, identified as amazons by both Forbes

King Gezo and his son Crown Prince Bahadou, who as king would take the name Glele. Between them they reigned seventy-one years. (A. Répin, "Voyage au Dahomey", *Le Tour du Monde*, VII, 2nd semester [1863], p. 85)

The "Tumulus of Courage," outside the Singboji palace. From atop the mound, just before the start of campaigns, kings fired up their army and amazon spokeswomen swore to outdo their male colleagues. (A. Le Hérissé, *L'ancien royaume du Dahomey*, Paris, 1911, opp. p. 336. Reproduction by courtesy of the Centre des Archives d'Outre-Mer, Aix-en-Provence, France.)

and Beecroft, received special honors. Unarmed, they had seized weapons from the enemy and taken prisoners.[18]

(One prisoner taken at Atakpamé was an elderly chief held responsible for killing many of Gezo's subjects. Blanchély saw him executed in an unusual manner outside Abomey: he was tied between two stakes and shot twice from a distance of about two meters by a cannon loaded with shot.)[19]

Nearly half a century later a German lieutenant, Rudolf Plehn, visited Atakpamé and talked to old men who as boys had survived Dahomey's capture of the town. They still remembered their surprise at seeing that some of the invaders killed were women.[20]

According to Le Hérissé, Gezo first tested his amazons against a Yoruba subgroup.[21] If so, it could have been one that had supported the Mahi of Hounjroto against Dahomey. But renewed and sustained warfare against the Yoruba seems to date from the early 1840s, i.e. a few years after the breakup of the Oyo empire. It would not end till the penultimate year of Dahomean independence.

Hostilities may have begun in 1841 against a town named Inubi where thousands of refugees from Oyo are said to have found asylum. Johnson says that nearly all were slaughtered by the Fon, who were doubtless still resentful of their long subjection to Oyo.[22]

Two years later came the turn of another big Yoruba community called Lefu-Lefu (or Refurefu). Here the Dahomeans took many prisoners and resettled them as slave labor on royal plantations in the area of Abomey. One plantation, which became known as Lefu-Lefu, was visited by Beecroft and Forbes. The consul reported "a fine Farm" of oil palms and maize; the naval officer found Lefu-Lefu "remarkable for the superiority of its cultivation and the industry of its denizens".[23] According to Dunglas, it also provided the king with a handy pool of potential sacrificial victims or slaves for export.[24]

Le Hérissé's principal informant, a court chronicler named Agbidinoukoun (he was a brother of Béhanzin), dates Gezo's

Tumulus of Courage to the Lefu-Lefu campaign. From atop the mound, he says, the monarch "singled out the Yoruba as our perpetual enemy; he cried out his hatred for them and knew how to pass it on to his people. The enthusiasm was immense. The warriors departed sure of victory" and overwhelmed Lefu-Lefu.[25]

That the amazons took part in these engagements against the Yoruba is suggested by a passage in Duncan. In the royal "collection of skulls" at Abomey in 1845, he

....found a number of them ornamented with brass, and rivetted together with iron. These were the heads of rival kings, who were killed by the King's women, or wives. Amongst these was the richly ornamented skull of the King of Nahpoo, in the Annagoo [Yoruba] country...His town was taken, and he himself made prisoner, by the female regiments, commanded by the female commander, Apadomey [Akpadume].[26]

Five years later Beecroft and Forbes saw an amazon who had been wounded in the head, nose and hand in the "ahnaa-goo war".[27]

Dahomey's fateful rivalry with the Yoruba of Abeokuta, the Egba, seems to go back to 1844. A chief named Sodeke had founded the city in 1830 and, according to tradition, assembled people from 153 villages displaced by internecine warfare in Yorubaland. The Yoruba had, and still have, a predilection for urbanization unusual in sub-Saharan Africa. By the mid-1840s Abeokuta had tens of thousands of inhabitants. In 1846 Christian missionaries began working there, starting with the Rev. Henry Townsend of the (Anglican) Church Missionary Society.

Initially, Gezo and Sodeke are said to have been allies. It is not clear why they fell out, but the growing power of each may well have inspired mutual fear. They had also become rivals in slave raiding and trading. Beecroft says that the main theme of amazon songs at the 1850 customs was for the king to allow them to go and attack Abeokuta. All the "Petty Nations" in the region had been conquered, they sang; only two "Great Nations" remained. "It was impossible for two Rams to feed out of the same Stall, their Horns must get entangled." So Dahomey and Abeokuta could not coexist.[28]

Many decades later, Agbidinoukoun explained it this way:

We no longer wanted any rival to Dahomey. Now Abeokuta threatened our power. All the Yoruba whose country we were devastating were taking refuge there and our enemies were thus concentrating at a single point, ever more numerous. Abeokuta was becoming a danger for Dahomey.[29]

In early 1844 the Egba were besieging a town called Ado belonging to another Yoruba group, the Egbado, who stood between them and the coast. Dunglas reports a tradition that the Egbado asked Gezo for help.[30] The king moved into the area with a force including many amazons. Whatever his intentions, the Egba besieging Ado felt threatened and decided on a pre-emptive strike.

The Dahomeans were camped near the village of Imojolu one morning, drying their things on bushes after an overnight rainstorm. The Egba caught them by surprise, inflicted heavy casualties, and routed them. Gezo barely escaped capture. Ellis says that the amazons lost most of their officers; Forbes specifies their general.[31] An historian of Abeokuta, Ajayi Kolawole Ajisafe, pays tribute to the amazons who, he says, made up most of the Dahomean force. "[T]hey dressed like men," he relates, "and were like the Spartans, very brave, powerful and smart. It was after the victory, when the Egba troops were searching the dead and examining the enemy, that they knew they had been fighting with women."[32]

Gezo mourned not only his amazons: the Egba had captured some of his regalia, including the royal war stool and an especially prized umbrella. Dunglas says that the latter was hung with sachets full of magic preparations.[33] Johnson describes it as "the standard of the Dahomian army" and heard that it was made of various animal skins.[34] Gezo negotiated for the umbrella's restitution, and reportedly was willing to pay any price, but alas the Egba, in celebrating their victory, had burned it. (According to Bowen and Burton, it was the stool that Gezo missed most of all.)[35] Traditions on both sides trace decades of Fon-Egba enmity to this incident, which was no flimsier a pretext for war than Spaniards cutting off Captain Jenkins's ear or the dey of Algiers striking the French consul with his fan.

The Imojolu defeat may have sparked the big buildup in the amazon corps that Europeans began to notice the following year. Suddenly there were thousands of women soldiers instead of the 800 Brue had estimated in 1843. One must assume that Gezo had launched an intensive recruitment and training program.

By April 1847 the king could tell British visitors that "he had sent four thousand [amazons] to battle a few days ago, and hoped they would return with plenty of captives."[36] Gezo may have been exaggerating, but plainly the women had now become a major factor in Dahomean warfare.

In 1848 Dahomey targeted the Egbado town of Okeadon whose leaders had made up with the Egba and become brokers for their slave trade to the coast. We know that amazons took part in this campaign because not long afterward Beecroft and Forbes saw a woman who had received two sword cuts on the head from an Okeadon man but still managed to capture him.[37] The Fon army marched past the town as if headed for Abeokuta, then doubled back at night and, with the help of a turncoat Okeadon chief, easily captured the place. Thousands of prisoners were taken.[38] The oral historian Agbidinoukoun makes the unusual assertion that Okeadon was attacked specifically to procure slaves for a ship off Whydah. He says 4,000 people were caught,[39] which is to say 3,000 more than the biggest slaver could handle. Bowen heard that 600 captives were supplied to a Brazilian slave dealer at Whydah, which *would* have made up a ship's cargo.[40] Forbes and Beecroft saw an octagonal or circular building they called a golgotha in the big square outside the Singboji palace. It was adorned with human skulls. Forbes counted 148 – Beecroft about 170 – "lately cleaned and varnished, the heads of some of the victims of the dreadful tragedy of Okeadon." [41]

17

ABEOKUTA 1851

The devastation of Okeadon moved the Fon closer to a showdown with Abeokuta. Their resolve could only have been strengthened by a series of Egba attacks which, according to a British consular report, destroyed more than twenty-five towns and large villages along Dahomey's border before the 1851 invasion.[1] At least one of them, Igbeji, was under Fon protection.[2]

When Forbes and Beecroft visited Abomey in May-July 1850, the die was already cast. Time and again, orators and singers, amazons prominent among them, appealed to Gezo to let them attack and destroy Abeokuta.[3] On one occasion, a chorus of female officers ridiculed alleged Abeokutan claims to be able to defeat Dahomey. The Yoruba, they sang, must be mad or drunk to tell such a lie, which would be exposed when they met. "If at night it will appear like day from the firing of their [the amazons'] Muskets. If it is day the Sun will be darkened with [gun] Smoke."[4] "It is too obvious", Beecroft commented in his journal on June 13, "that they [the amazons] are fully bent and determined on the downfall of Abbeo Kutta."[5]

If there was any doubt about Gezo's intentions, it was dispelled on July 4 at his final meeting with the British emissaries. Habitual Dahomean secrecy about military plans was abandoned. The monarch bluntly announced that he was going to attack Abeokuta and advised Beecroft – who said he would soon visit the place – to remove the white missionaries. (The Meu complained that the clerics had no right to teach the Egba how to read and write, implying

174

that this would give them an unfair advantage over the Fon.)[6]

In January 1851 Beecroft traveled to Abeokuta, "met the chiefs and people in a grand council", and alerted them to a Dahomean invasion.[7] He did not get the missionaries out; instead, he supplied the Rev. Mr Townsend with ammunition for defense of the city.[8]

Around mid-February, after haranguing his army from atop the Tumulus of Courage, Gezo set out for Abeokuta with between 10,000 and 16,000 troops, including as many as 4,000 amazons.[9] The army was commanded by the Gau Akati, who is said to have distinguished himself at Okeadon.[10] No effort seems to have been made to mask the goal of the expedition.

On March 1 the Fon reached the Yoruba town of Ishagga, 16 miles west of Abeokuta. The chief, Oba Koko (*oba* being the Yoruba word for king or paramount chief), pretended to cooperate with the Dahomeans but sent word to the Egba of their approach. (That same day, Townsend reported, Abeokuta's leaders, alerted to the invasion, met to plan the city's defense.)[11] Oba Koko also gave Gezo's military leaders some very bad advice. He suggested that they attack at midday instead of before dawn, because Egba men would then be either taking a siesta or working in their fields. He persuaded them to attack the southwestern, or Aro, gate of the city, which had just been fortified, instead of the northwestern gate, which had been left in a dilapidated state. And he told them to ford the Ogun River, which runs just to the west of Abeokuta, at a place so deep that some of their powder would certainly get wet. Implausibly, the Fon followed Oba Koko's counsel to the letter, though presumably they had better information from at least one spy, remembered by name, who had scouted the city. Ishagga would eventually pay a terrible price for this deception which, according to a Fon oral tradition, was confirmed by Dahomeans captured at Abeokuta who either by ransom or escape made it back to Abomey. It was also amply confirmed on the Abeokuta side.[12]

Apart from this disinformation, the Dahomeans seem to have been unaware, or incautiously dismissive, of the sheer size and defensive advantages of their enemy. Abeokuta, meaning "under stone", was named for a cluster of huge granite slabs rising 200 feet or more on a broad plain. The city grew between and around these natural defenses. The Ogun, about 100 yards wide, gave further protection. By 1851 the population had reached at least 50 or 60,000; some visitors estimated it at 100,000 or more. Bowen reported the city to be close to 4 miles long, 2 to 3 miles wide, and at least 10 miles in circuit. It was surrounded by an earthen wall about 15 miles long which also enclosed much open space.[13] The wall is variously described as 2 to 5 meters high; Dunglas says a gentle slope led to the top from inside.[14] Outside the wall was a ditch, its dimensions 3 to 5 meters wide and perhaps 3 deep. Dunglas adds that the outer slope of the ditch was thickly planted with thorny acacia.[15]

Bowen, who had had military experience fighting Indians in Georgia and Mexicans in Texas, estimated Abeokuta's forces at perhaps 15,000 men, all armed with muskets.[16] As the Fon approached, Townsend distributed bullets, and Bowen "exhorted the people to stand firm, to reserve their fire, and take good aim".[17]

Toward noon on March 3, the Dahomeans struck. Bowen watched from the wall, and Townsend, his wife and other missionaries from a high rock within the city, using a telescope. As far as we know, it was the first time whites had ever seen the amazons in combat.

The Fon advanced across the prairie to the west of the river "in heavy squadrons, with flying colors".[18] Egba soldiers sent out to meet them were driven back. The Dahomeans divided into two formations that crossed the river at two points in compact masses. According to Dunglas' reconstruction, the Dahomeans passed over the thornbushes as if traversing a meadow.[19] One formation, led by amazons, charged

right up to the Aro gate, where the foe held fast. Some
women managed to get over the wall but were cut down.
Most of the Egba retreated into the city and took up positions
along the rampart. Their musket fire was so intense that
the Fon spread out, probing for weak spots in the wall,
until their front extended for a mile or more.

Neither Bowen nor Townsend offers evidence for an
Egba tradition, first written down long afterward, that the
tide of battle turned after the defenders realized that women
were spearheading the assault. Burton, who visited Abeokuta
a decade after the battle, did hear that the Egba, "enraged
by being attacked by women", hotly pursued the retreating
foe once the issue was decided.[20] But he is silent on traditions
that he would surely have savored had he known about
them.

According to one version, a Dahomean soldier, mortally
wounded, fell at the feet of an Egba chief, who glimpsed
a female breast under a tattered tunic. The chief spread the
word that the Egba were being pushed back by women.[21]
Other sources say the Yoruba customarily decapitated and
emasculated the first enemy captured, or slain, and sent the
head and genitals as trophies to their leader.[22] Or the first
prisoner was sent alive to the leader and sacrificed, by beheading and emasculation, to the tutelary spirits of the town.[23]
In either case, the victim's sex was immediately apparent.
Examination of attackers who had crossed the wall and been
killed confirmed that all were women.

This discovery was said to shame, insult, revolt and so
infuriate Egba men that they redoubled their efforts and
carried the day. However, this story may be apocryphal.
We have already noted a tradition that after the battle of
Imojolu in 1844, the Egba learned by examining the dead
that they had been fighting women. Even if that tradition,
too, was questionable, it is hard to believe that Abeokutans
would not have heard of the amazons of Dahomey in the
previous two decades. Bowen indicates as much when he
writes that for twenty-five years Dahomey's regular army,

"nearly half...composed of women, trained to war from their youth...had been the scourge and terror of the whole surrounding country, always at war and generally victorious."[24] In a letter dated March 4, Townsend reports that the first prisoner brought in was "one of the renowned women soldiers". (He followed her to her captor's house, where she spoke to him "as freely as our ignorance of each other's language would admit of.")[25] Finally, it is unlikely that Beecroft failed to mention the amazons when he briefed Abeokutans on Gezo's plans. In any event, Dahomean attacks tapered off and the invaders camped a safe distance from the wall. They had suffered heavy casualties. An Egba slave of the Fon, who later escaped, reported that when Gezo's warriors gathered that night, they "were struck dumb at the loss they had sustained, especially of their female soldiers".[26] The Gau Akati himself had died fighting. The king moved off during the night, presumably with amazon bodyguards. At daybreak the bulk of the army began an orderly retreat, turning at times to fire at the closely pursuing Egba.

When they reached Ishagga, another major battle erupted, as the Abeokutans and local townspeople joined forces. Townsend heard that Gezo lost some personal baggage and had to flee on foot[27] (instead of in a hammock or palanquin). Fon casualties at Ishagga may have been even higher than at Abeokuta. The pursuit ended soon after, and the survivors returned to Abomey.

Townsend's fellow Anglican missionary, a Yoruba named Samuel Ajayi Crowther (later to become a famous bishop), walked around the Abeokuta battlefield on March 4 and saw great numbers of corpses. In the space of a few yards between the city wall and the Ogun River he counted eighty, all but five of them female.[28] Next day Townsend sent out two persons for a more thorough body count; on only one part of the battlefield they tallied 1,209 slain Dahomeans, the majority of whom were women. Townsend put the total Dahomean dead outside Abeokuta at "not less than 1800".[29] All told, counting casualties suffered during the retreat, the Fon may have lost more than 3,000 troops, including as many as 2,000 amazons.[30] Egba losses, too, were substantial, but apparently these were not tabulated. Of several hundred prisoners taken by the Abeokutans, many were women and some were killed rebelling against their captors. "This affair" Bowen observed, "spoiled the terrible name of the Dahomies."[31]

The reasons for the debacle are rather obvious. Gezo and his generals clearly underestimated enemy strength. They had never faced so many men, so well equipped with firearms and ammunition, and in such an advantageous position. British help and the very presence of the missionaries probably boosted Egba morale: Townsend wrote to Beecroft that "the bullets were very useful" and advised the Church Missionary Society that "people everywhere here seem to ascribe their deliverance to God and the white men."[32] Moreover, the Abeokutans had nowhere to retreat, most of their Yoruba neighbors being hostile.

Just as clearly, the Fon were overconfident. "They must have believed their own propaganda," Maroukis suggests; "they must have been convinced of their own invincibility."[33] Hence the fact that they did not trouble to conceal their intentions, and attacked in broad daylight. In Abomey Forbes and Beecroft had been told that Gezo had or would make a "fetish" to send to Abeokuta. It would cause civil strife and make the city easy pickings, like Okeadon.[34] Such a belief would go far toward explaining the Dahomeans' behavior.[35]

18

ABEOKUTA 1864

Gezo quickly rebuilt his female corps. As mentioned earlier, less than four months after the disaster, Bouët visited Abomey and reckoned amazon strength at 4,000 to 6,000. Fraser followed him two months later. He watched amazons dance in "dingy war dress", doubtless what they had worn in battle. They "talked a great deal about [Abeokuta]...saying they had lost a great many friends there, and ought to weep for them." In effect, they asked permission to avenge their comrades, and vowed to "break" the city next time. Fraser counted roughly 5,000 female soldiers but decided that the same women had gone past four times and that there were no more than 1,250 in all. (The Briton's judgment may have been influenced by a visceral antipathy toward the Dahomeans. He found the amazons "an ill looking lot [who seemed] to vie with each other in ugliness", and the whole army "a wild cut-throat set of fiends".)[1] Later in the 1850s Répin and Vallon, both careful observers, agreed on a figure of about 4,000 amazon paraders and Vallon put the total at 5,000.[2]

Gezo seems to have resumed annual campaigns but never felt strong enough to return to Abeokuta. Répin and Vallon were told of an expedition against another, unidentified Yoruba town, apparently around 1855, led by the new Gau. The town turned out to be well fortified, and the Dahomean attack was beaten off with heavy casualties. The Gau talked of pulling out, but the head of the amazons said that her troops would continue the siege alone if they had to. "This bold resolution of the women shamed the men," who joined in a new attack that subdued the town but cost the Gau's life. When asked if he regretted the general's loss, Gezo is said to have replied, "Yes, indeed, because I won't be able to have his head cut off to punish him for his cowardice."[3]

On another expedition into Yoruba country in 1858, when Gezo was well into his sixties, he was ambushed and mortally wounded by a local youth. In retaliation, the Dahomeans wiped out the village of Ekpo, near Ketu, and carried off between 1,400 and 1,500 prisoners.[4]

Glele took power determined to avenge his father's defeat at Abeokuta. But first there was a score to settle with Ishagga. One night in March 1862, eleven years after Oba Koko's alleged perfidy, Dahomean forces silently surrounded Ishagga and blocked all the exits. Father Noël Baudin, of the French mission at Whydah, later heard that they were "preceded by the fierce battalion of amazons".[5] It was a classic Dahomean operation, a predawn attack that caught the inhabitants off-guard and met little resistance. According to Charles Andrew Gollmer, an Anglican missionary then stationed in Abeokuta, 1,000 people were slain and 4,000 captured.[6] At Whydah Dawson heard that 3,000 or more had been taken.[7] (The few that escaped fled to the Egba capital and settled there.[8]) Several Ishagga chiefs were killed and their heads hung from the necks of Dahomean chiefs' horses for the march back to Abomey.[9] (Another version says they were taken alive to the capital and executed there, whereupon their skulls were displayed throughout the kingdom hanging from their own horses.)[10] A Christian convert, one of eighteen caught at Ishagga, was crucified in Abomey.[11] In one Fon village an amazon named Hounsi is remembered to this day for bringing back a prisoner and two skulls from Ishagga.[12]

Ordinary prisoners were attached to chains by iron collars in groups of twelve, men, women and children intermingled. They would be seen by Baudin and other Europeans in the Whydah market for sale as slaves. It was understood that unsold captives would be taken to Abomey for sacrifice; Borghero bought several children to save them from that fate.[13]

As for Oba Koko, he was brought to Abomey, and decapitated. Not long after, Burton saw his "well boiled" skull embellished with brass. It was surmounted by a helmet-like drinking cup.[14] Dunglas explains that in 1851 the Oba had offered the Dahomeans "pure water as a sign of friendship and loyalty" while at the same time betraying them. Now they drank water from his head.[15]

In March 1863 the Dahomeans struck even closer to Abeokuta, destroying the town of Ibara just 9 miles to the west. For sixteen days they camped on a rise within sight of the city, but failed to attack.[16]

A year later Glele was ready, but he seems not to have learned the lessons of his father's defeat. Again the British were forewarned of the planned attack. "I must go to Abbeokuta," Glele told Wilmot, "I must punish them.[...] [W]hy interfere in black man's wars?[...][L]et every [white man] go out of Abbeokuta, and see who will win...see which are the brave men!"[17] The Fon had found a scapegoat for their 1851 failure in the missionary presence. (Unlike Beecroft, Wilmot actually advised the missionaries to leave, but they stayed.)[18]

If anything, Abeokuta had grown bigger in the interval. In 1861 Burton put the circumference of its defenses at 17 to 20 miles, although he scoffed at its wall and ditch, which he gauged, respectively, at 5 to 6 feet high and 5 feet broad.[19] In 1863 Wilmot, more conservatively, thought the wall to be about 12 miles round and only 4 to 5 feet high and, skeptically it must be said, cited population estimates of 100,000.[20]

On February 22, 1864, an estimated 10,000 to 12,000 troops left Abomey, including perhaps 3,000 amazons. It took them twenty-two days to cover the 100 miles. Dunglas explains that they made a long detour to try to catch Abeokuta unawares, but the Egba had advance notice and were ready and waiting.[21] They had repaired their wall, mounted two or three field-guns on it, and deepened the ditch. Instead of sallying out to meet the Fon in the field, where the latter's discipline and experience gave them an advantage, the Egba largely remained behind the rampart. And this time they were reinforced by contingents from two other Yoruba subgroups.

The long march had only wearied the Dahomeans, and caused them to run short of food. The night of March 14–15, they marched to the Ogun River by moonlight and refreshed themselves in its waters at daybreak. As noted earlier, Burton reported that a ration of rum laced with gunpowder raised their spirits. The Fon crossed the river under cover of fog, coming into view when they reached the east bank. With typical bravado, the attackers threw their muskets into the air and caught them with one hand, and the amazons sang and danced. They then formed into three columns 200 meters from the city wall, hoisted their flags and, toward 7 o'clock, at a signal from the Gau, charged along a front of about 700 meters. One column headed for the Aro gate, the others to the left of it, braving withering enemy fire.

Again the amazons distinguished themselves. Many reached the ditch under cover of gunsmoke, and some managed to scale the wall. They fired their muskets at almost point-blank range and even hurled large stones. Some pushed enemy muskets aside with their left hand and slashed the gunmen with the machete in their right. One woman whose arm was cut off shot her adversary dead with the musket in her other hand, before being run through with swords and thrown back into the ditch. Three amazons succeeded in planting banners atop the wall; they were quickly cut down. Their heads and hands were fixed to the ends of poles and paraded through the city to shouts of "Victory". Some women soldiers crept through narrow tunnels in the wall that the Egba had dug for possible sorties. But enemies were waiting at the other end and decapitated them as they emerged. Only four Dahomeans got all the way through Abeokuta's defenses before being killed; all were women.

Dunglas relates a tradition that at one point in the battle

an amazon, "to show her scorn for the Egba [and, Amélie Degbelo adds, keep 'even the most cowardly male soldiers' from breaking Dahomean ranks], stopped not far from the ramparts, sat down on a copper caldron and, disdainfully turning her back to the enemy, tranquilly began smoking a long pipe." When enemy bullets failed to hit her, a sharp-shooting hunter was summoned. "Taking his time, he aimed carefully and slew the warrioress with his first shot." The Egba made a sortie to cut off her head, which one of their women displayed around town.[22]

Despite amazon heroics, the Fon gave up after only an hour and a half, and began an orderly retreat. The Egba pursued them. After further fighting at Ibara and Ishagga, the retreat turned into a rout. Glele escaped with his women protectors but, according to one report, lost his tent, his throne and his sandals.[23] The Fon also lost many weapons, including three bronze cannon and a few of the giant amazon razors. Estimates of casualties vary greatly, but there is general agreement that the amazons suffered fewer, both absolutely and relative to their male comrades, than they had in 1851. Of perhaps 2,000 Dahomean dead, 700 may have been women, but only about 140 female bodies were counted outside Abeokuta's wall. As many as 1,000 prisoners were taken, including many women. The Egba admitted to only fifty dead and 100 wounded.[24]

Dahomey never lost hope of obliterating Abeokuta. Revenge became an obsession during Glele's reign. "As long as the monarchy existed and Abeokuta subsisted," Djivo tells us, "how to destroy that city would remain the major preoc-cupation of everyone."[25] Townsend heard a rumor that Glele could not "enjoy the full honours of king" until he had fulfilled a pledge to his father to bring down the Egba metropolis.[26] As already noted, Skertchly saw an amazon unit armed with axes that were intended to be used against Abeokuta's gates – and never were. (The women wore gray togas and red crossbelts, and a skull was affixed below each axe-head.)[27] A missionary source counted a total of seven Fon invasions of Egba country between 1851 and 1876.[28]

One incursion was in 1873, when the Dahomeans camped within sight of Abeokuta for thirteen days and then withdrew. The Egba had three different explanations for their deliverance: traditionalists believed a certain sorcerer had put a hex on the expedition, or had caused a smallpox epidemic to strike the Fon; Christians thought that God had answered their prayers.[29] In 1875 the Dahomeans came again, and stayed in the area for two months. There were several small-scale clashes, including at least one that the Egba remember as a victory.[30] Yet another invasion was reported in 1890, under Béhanzin, when the Fon are said to have destroyed eleven towns in the vicinity of Abeokuta.[31] And as late as May 1891, only eighteen months before Dahomey's final defeat by the French, the Fon were still raiding Egba villages.[32]

Even after the French conquest, resentment against the Egba lingered. Agbidinoukoun told Le Hérissé that that conquest would have been easier to bear had the Fon previously defeated Abeokuta. "Nevertheless we have one consolation," he added. "[T]he inhabitants of Abeokuta too are under the domination of the whites [i.e. the new British colony of Nigeria]."[33]

19

YEARS OF SUCCESS

If Glele never achieved his primary goal, his army scored a string of successes against other targets, often with amazon participation. In April 1878 a French naval officer, Commander Paul Serval, heard at Whydah that the king had just returned to Abomey after taking six villages by storm. "[T]he largest is said to have been captured by the amazons", he reported, "after very sharp resistance." He did not locate the villages, but was told they had been tributary to Dahomey and "had manifested some symptoms of rebellion".[1] We do know that Glele's forces carried out punitive expeditions against Mahi communities to the north. Agbidinoukoun reeled off the names of thirty-three that were successively attacked.[2] A bas-relief in Glele's palace shows two amazons on a hill in Mahi country drinking to celebrate a victory;[3] conceivably it was the one Serval heard about.

Glele also sent troops against the Atlantic port of Grand Popo west of Whydah. Protected by lagoon waters, Grand Popo repelled a Fon attack dated to 1869.[4] Six years later the Fon returned, and triumphed. A salt tribute was imposed,[5] but Grand Popo's subjection to Abomey does not seem to have lasted long. By the 1880s German firms were active there, apparently outside Dahomean control.[6]

Still another victim of Glele's wrath may have been the Ouémé people southeast of Abomey, first conquered in the early eighteenth century. Ellis says that the Dahomeans invaded and pillaged "Ewemi" in 1882.[7] Toward the end of that decade, according to an oral tradition collected by Degbelo, Glele sent an amazon detachment to crush a village called Banigbé Poto-Poto in the same general area. He ordered them to bring back only ablebodied females fit to become soldiers. The first amazon attack was repelled; the second resulted in the disemboweling of all local men who could be caught, and the roundup of girls and women who were taken to Abomey for military training.[8]

However, the main thrust of Glele-era campaigning was against Yoruba communities other than the Egba. The Fon actually struck deeper into Yorubaland than ever before. After the Oyo empire disintegrated around 1836, a successor kingdom was founded by fugitives at a place that would also be called Oyo 140 miles northeast of Abomey. In 1881 the ruler of this new Oyo sent a letter to Lagos appealing for British help against the Dahomeans. He complained that they had recently overrun seven towns in his kingdom, were threatening an eighth, and "the next turn might be to my own royal city."[9]

Even the area of Lagos, 110 miles southeast of Abomey, a British colony since 1861, seems to have been menaced. Ellis reports that in 1886 a town only about 16 miles from Lagos was abandoned in the face of a Fon invasion.[10]

The Yoruba town of Meko (also known as Imeko, Mek-kaw) northwest of Abeokuta was destroyed in 1879. This is where two amazon spies are reputed to have seduced the war chief and stripped him of his occult powers. In any event, women soldiers are credited with a key role in taking Meko. It was a major prize. John Milum, a British Wesleyan missionary who visited Abomey not long afterward, was told that Dahomean troops had brought back more than 17,000 captives and 7,200 heads from Meko.[11] More credibly, a French document speaks of about 3,000 prisoners and more than 4,000 heads.[12]

Another Yoruba town, Okeadon, which had risen from the ashes of 1848, was attacked and destroyed once again in 1884. Agbidinoukoun explains that Okeadon had been raiding outlying parts of the coastal kingdom of Porto-Novo, which Dahomey considered to be under its protection. The

Porto-Novo monarch, Tofa, who had ascended the throne ten years earlier with Glele's support, now asked him for help, and Glele obliged by wiping out Okeadon.[13] (The subsequent deterioration in relations between Dahomey and Porto-Novo would offer a pretext for French intervention.)

Glele's victims included two of the oldest towns in Yorubaland, Savé (or Shabe), some 70 miles northeast of Abomey, and Ketu, 50 miles to the east. They were the capitals of kingdoms founded, according to legend, by dispersal of princes from Ife, the cradle of Yoruba civilization. Since Ife is more than 1,000 years old and the princes are said to have been sons or grandsons of *its* founder, Oduduwa, Savé and Ketu almost surely go far back into what Westerners call the Middle Ages. (In the mid-twentieth century a British scholar, Geoffrey Parrinder, recorded a meticulous Ketu king list of forty-eight names, which suggests tenth-to-twelfth-century origins.)[14]

Some time between 1825 and 1830, Gezo sacked Savé and killed its king. Since this happened not long after Dahomey threw off the yoke of Oyo, it may be that Savé had sided with the old Yoruba empire. According to Fon tradition, the king of Savé had boasted that he would kill Gezo and twirl his head like a spindle. A bas-relief in Gezo's palace shows the Savé ruler's head squeezed between two parts of a spindle.[15]

Amazons probably did not take part in that campaign, but they surely did in one that ravaged Savé again in 1887. A bas-relief in Glele's palace shows an amazon who has felled a Savé warrior and is about to open his belly with a hoe.[16] Conceivably the heroine is Tata Ajachê, the warrioress who eviscerated a farmer with his own hoe and was rewarded by Glele with two female slaves.

Of all the Yoruba towns targeted by Glele after his defeat at Abeokuta, Ketu may have been the most important, with a population of up to 20,000, a wall perhaps 4 miles in circumference and a ditch put at 5 meters deep and 15 wide. It is also the one about which oral historians have preserved the most details. Dahomey defeated Ketu twice: in 1883 and again in 1885. On the first of these occasions, typical Fon ruses hoodwinked the town. Presents were sent, friendship was offered and false word was spread that Dahomey had suffered a serious defeat against the Mahi. Ketu felt safe enough on its western side to dispatch its main forces east against Yoruba rivals. The Dahomeans, marching at night, surprised the town at dawn and overpowered it. Ketu was sacked and burned, and its king and many of his subjects were beheaded, and others led off as prisoners. Some residents escaped, and when Ketu's troops returned from the east the town was quickly rebuilt.[17]

It is not known whether the amazons took part in this first conquest of Ketu, but they did in the much more difficult campaign two years later.[18] This time Dahomey had the help of one of its most famous spies, a Ketu native named Arepa (or Arekpa) who, it is said, had a deep grievance against the town fathers: they had married off the girl he loved to a higher-ranking man.[19] But initially the Fon were thwarted. Ketu had strengthened its defenses, and its musketeers stood ready behind the town wall when Dahomey attacked. According to one account, amazons led the early-morning assault. Half of them were shot down in the ditch, and the rest tried but failed to scale the wall.[20] A male gate-opening company was all but wiped out. Dahomey's war chiefs, including an amazon "colonel" named Goubé, gave up the idea of frontal attacks and opted for a siege.[21]

The Fon army camped on a plateau a mile from Ketu and blocked all paths out of town. The siege lasted three months. Ketu ran out of provisions; old people and children began starving to death. Defectors were well received and well fed by the Dahomeans, who then sent them back to town with offers of peace. After some hesitation, Ketu's chiefs put on their best clothes and went to the enemy camp preceded by drums. Invited to dine individually in officers' huts before the promised negotiations, they were easily overpowered, bound and gagged. Arepa is said to have looked them over to see who was missing, and the Ketu musicians were forced to summon those few with drum talk.

The Fon then attacked the leaderless town. According to one tradition, their victory was swift; another has Ketu resisting quarter by quarter for three days.[22] In either case, the population was slaughtered or taken prisoner, and the town totally destroyed. Glele is said to have decreed that no one ever live there again. After the march back to Abomey, twenty-three Ketu officers were executed. The town lay in ruins for eight years, but was then revived by returning prisoners freed by the French conquest of Dahomey. Even Arepa eventually returned to Ketu from Abomey, in 1926, "trusting that time and the French peace would keep him from harm", but he soon died in mysterious circumstances.[23]

20

FRANCE VS. DAHOMEY, 1890

When in Paris, I stay in a modest hotel on the rue Bobillot in the thirteenth *arrondissement*. The street is named for a forgotten hero of a forgotten nineteenth-century colonial war in Indo-China. A bust of Sergeant Jules Bobillot stands ignored in a forlorn patch of park with benches used by *clochards*. He is of interest to almost no one in the postcolonial world.

I think of Bobillot when contemplating the genesis and details of the French conquest of Dahomey. They were ripples in the tide of European imperialism that swept across Africa in the last decades of the nineteenth century. The complex sequence of events that extinguished the Fon kingdom is not important; a wholly different set of circumstances would have led to the same inevitable outcome. Autonomous Africa was doomed.

Succinctly, in 1841 the Marseille commercial house of Régis decided to set up an establishment in the old French fort at Whydah that had been abandoned at the end of the eighteenth century. Two years later Gezo gave his blessing to the plan and obliged Régis to pay substantial annual charges. A Franco-Dahomean friendship treaty of 1851 imposed rules on European merchants and allowed missionaries to enter the country; a mission was opened at Whydah ten years later.

The small kingdom of Porto-Novo east of Whydah traced its origins, like Dahomey, to Tado in Togo (although it did not acquire its Portuguese name – meaning "new port" –till the mid-eighteenth century) and considered the Fon as cousins. According to Porto-Novo traditions, the kingdom

successfully fought against Dahomey during the reign of
Tegbesu (1740-74).[1] Yoruba began settling in the area at
the same time, and it may be that Porto-Novo was able to
solidify its independence *vis-à-vis* Dahomey as a protégé of
the Oyo empire. In Gezo's time Abomey and Porto-Novo
seem to have maintained friendly relations.

In 1861 British ships from Lagos, where the Royal Navy
had been established for a decade, shelled and burned Porto-
Novo. The British believed that under pressure from Dahomey the little kingdom had been diverting palm-oil trade
from Lagos to Whydah. Porto-Novo's participation in the
Atlantic slave trade in defiance of Britain's antislavery patrol
was also a factor. As a result of the British attack, Porto-Novo
asked for French protection and a treaty to that effect was
concluded in 1863, the same year that France opened a
consular agency at Whydah. The French protectorate actually
lasted less than two years because the king who signed the
treaty died and his successor opposed it. Glele, who apparently
regarded the ruler of Porto-Novo as his vassal, was also
hostile.

At the same time, however, the king of Dahomey permitted
certain rights to French traders at the port of Cotonou,
between Whydah and Porto-Novo. According to the French,
he verbally "ceded" part of the town, and a treaty ratified
that cession in 1868. A second treaty ten years later confirmed
French rights in Cotonou. The treaties were signed not by
the king but by his representative in Whydah, and Glele
would subsequently deny that he had approved either one.
He dispatched troops to Cotonou in 1885, and continued
to collect customs there.

Tofa took power in Porto-Novo in 1874, and the French
protectorate over that kingdom was re-established by mutual
agreement in 1882-3 after Dahomey began raiding villages
in the Ouémé River valley that was claimed by both Porto-
Novo and Abomey. Such raids continued through the decade.
Events were now moving inexorably toward an armed con-
frontation between France and Dahomey.

Alfred Barbou, a French chronicler of the Franco-Dahomean wars, tells of an incident in 1887 which, he says, "set fire to the powder". Dahomeans attacked a village on the Ouémé where a Senegalese, sponsored by the French, ran a trading post that flew the tricolor. Have no fear, he is said to have told his employees, the French flag will protect us. But the Dahomeans killed or wounded his whole staff, and wounded and captured the Senegalese. "So you like this French flag?" said the Dahomean war chief. "*Eh bien*, it will serve you." He gave a signal to an amazon, who then beheaded the Senegalese with one blow of her cutlass. The head was wrapped in the flag, and the wife of the victim was forced to carry it to Glele himself. Barbou gives no source for the anecdote.[2] A more reliable author, Major Léonce Grandin, says that the incident took place in March 1889 and that the man who thought the tricolor would save him was a village chief. He does not mention the victim's wife, but reports that a woman soldier carried out the execution.[3]

In November 1889 France sent a mission to Abomey to assert its claims to Cotonou and offer to pay an annual rent. Glele was dying. The mission, led by Jean Bayol, was received by the crown prince, soon to ascend the throne as Béhanzin at the year's end. The French, already preparing to garrison Cotonou and contemplating military operations against Dahomey, succeeded only in antagonizing Béhanzin.

A token French contingent was already quartered among French merchant houses in Cotonou. In the early weeks of 1890 it was built up into a force of 359 men. The great majority – 299, or 83 per cent – were Africans (Senegalese and Gabonese *tirailleurs*) trained and led by French officers. They were equipped with eight-shot Lebel repeating rifles. French weaponry also included four field-pieces that fired canister or grape shot. On February 21 the French arrested senior Fon officials in Cotonou, began setting up a fortified 800-meter perimeter in front of the trading posts, and skirmished with local militia. The first Franco-Dahomean war had begun.

The war lasted two months and included two major engagements, in both of which the amazons played a salient part. What became known as the Battle of Cotonou started before dawn on March 4. During a rainy night a Dahomean force of several thousand, including what the French described as a "regiment" of women, silently approached the French perimeter. Around 5 a.m. amazons opened the attack by leading a charge against a log stockade. Some prised the stakes apart and thrust their musket barrels through to fire on the defenders. In hand-to-hand fighting, some women were impaled on bayonets; it was the first time the Fon had ever faced such weapons.

The chief gunner in the stockade, apparently a white sergeant, was killed and decapitated by an amazon aged about sixteen, who in turn was slain. Bayol later recognized her as Nansica, the "ravishing" girl he had seen in Abomey not three months earlier executing a man with her sword. Nansica "lay on her back, arms extended", he reported.

She wore a white cap, scarlet pants covered by a snug pagne, a flowered vest which, partly open, let one glimpse the nascent and pure shapes of the Dahomean vestal. The cleaver, its curved blade engraved with fetish symbols, was attached to her left wrist by a small cord, and her right hand was clenched round the barrel of her carbine covered with cowries.[4]

Another amazon was said to have beheaded a Senegalese corporal and then fallen dead over his body. And according to Fon tradition, another *tirailleur*, possibly Gabonese, disarmed a woman soldier who then tore his throat open with her teeth[5] (for the amazons fighting tooth and nail was no mere metaphor).

The struggle raged for some four hours. French firepower, augmented by shells from a gunboat offshore once day had dawned, was simply too much for the Dahomeans. They broke off their attacks, leaving the bodies of 120 men and

Engraving of amazons, said to be based on an eyewitness sketch. Note the heads adorning the walls. The presence of a European is not explained. (H. Morienval, *La Guerre au Dahomey*, Paris, 1893, p. 27)

Béhanzin, last independent king of Dahomey, puffing on his long pipe. (A.L. Albéca, "Au Dahomey", *Le Tour du Monde*, 1894, 2nd semester, p. 99)

seven women within French lines. Several hundred other Dahomean dead and wounded were said to have been found on the plain and in the woods outside the French camp. Among the dead was the amazon commander, described by the French as a colonel. Bayol claims that "a great number" of Dahomean male warriors fled eastward toward Porto-Novo and Lagos, and that amazons were sent to stop them.[6] French losses were announced as eight dead and twenty-six wounded.[7]

The other major engagement of the first Franco-Dahomean war was the Battle of Atchoupa on April 20. By then the French had received reinforcements, including marines and *disciplinaires* (army convicts), but African *tirailleurs* still comprised the bulk of the expeditionary force. Hearing that the main Dahomean army was moving toward Porto-Novo, the French command sent some 350 or 400 men and three field-guns north to intercept it; 500 Porto-Novo warriors contributed by King Tofa provided them with cover. At the village of Atchoupa about 4 miles north of Porto-Novo, toward 7.30 a.m., the Dahomeans opened fire, killing the royal prince who led Tofa's men and routing them. But a Senegalese company alongside them held its ground, giving the French time to form a defensive square.

The French (who were prone to exaggerate the odds against them) would later put the attacking force at 6,000 male soldiers and 2,000 amazons. But the indubitable Dahomean manpower advantage was again more than offset by enemy firepower. Repeated charges against the square were shredded by rifle and artillery fire before the Fon could get within musket range. French breech-loaded rifles could not only be fired rapidly but had an effective range of at least 300 yards, compared with less than 100 for the single-shot, muzzle-loaded Dahomean flintlocks. When the Dahomeans tried to outflank and cut off the French from their Porto-Novo base, the square began moving backwards, pausing frequently to beat off the attackers with salvos of gunfire.

The French later testified that their fiercest, most determined adversaries were the amazons. Some managed to reach the square and fight hand to hand, falling to bayonet thrusts. One woman was disemboweled as she tried to saw off a wounded corporal's head. Some amazons grabbed *tirailleurs* by the legs, trying to bring them down and then stab them.

The fighting ended around 10 a.m. as the square came within sight of Porto-Novo. French estimates of Dahomean casualties ranged from 600 to 1,500; amazon losses were thought to have been especially high. The French admitted to eight dead, all of them Tofa's auxiliaries, and fifty-seven wounded.[8]

The Battle of Atchoupa was followed by peace negotiations, culminating in a treaty signed on October 3, 1889. Dahomey recognized France's protectorate over Porto-Novo and its occupation of Cotonou. Béhanzin was to receive 20,000 francs a year for giving up customs rights at Cotonou. But both sides anticipated a renewal of the conflict.

The first Franco-Dahomean war had brought the female warriors of the Fon kingdom to Europe's notice, and in the age of P.T. Barnum it was perhaps inevitable that some showman would try to capitalize on the curiosity they had aroused. In February 1891 (the year, as it happened, that Barnum died) a British entrepreneur named John Wood brought a "Dahomean" dance troupe to Paris. They were installed in the exhibition hall of the Jardin d'Acclimatation in the Bois de Boulogne, well heated for the occasion.

The troupe included twenty-four women billed as amazons, but a careful French reporter discovered that ten were Egba from the Abeokuta area (of all places); the rest were Dahomeans who may have originated in Whydah. They were dressed as no amazons had ever been dressed, with leather diadems and snug bodices, both adorned with cowries, and rings lined with little bells round their knees. Their hair was arranged in cornrows of tied little braids that met at the top.

If, as is likely, there were no real amazons among them, their dances seem to have been good imitations. (It is easy to imagine that any little girl growing up in Dahomey would have taken delight in copying the steps of her illustrious elders.) The dances at the Jardin d'Acclimatation were military exercises: marches and countermarches, manipulation of swords and muskets, simulation of murderous hand-to-hand combat. Two Dahomean male drummers pounded out the rhythms. The amazons' faces, said the reporter, "at first calm and almost smiling, gradually become severe and hard, and end up reflecting a sort of martial ecstasy resembling delirium." He predicted that the women would "attract to the Jardin...all those who, avid for novelty, will be curious to witness the dances and sham fighting of a female army who will transport them painlessly to the Slave Coast."[9]

After Paris, the troupe toured Europe. Two years later it was still touring, even after France had put an end to the women soldiers of Dahomey. We know this from the obituary of a young "amazon" named Goutto who died in Prague of some unstated cause and was buried by her fellow dancers in a local cemetery.[10]

Béhanzin had taken an active military role in the 1890 war and was well aware that Dahomey could not hope to stave off the French without modern weapons. He began buying them from German merchants at Whydah and elsewhere, paying at least in part with slaves (who were shipped to European colonies in Africa ostensibly as contract workers).[11] As mentioned earlier, by the time of the second war with France, Dahomey had some 4,000 to 6,000 rifles of many makes (French estimates were as high as 8,000). The amazons specifically were equipped with Mannlichers, *chassepôts* and particularly Winchester carbines, which may have been the best rifles in the Dahomean arsenal. The Winchesters had magazines holding eight or fifteen cartridges;[12] a simple movement of a lever carried a cartridge to the barrel chamber and cocked the hammer. Béhanzin also bought some machineguns and Krupp cannons for the showdown with France.

21

FRANCE VS. DAHOMEY, 1892

The second Franco-Dahomean war was sparked by a relatively minor incident. In March 1892 Fon warriors raided villages on the Ouémé claimed by the kingdom of Porto-Novo. The French Resident, Victor Ballot, went upriver on the gunboat *Topaze* to investigate. The ship was attacked and five soldiers were wounded. The *Topaze* returned to Porto-Novo and the Fon resumed their raids. Béhanzin rejected a protest by Ballot, claiming the Ouémé valley as Dahomean territory. On receiving news of these events, Paris declared war. Béhanzin was defiant. "The first time", he wrote, "I was ignorant of how to make war, but now I know. [...]If you want war, I am ready. I wouldn't stop even if it lasted 100 years and killed 20,000 of my men."[1]

The French had realized that it would take more than a few hundred troops to topple the kingdom of Dahomey. The military buildup and campaign of conquest were entrusted to an octoroon from Senegal, Marine Colonel Alfred-Amédée Dodds, who arrived at Cotonou in May. Foreign Legionnaires, naval infantry (marines), engineers, artillery and cavalry (mostly Senegalese *spahis*) were added to French forces. More Senegalese *tirailleurs* were brought in, as well as "Hausa" riflemen, who included many other African ethnic groups, notably Yoruba. Africans would still comprise nearly half the fighting force (930 out of 2,164) that would set out to conquer Dahomey, and more than half by the time the deed was done (830 out of 1,455). (The African component was doubtless larger than French figures indicate: Foreign Legion enlisted men, whose origins were not detailed, included Africans.) In addition, up to 2,600 porters from Porto-Novo would accompany the expedition.

On June 15, 1892, France imposed a naval blockade along the coast of Dahomey in order to prevent more arms and munitions from reaching the Fon. Hostilities began with gunboats shelling villages along the lower Ouémé on July 4. In mid-August the French invasion force began moving up the valley; by September 14 it had assembled at the village of Dogba, some 50 miles upriver, on what the kingdom of Porto-Novo considered to be its northern border with Dahomey.

At 5 a.m. on September 19, the French bivouac at Dogba was attacked by an estimated 4,000 to 5,000 Fon soldiers. This was the first in a series of battles that would go on for nearly seven weeks and destroy the army of Dahomey. The amazons were conspicuous in nearly all the engagements – Degbelo counts twenty-three in which they took part[2] – and fought to the very end. Every account by French eyewitnesses rated them as first-class troops.

It is impossible to say exactly how many women soldiers participated in the final campaign. Just before the first Franco-Dahomean war, Bayol estimated their number at more than 3,000.[3] The French guessed that 2,000 fought in the Battle of Atchoupa.[4] Chaudoin, who spent nearly ten weeks in inland Dahomey in the spring of 1890 (as one of eight French hostages seized at Whydah in retaliation for the arrest of Fon officials in Cotonou), claimed to have seen 4,000 armed "black virgins" but reckoned amazon regulars at 2,000 "in ordinary times".[5] A year later an official French mission to Abomey saw only 900 women soldiers massed around the king.[6] Immediately after the fighting ended in November 1892, as mentioned earlier, a Dahomean official said that 1,200 women had taken the field.

On the other hand, French estimates of the size of the Dahomean army facing them in 1892 ranged from 10,000 to 15,000.[7] More detached, Garcia makes an educated guess of 8,000 at the start of hostilities, rising toward 10,000 with reinforcements. Even the former figure would suggest an amazon total of close to 2,500 since Garcia himself states that in 1890 women composed at least 30 per cent of the army and gives no grounds for supposing that the percentage had appreciably changed in the interval.[8] The prominence of the amazons in French reports on the campaign also argues for a fairly high level of participation, although certainly the novelty of fighting against women must have earned them disproportionate attention. Whatever the number of female soldiers, most would make the supreme sacrifice for their king.

Captain Demartinécourt (if it was he) caught the mood of French troops about to duel with young women. "Oh those amazons, how they excited the soldier's curiosity!" Visions of "black virgins armed with bows and arrows", their fingernails "red with the blood of victims", danced in flickering campfires. To fight women was "neither very chivalrous nor very French", but not since remotest antiquity had warriors been so "fortunate". Enemy bodies were subjected to "the most shameless search", but no female ones would be found at Dogba.[9]

The Battle of Dogba lasted three or four hours and involved six separate assaults on French positions. The Foreign Legionnaire Bern, an eyewitness, said the Fon "fought with ferocious rage, spurred into action by their fetishers [priests] and the amazons", who themselves "gave proof of incredible courage and audacity".[10] When the fight was over, hundreds of Dahomeans lay dead on the battlefield while other bodies, including apparently all the women, had been carried off; the French lost five men.[11]

Bern says that a Senegalese spahi was captured and "the amazons made him suffer horrible [and fatal] mutilations" (he fails to explain how this information was obtained).[12] In reprisal, the French are said to have shot some Dahomean prisoners, including two women.[13] Barbou claims (without giving a source) that Béhanzin had ordered all black prisoners killed but white ones spared to be used as hostages.[14] But

Gen. Alfred-Amédée Dodds, octoroon conqueror of Dahomey. (Ed. Aublet, *La guerre au Dahomey*, 1888-1893, Paris, 1894, frontispiece.) The portrait originally appeared on the front page of *L'Illustration*, LI, no. 2621, May 20, 1893. Reproduction by courtesy of the Centre des Archives d'Outre-Mer, Aix-en-Provence, France.)

An artist's view of the Battle of Dogba, Sept. 19, 1892, showing amazons firing at French soldiers. (A.L. d'Albéca, "Au Dahomey", p. 93)

Artist's impression of the night of Nov. 16-17, 1892, when the French invasion force paused in slight of Abomey, set aflame by its fleeing defenders. (H. Morienval, *La Guerre du Dahomey*, p. 197.

Two amazon survivors photographed at Abomey, 1942. (E.L.R. Meyer-owitz, " 'Our Mothers': The Amazons of Dahomey", *Geographical Magazine*, vol. XV [1943], p. 446.

the Senegalese cavalryman seems to have been the only member of the French expeditionary force who fell into Dahomean hands. There is good evidence (though not in official records) that some Dahomeans who fell into French hands fared little better.[15]

It was with the Battle of Dogba that the devastating effect of the state-of-the-art Lebel rifles, adopted by the French Army in 1886, began to be noted. A particularly small bore gave bullets greater velocity than previous arms. An officer reported that the projectiles went clear through big palms, and Dahomean soldiers concealed behind them. The bullets left a small entry hole in the body but a funnel-like exit wound, churning flesh to pulp.[16]

The French column moved 15 miles farther north up the Ouémé valley, then turned west in the direction of Abomey. It was now entering the Fon heartland and its progress would be contested day after day. The first major clash was the Battle of Poguessa (otherwise known as Pokissa or Kpokissa) on October 4. The French put the number of Dahomean attackers at more than 10,000, including many amazons, who were said to have been commanded personally by Béhanzin.[17] In a period of two to three hours the Fon staged several furious charges. The French responded with their first bayonet charge, a highly successful tactic they would use through the rest of the campaign. Like boxers with longer arms than their foes, soldiers wielding French rifles with fixed 20-inch bayonets outreached enemy swords and machetes. (The giant razors were no longer mentioned.)

The fighting spawned a number of anecdotes about the amazons (the details of which usually vary with the telling). A Hausa company was hit in the flank by a band of women suddenly appearing out of high bush, and saved in extremis by a Senegalese company.[18] An amazon "battalion" ran head on into a Senegalese company and was stopped in its tracks by bayonets.[19] A French cavalry captain reared his horse just as an amazon fired at him; the mount took the bullet instead. The woman then clutched at the officer's sword to pull him toward her, but a Senegalese corporal dispatched her with *his* sword.[20] A marine grabbed a female warrior, who thereupon bit off his nose. Hearing him scream, a lieutenant turned and cut her down with his sword.[21]

The Dahomeans left more than 200 bodies on the field, including some thirty amazons; other dead were carried off. The French suffered forty-two casualties, including five Europeans killed and twenty wounded. Fallen amazons, Winchesters still clenched in their hands, were concentrated in the area where one French officer had been shot dead and two fatally wounded.[22] Schelameur said "débris of cheap finery" littered the ground, and the grass was "steeped in blood". He wrote that he could still see

....a little amazon, quite young, almost pretty, her big eyes open, glazed by a short agony. A Lebel bullet has fractured her right thigh, turning the limb completely inside out, chewing up the femur and detaching a hundred splinters. A very small hole can be seen on the inside edge of her left breast, while below her shoulder blade on the same side is a gaping wound.[23]

Nuëlito counted up to a dozen corpses behind a big tree, victims of Lebel rifles.

The wounds were horrible to see: when the bullet encounters a bone, the latter is pulverized, shredded; the flesh around it is chewed up. It was a heartrending spectacle. Men, women, pell-mell, were lying on the bloody ground, in part hidden by the grass. I picked up beside one dead amazon some cartridges and a little bracelet of glass beads.[24]

From Poguessa to Cana, where Dahomey would make its last stand, was only about 25 miles, but it would take the French a month's hard fighting to get there. As the Fon fell back, they dug foxholes, then trenches, in their effort to stem the foe. Major Pierre-Auguste Roques, head of an army engineers' unit, described the holes as about 1.4 meters deep. The crouching occupant rose only to fire his or her rifle then ducked back down. Many foxholes contained small three-legged stools; Roques thought these were reserved for amazons or male officers. Trenches were 5 to 6 meters long, about 1.5 meters deep and in two parallel rows.[25]

Out on reconnaissance patrol on October 5, Nuëlito was knocked off his horse by a bullet in the shoulder. He found himself in high grass, with an amazon bearing down on him, a carbine in her hand and a machete between her teeth. She "roar[ed] like a wild beast", he writes. He had time to fire and "shatter her head with a revolver bullet".[26]

Next day a battle was fought at the village of Adégon, near Poguessa. French sources say relatively little about it. Alexandre Librecht d'Albéca, a colonial official, reported a bayonet charge there, which he thought was the first.[27] Nuëlito says an amazon captured a Legionnaire during the fighting and tied him up. But he was quickly rescued by a *tirailleur*, who killed the woman with a bayonet thrust.[28] The French said the Fon left ninety-five bodies behind, including sixteen amazons, and that more were later found in the woods. They admitted to six dead, one an officer, and thirty-two wounded, including four officers, a total suggesting almost as fierce a struggle as at Poguessa.

According to a royal Fon tradition, Adégon was a bloodbath for the women soldiers. Sagbaju Glele told Luc Garcia that of 434 amazons committed to the October 6 fighting, only seventeen returned. He singled out the battle as a moment of epiphany: the royal court now understood, he said, that Dahomey would be crushed.[29]

The French then moved 15 miles farther to the village of Akpa, where they bivouacked to await new supplies and reinforcements. They were attacked daily. Amazons are not mentioned in most reports on the fighting at Akpa; they may have been regrouping. But Bern describes a battle on October 15, showing that some women were still in the front lines. His Legion battalion met intense resistance as it tried to seize control of some vital fresh-water springs. A bayonet charge, he says, left "hundreds" of enemies dead. "At that moment a disheveled amazon, marching at the head of a group of Dahomeans, fired her Winchester from less than 15 paces" at the battalion commander, a captain, and hit him squarely in the chest. "The amazons numbered a dozen in the enemy's first rank." A Legion section knelt and fired a salvo that "demolished the whole rank".[30]

The women soldiers reappear conspicuously in the records for October 26 and 27, when the French column moved out of Akpa, crossed lines of enemy trenches with bayonet charges, fought its way across a stream called the Coto (or Koto), and captured the large village of Cotopa (or Kotopka) on the approaches to Cana.

Morienval, a marine second lieutenant, reports that driven out of their trenches, the amazons staged two counterattacks, "uttering terrible cries and making their big cutlasses whistle", to no avail.[31] In another incident, related by Bern, Dahomean troops "in the midst of whom one heard the wild cries of the amazons" penetrated the French camp and surrounded Colonel Dodds's tent before being dispersed by a Senegalese bayonet charge.[32] Garcia tells us (at second hand) of amazons crawling silently through grass to approach French troops having lunch in a bean field. Something alerted the French, who mowed down the first rank of ten women with a burst of gunfire. Those behind them backed off.[33]

In three days of fighting on the outskirts of Cana, November 2, 3 and 4, the invasion force broke the back of Fon resistance; in Dodds's words, it "dealt a decisive blow at Dahomean power".[34] For his last-ditch stand, Béhanzin assembled what was left of his army, now believed by the French to number no more than 1,500. He is also said to have enrolled slaves and convicts. On November 3 the king directed a furious mass attack on the French bivouac. Morienval says the assault on his marine unit's sector was carried out mainly by amazons.[35] After more than four hours of combat, the Dahomeans withdrew, leaving the battlefield strewn with bodies.

In comments on this battle Dodds asserted that Fon troops had received gin "in abundance" beforehand, which might have accounted for their audacity.[36] Maroukis insists that the colonel "confused a ritualistic imbibement with bravery from alcohol",[37] but the evidence suggests that in the final weeks of fighting, from Poguessa to Cana, the Fon were at times steeling themselves with drink for the unequal combat. Obviously some of them carried it too far. Nuëlito's anecdote about the amazon and two male warriors found dead drunk in a foxhole was not unique. Schelameur tells of another Senegalese spahi who found another woman soldier *ivre-morte* in a hole and brought her in slung across the back of his horse.[38] Dodds, in a communiqué, cites two amazons discovered in the same condition in a trench beside empty gin bottles. They were sobered up and grilled about Fon troop movements and numbers, but refused to answer.[39] Passaga recalls that the three dead amazons he examined (and stripped of their shorts) had "half-empty flasks of alcohol, which had served as a prelude to the fighting".[40] Empty bottles were said to litter battlegrounds and abandoned Dahomean camps and defensive positions.[41]

November 4, 1892, the last day of fighting, was, according to Dodds, "one of the most murderous" of the campaign. It was marked, he reported, by the entrance into action of "the last amazons...as well as the elephant hunters whose special assignment was to direct their fire at the officers".[42] The colonel's wording, including use of the masculine form of "hunters" (*chasseurs*), suggests that he got his information slightly garbled. Some historians think he referred to the *gbeto*, who therefore may have been not only the first amazons but the last.[43]

The final battle was fought at the village of Diokoué (or Diohoué), site of a royal palace outside Cana. After day-long fighting, a French bayonet charge overran Dahomean defenses, and the war was effectively over.[44]

Next day a Fon truce mission entered the French camp, and on November 6 Cana was occupied. Subsequent peace negotiations broke down, and on the 16th Dodds, newly promoted general, ordered a march on Abomey. Béhanzin burned and evacuated his capital, fleeing north. On November 17 the French entered Abomey, hoisted the tricolor over the largely intact Singboji palace, and camped in the main courtyard.

In less than seven weeks of fighting, the army of Dahomey had lost between 2,000 and 4,000 dead. The lower figure was offered by Candido Rodrigues, a literate "Brazilian" from Whydah who was Béhanzin's private secretary. The historian Dunglas, relying on oral sources, came up with the higher figure. Rodrigues reckoned that more than 3,000 troops had been wounded, Dunglas 8,000.[45] Dunglas' total of 12,000 casualties seems excessive, although as careful a student as Maroukis thinks it is not far off.[46]

French casualties were few by comparison but still substantial considering the size of the expeditionary force and losses suffered in other African conquests. Fifty-two Europeans, including fifteen officers, and thirty-three Africans were killed; 224 Europeans, including twenty-nine officers, and 216 Africans were wounded. In addition, 173 Europeans and thirty-two Africans died of disease, notably dysentery and malaria.

As mentioned earlier, the head of the Dahomean peace delegation told Schelameur that fifty or sixty amazons remained out of an original 1,200. I presume he referred to those still able to bear arms, and that several hundred, including wounded, would survive the war.

Béhanzin retreated to the town of Atcheribé 30 miles north of Abomey and tried to rebuild his army. Some amazons rallied round him, and it is said that a start was made on recruiting girls to make up the losses.[47] But there was no more fighting. Béhanzin managed to elude capture till January 1894, when his brother, the ex-Gau Goutchili, was chosen king of the new protectorate of Dahomey with French approval. Béhanzin surrendered and was packed off with five wives and perhaps unintended irony to exile in Martinique, a place where his ancestors had sent many slaves. The new king, who took the royal name of Agoli-Agbo, chafed under French controls until, in 1900, France abolished the monarchy and instituted direct rule.

The epitaph on the women's army corps of Dahomey was written by French military men, who unanimously rated them worthy foes. Bern the Legionnaire could not praise them highly enough. "These warrioresses", he wrote, "fight with extreme valor, always ahead of the other troops.[...][They are] outstandingly brave...well trained for combat and very disciplined."[48] A Foreign Legion major named Drude attested to the amazons' "savage tenacity".[49] Morienval the marine found them "remarkable for their courage and their ferocity.[...] [They] flung themselves on [our] bayonets with prodigious bravery... [N]either the cannons, nor the canister shot, nor the salvo fire stops them.[...]It is really strange to see women so well led, so well disciplined."[50] Nuëlito the cavalryman recalls how in "terrible hand-to-hand fighting, the amazons, always in front, uttered their war cries and came to die at the foot of our men."[51] When Schelameur the veterinarian looked at amazons left on a battlefield, their faces "preserved the expression of fierce savagery they wore when death surprised them".[52] Forty years later, General Passaga remembered that the women "gave proof of very great bravery".

Major Grandin, whose two-volume work on the Franco-Dahomean wars, published in 1895, drew on a variety of military and civilian sources, assured his readers:

The valor of the amazons is real. Trained from childhood in the most arduous exercises, constantly incited to war, they bring to battle a veritable fury and a sanguinary ardor...inspiring by their courage and their indomitable energy the other troops who follow them.[53]

He need only have put the encomium in the past tense.

EPILOGUE

According to oral traditions collected by Degbelo, not all surviving amazons went north with Béhanzin. Some stayed behind in Abomey to the misfortune of certain French officers. The latter allegedly sought "the repose of warriors" in the arms of royal or ministerial wives. The women soldiers "cleverly substituted themselves" and "silently exterminated a good number of French officers" with their swords.[1] There is no corroboration for this in French records, but then it is likely that any such deaths would have been officially attributed to other causes.

A couple of months after the French conquest, Father Ignace Lissner visited an empty Dahomean camp near Allada. Screened by a thick belt of giant trees, it may have stood on the same site as the one Snelgrave saw 166 years earlier. It was a "huge military town", the priest reported, "more than a kilometer square: fifteen thousand men could easily live there." Thousands of two-man huts surrounded a big open space. Here and there stood the taller huts of chiefs, adorned with their insignia. At one end "immense verandas formed the quarter of the king and the amazons."[2] Three years later, another priest passed by. Only a few stakes showed where the camp had been.[3]

Only four months after the fall of Abomey an impresario brought another troupe of Dahomeans to Paris. They were advertised as amazons and male warriors of Béhanzin, and were said to number 150. They were exhibited on the Champ-de-Mars, behind the Eiffel Tower — like two-headed calves, in the words of a satirical French columnist. He found the women "neither fierce, nor sinister, nor even ugly. [...]They have left their atrocious savagery in Africa [and] would easily become *boulevardières.*" They had, according to the commentator, already learned how to cadge *sous* from spectators, yet it was clear from their military drills what redoubtable adversaries General Dodds's men had faced. The show was scheduled to go on to Brussels and Chicago.[4]

Degbelo traced the lives of some amazon survivors. She names seven who married but remained sterile, and thirteen who married and had children. "But even when they successfully rejoined society", she says, "they exhibited, especially in squabbles, virile and very energetic behavior that showed the depth of the change they had undergone. They often beat up men who dared to affront them...[and] inspired fear among their co-wives as well as in their husband."[5] Le Hérissé, a contemporary observer, wrote: "They seem to have preserved from their former condition only a certain bellicose temper...directed especially against their husbands."[6]

Some amazons were unable to readjust. They preferred to remain single, says Degbelo, "cherishing the memory of their past glory and above all of their prowess against the whites". A Fon princess, Assangan Adonon Glele, told Degbelo that such veterans considered marriage servitude of woman to man. Believing themselves superior to men, they could not countenance such humiliation.[7]

Some of these *célibataires*, again according to oral sources, rejected any sort of family ties and joined the new king in Abomey. They formed a "discreet" palace guard, posing as true royal wives of Agoli-Agbo while protecting his person.[8]

In February 1894 the king invited French officers to witness an amazon dance. Maire, an infantry captain who had just arrived in Dahomey, was curious to see these females "who had done us so much harm and had battled us to the bitter end". But Agoli-Agbo trotted out six old women, presumably long-retired amazons. They performed authentic dances but hurt each other in the mock hand-to-hand and eventually dropped from exhaustion.[9]

As decades passed, the women soldiers, like old soldiers

everywhere, gradually faded away. A friend of d'Almeida-Topor tells of an ancient woman he and his playmates used to see on the streets of Cotonou around 1930:

Sometimes [she] stopped and looked at us. [...]Half bent over, she leaned on a stick and muttered incoherently.[...]

One day, one of us throws a stone that hits another stone. The noise resounds; a spark flies. We suddenly see the old woman straighten up. Her face is transfigured. She begins to march proudly, in step.[...] Reaching a wall, she lies down on her belly and crawls on her elbows to get round it. She thinks she is holding a rifle because abruptly she shoulders and fires, then reloads her imaginary arm and fires again, imitating the sound of a salvo. Then she leaps, pounces on an imaginary enemy, rolls on the ground in furious hand-to-hand combat, flattens the foe. With one hand she seems to pin him to the ground and with the other stab him repeatedly. Her cries betray her effort. She makes the gesture of cutting to the quick and stands up brandishing a fictive trophy. I was told later that she was doubtless thinking she had cut off the sex organs of the vanquished.

She intones a song of victory and dances:

> The blood flows,
> You are dead.
> The blood flows,
> We have won.
> The blood flows, it flows, it flows,
> The blood flows,
> The enemy is no more.

But suddenly she stops, dazed. Her body bends, hunches. How old she seems, older than before! She walks away with a hesitant step.

She is a former warrior, an adult explains.[...] In the time of our former kings, there were women soldiers. Their battles ended long ago, but she continues the war in her head.[10]

In 1934 a British traveler, Geoffrey Gorer, visited the Singboji palace. Seated against a wall near Glele's tomb, he relates,

....was an incredibly old and withered hag spinning cotton; her name was Yahi, and she was the last of the Amazons who had fought with Glélé against the Yoruba and with Béhanzin against the French.

There was something very pathetic and romantic about this battered old relic of a completely dead age; she who had once proudly boasted that she was no woman, but a man, was now reduced to the degradation of spinning; she who had once captured her own booty with her musket and cutlass was happy for a few sous to hobble into the sun and be photographed. She must have been well over eighty.[11]

Passing through Abomey eight years later, the British Africanist Eva L.R. Meyerowitz (who was to become known for her writings on the Akan peoples of Ghana) saw "the only 'Amazon' still alive. In her youth she fought against the French...and is now a very old woman, hanging around the courtyards of the former royal palace. She has a terrible face, and one wonders what memories lie behind it."Curiously, Meyerowitz's article contains a photo of *two* elderly ex-amazons.[12]

Thereafter all is silence.

It is unlikely that either Gorer's or Meyerowitz's "last amazon", who may have been the same person, was indeed the last. A woman who had fought the French in her teens would have been no older than sixty-nine in 1942 and possibly in her mid-sixties. Almost surely one or more lived to see the French colony of Dahomey (embracing much more territory than the old kingdom) become an independence republic in 1960.

Amélie Degbelo is certain that some amazons survived beyond independence. In 1978 she met a very old woman named Nawi in the village of Kinta who convincingly claimed to have been one. Nawi died in November 1979.[13] If she had been sixteen in 1892, she lived to the age of 103.

The *gbeto* and their comrades-in-arms have gone the way of the local elephant. No monument has been raised to the memory of that unique human experience. The non-Fon peoples who compose the majority of the people of the former colony, and changed its name from Dahomey to Benin in 1975 for that reason, might prefer to forget the amazons. But the documentary testimony ensures that, unlike the women warriors of old, they will never be relegated to myth.

NOTES

Abbreviations used

APF   *Annales de la Propagation de la Foi* (Lyon)
CAOM   Centre des Archives d'Outre-Mer (Aix-en-Provence)
CMS   Church Missionary Society (archives in Birmingham)
DFC   Dépot des Fortifications des Colonies (Aix-en-Provence)
ED   *Etudes Dahoméennes* (Porto-Novo)
FO   Foreign Office (London)
HA   *History in Africa* (Atlanta)
IUP   Irish University Press (Shannon)
JAH   *The Journal of African History* (Cambridge, England)
MAE   Ministère des Affaires Etrangères (Paris)
MC   *Les Missions Catholiques* (Lyon)
PP   Parliamentary Papers (British Library)
PRO   Public Record Office (Kew)

Introduction

1. Antonia Fraser, *The Warrior Queens* (New York, 1989), 307-22.
2. P.L. Shinnie, "The Nilotic Sudan and Ethiopia, *c*. 660 BC to *c*. AD 600", *Cambridge History of Africa*, vol. 2 (Cambridge, 1978), 237-49; J. Leclant, "The Empire of Kush: Napata and Meroe" in *Unesco General History of Africa*, vol. 2 (Berkeley, 1981), 289-90; *ibid.*, A.A. Hakem, "The Civilization of Napata and Meroe", 302-4.
3. Acts of the Apostles, 8:26-8.
4. Olfert Dapper, *Naukeurige beschrijvinge der afrikaensche gewesten* (Amsterdam, 1668), 611-13; John Ogilby, *Africa* (London, 1670), 563-5 [English translation of Dapper]; Dapper, *Description de l'Afrique* (Amsterdam, 1686), 369-70 [French translation]; Jan Vansina, *Kingdoms of the Savanna* (Madison, 1966), 134-7, 142-4; Douglas L. Wheeler and René Pélissier, *Angola* (New York, 1971), 39; Joseph C. Miller,

212

"Nzinga of Matamba in a New Perspective", *JAH*, XVI, 2 (1975), 201-16.

5. 2 Samuel 15:16, 16:20-2, 20:3.
6. *Bulletin de la Société de Géographie* (Paris), 2nd series, XVII, November 1842, 375-6; *ibid.*, December 1842, 533.
7. G.I. Jones, 'Olaudah Equiano of the Niger Ibo" in Philip D. Curtin, ed., *Africa Remembered: Narratives by West Africans from the Era of the Slave Trade* (Madison, 1967), 66, 77.
8. Dixon Denham, Hugh Clapperton and Walter Oudney, *Narrative of Travels and Discoveries in Northern and Central Africa in the Years 1822, 1823, and 1824* (London, 1826), 132.
9. Richard F. Burton, *A Mission to Gelele, King of Dahome*, ed. C.W. Newbury (New York, 1966), 259.
10. Lauren Cook Burgess, ed., *An Uncommon Soldier* (New York, 1995), xi, 2.
11. My sources for the Libyan amazons have included Donald J. Sobol, *The Amazons of Greek Mythology* (South Brunswick, NJ, 1972), 19-31; J.O. de G. Hanson, "The Myth of the Libyan Amazons", *Museum Africum* (Ibadan), III (1974), 38-43; Pierre Samuel, *Amazones, guerrières et gaillardes* (Grenoble, 1975), 52-5.
12. My sources for the amazons of Asia Minor have included Guy Cadogan Rothery, *The Amazons in Antiquity and Modern Times* (London, 1910), 24-45, 55-61; Sobol, *Amazons*, 32-147; Samuel, *Amazones*, 43-82; William Blake Tyrrell, *Amazons: a Study in Athenian Mythmaking* (Baltimore, 1984); Fraser, *Warrior Queens*, 19-22.
13. Tyrrell, *Amazons*, 24, quoting from Plutarch, *Alexander*, 46.2. See also Sobol, *Amazons*, 87-8; Samuel, *Amazones*, 45, 51.
14. A.C. Moule and Paul Pelliot, *Marco Polo: the Description of the World*, 2 vols (London, 1938), I, 424-5.
15. Sobol, *Amazons*, 118; Samuel Eliot Morison, *Admiral of the Ocean Sea: a Life of Christopher Columbus* (Boston, 1942), 315-6.
16. Samuel, *Amazones*, 233.
17. *Ibid.*, 33-4.
18. Filippo Pigafetta, *A Report of the Kingdom of Congo and of the Surrounding Countries, Drawn out of the Writings and Discourses of the Portuguese Duarte Lopez in 1591*, tr., ed. Margarite Hutchinson, reprint of 1881 edition (London, 1970), 118-9.
19. Sobol, *Amazons*, 157.
20. Samuel, *Amazones*, 22-5.
21. Dalzel, *History of Dahomy*, reprint of 1793 edn (London, 1967), x-xi.
22. Frederick E. Forbes, *Dahomey and the Dahomans, Being the Journals of Two Missions to the King of Dahomey and Residence at His Capital in the Years 1849 and 1850*, 2 vols, reprint of 1851 edn (London, 1966), II, 15. Forbes based vol. II on a 139-page journal that he

kept on his second visit to Dahomey. It is preserved in PRO, FO 84/827, Fanshawe to Admiralty, July 19, 1850. On p. 70 [my pagination] an amazon officer declares "that Gezo alone of all the Kings of the Earth has an Army of Women, there is no King like him." This document will hereafter be referred to in the notes as Forbes's journal, and cited when it differs from the printed version. A dozen years after Forbes, a merchant named Joseph Dawson quoted Gezo as saying he founded the amazons early in his reign not only to strengthen Dahomey but "that he might have a name above all others for having introduced a thing which was not to be found in any other part of the world." CMS, CA2/016/34, extracts from Dawson's journal and from his letters to Fitzgerald, Nov. 17, 1862, p. 21 of journal.

23. A. Vallon, "Le royaume de Dahomey" (1st part of 2-part article), *Revue Maritime et Coloniale*, II, Aug. 1861, 338.

24. *Larousse du XXe siècle*, 6 vols (Paris, 1928), I, 178.

25. Burton, *Mission*, 322. For the same reasons, Dahomey has also been called "this West African Prussia". Robert S. Smith, *Kingdoms of the Yoruba*, 3rd edn (London, 1988), 133.

Chapter 1: A Mock Battle

1. Francesco Saverio (a.k.a. François-Xavier) Borghero, "Missions du Dahomey", *Annales de la Propagation de la Foi*, XXXV, no. 206 (Jan. 1863), 31-4. (From 1861 to 1867 this monthly organ of the Missions Africaines of Lyon published reports and letters addressed by Borghero to Augustin Planque, superior of the congregation. After initial references, they are identified in the notes by the number of the issue.) An account of the same spectacle, with minor changes (including the exact date) and some added details, can also be found in Borghero's recently published journal: Renzo Mandirola and Yves Morel, eds, *Journal de Francesco Borghero, premier missionaire du Dahomey (1861-1865)*, (Paris, 1997), 76-9. The manuscript was completed in 1876. See also Jean Laffitte, *Le Dahomé. Souvenirs de voyage et de mission* (Tours, 1873), 87-90. Borghero originally called the barrier thornbush "cactus" and Laffitte, a fellow missionary, persuaded him it was "bombax", but almost surely it was acacia (*A. ataxacantha*), the typical spiny plant of the region.

Chapter 2: Origins of Dahomey

1. Edouard Dunglas, "Contribution à l'histoire du Moyen-Dahomey (royaumes d'Abomey, de Kétou et de Ouidah)" (1st of 3 tomes

under same title), *ED*, XIX, 1 (1957), 75; Henri Labouret, *Africa Before the White Man*, tr. Francis Huxley (New York, 1962), 109; Jacques Bertho, quoted in W.J. Argyle, *The Fon of Dahomey: a History and Ethnography of the Old Kingdom* (Oxford, 1966), 4; Paul Mercier, "Guinée centrale et orientale" in Hubert Deschamps, ed., *Histoire générale de l'Afrique noire, de Madagascar et des archipels, I: Des origines à 1800* (Paris, 1970), 319; Roberto Pazzi, "Aperçu sur l'implantation actuelle et les migrations anciennes des peuples de l'aire culturelle Aja-Tado" in *Peuples du Golfe du Bénin (Aja-Ewé)*, ed. François de Medeiros (Paris, 1984), 18 n. 20 (see also p. 323 of the same book).

2. For details of these myths see Henri Labouret and Paul Rivet, *Le royaume d'Arda et son évangélisation au XVIIe siècle* (Paris, 1929), 11-13; Melville J. Herskovits, *Dahomey, an Ancient West African Kingdom*, 2 vols (New York, 1938), I, 166-9; A. Akindélé and C. Aguessy, *Contribution à l'étude de l'histoire de l'ancien royaume de Porto-Novo* (Dakar, 1953), 20-6; Dunglas, "Contribution," tome 1, 80-1; Robert Cornevin, *La République populaire du Bénin: des origines dahoméennes à nos jours* (Paris, 1981), 74-8; Maximilien Quénum, *Au pays des Fons (us et coutumes du Dahomey)*, 3rd edn (Paris, 1983), 11-12.

3. Robin Law, *The Slave Coast of West Africa 1550-1750: the Impact of the Atlantic Slave Trade on an African Society* (Oxford, 1991), 32 n. 68.

4. A.F.C. Ryder, *Benin and the Europeans 1485-1897* (London, 1969), 73.

5. Robin Law, "Problems of Plagiarism, Harmonization and Misunderstanding in Contemporary European Sources: Early (Pre-1680s) Sources for the 'Slave Coast' of West Africa" in Beatrix Heintze and Adam Jones, eds, *European Sources for Sub-Saharan Africa Before 1900: Use and Abuse* (Stuttgart, 1987), 341.

6. Richard Hakluyt, *The Principall Navigations, Voiages, and Discoveries of the English Nation...*, 10 vols (London, 1927-8), IV, 302-3.

7. Pieter de Marees, *Description and Historical Account of the Gold Kingdom of Guinea (1602)*, tr., ed. Albert van Dantzig and Adam Jones (Oxford, 1987), 224.

8. The first printed reference to the "Slave Coast" dates to a 1697 book by a Dane, Erick Tilleman: *A Short and Simple Account of the Country Guinea and Its Nature*, tr., ed. Selena Axelrod Winsnes (Madison, 1994), 32.

9. Cited in Law, *Slave Coast*, 231, 261, 263, 354.

10. Labouret and Rivet, *Royaume d'Arda*, 16-30.

11. Cited in Ray A. Kea, *Settlements, Trade, and Polities in the Seventeenth-Century Gold Coast* (Baltimore, 1982), 401 n. 168.

12. Jean-Baptiste Ducasse, "Mémoire ou relation du Sr du Casse sur son voyage de Guynée avec 'La Tempeste' en 1687 et 1688" in Paul

Roussier, *L'établissment d'Issiny 1687-1702: voyages de Ducasse, Tibierge et d'Amon à la côte de Guinée...* (Paris, 1935), 15.

13. Cited in Robin Law, "Dahomey and the Slave Trade: Reflections on the Historiography of the Rise of Dahomey", *JAH*, XXVII, 2 (1986), 242 nn. 38 and 39.

14. William Smith, *A New Voyage to Guinea*, reprint of 1744 edn (London, 1967), 171-89. Lamb's letter can also be found in Forbes, *Dahomey*, I, 181-95.

Chapter 3: Origins of the Amazons

1. J.A. Skertchly, *Dahomey as It Is; Being a Narrative of Eight Months' Residence in That Country* (London, 1874), 256-7. See also Burton, *Mission*, 247.

2. A. Répin, "Voyage", *Le Tour du Monde*, VII, 2nd semester (1863), 92. Vallon, who accompanied Répin, describes the same mimed hunt in the second part of his previously cited article, "Le royaume de Dahomey", *Revue Maritime et Coloniale*, III, November 1861, 349. See also a secondhand description of an amazon elephant hunt in Forbes, *Dahomey*, I, 157-9. Forbes called the women "rangers of the forest", said they numbered two "regiments", and that they shot "African wolves" (*ibid.*, I, 161) – presumably hyenas – as well as elephants. He said lions and leopards were also killed but did not specify by whom.

3. Répin, "Voyage", 88.

4. Vallon, "Royaume" (1st part), 345. Vallon, whose full Christian name was Aristide-Louis-Antoine-Maximilien-Marie, visited Abomey twice, in 1856 and 1858. A lieutenant-commander at the time, he would rise to admiral and later become a member of the French parliament from Senegal.

5. Répin, "Voyage", 90.

6. Skertchly, *Dahomey*, 456.

7. Edouard Foà, *Le Dahomey. Histoire, géographie, moeurs, coutumes, commerce, industrie, expéditions françaises (1891-1894)*, (Paris, 1895), 258.

8. See, e.g., Pierre-Eugène Chautard, *Le Dahomey* (Lyon, 1890), 10; CAOM, Dahomey, III, 2, journals of artillery captain Henri Decoeur (p. 10) and Midshipman Joseph d'Ambrières (p. 42), members of a French mission to Abomey in February-March 1891; Ed. Aublet, *La guerre au Dahomey, 1888-1893, d'après les documents officiels* (Paris, 1894), 95; Victor-Louis Maire, *Dahomey: Abomey – la dynastie dahoméenne. Les palais: leurs bas-reliefs* (Besançon, 1905), 53.

9. Marie-Madeleine Prévaudeau, *Abomey-la-mystique* (Paris, 1936), 93.

10. For details of the Ahangbé legend see Auguste Le Hérissé, *L'ancien royaume du Dahomey. Moeurs, religion, histoire* (Paris, 1911), 6-7, 15,

294-5; Anilo G...(presumably Glele), "Histoire des rois du Dahomey," *Grands Lacs* (Namur), 61st year, new series, nos. 88-90, July 1, 1946, p. 47; Anatole Coissy, "Un règne de femme dans l'ancien royaume d'Abomey", *ED*, II (1949), 5-8 (source of the story about Ahangbé's dramatic abdication); Dunglas, "Contribution", tome 1, 96, 99; Cornevin, *République populaire*, 100-1; Maurice Ahanhanzo Glélé, *Le Danxome du pouvoir aja à la nation fon* (Paris, 1974), 89; Edna Grace Bay, "The Royal Women of Abomey", Ph.D. thesis, Boston U., 1977, 125-6; Amélie Degbelo, "Les amazones du Danxomè 1645-1900", master's thesis, Université Nationale du Bénin, 1979, 36-7, 39.

11. *Ibid.*, 35. The Ouéménou are said to have been so impressed by Akaba's female militia that they started one of their own but it fizzled out.

12. *Ibid.*, 174.

13. Cited in Degbelo, "Amazones", 35-6; Hélène d'Almeida-Topor, *Les amazones. Une armée de femmes dans l'Afrique précoloniale* (Paris, 1984), 33-4.

14. Maire, *Dahomey*, 43.

15. Robin Law, "The 'Amazons' of Dahomey", *Paideuma* (Stuttgart), 39 (1993), 250.

16. Robin Law, "Further Light on Bulfinch Lambe and the 'Emperor of Pawpaw': King Agaja of Dahomey's Letter to King George I of England, 1726", *HA*, 17 (1990), 217.

17. Forbes, *Dahomey*, II, 135. In Forbes's journal, 71, he says Adono's "name is now a title in the royal Family." Presumably his printed version is more accurate.

18. A. de Salinis, *La Marine au Dahomey. Campagne de 'la Naïade' (1890-1892)*, (Paris, 1901), 98.

19. Paul Mercier, "The Fon of Dahomey" in *African Worlds: Studies in the Cosmological Ideas and Social Values of African Peoples* (London, 1954), 232.

20. William Bosman, *A New and Accurate Description of the Coast of Guinea*, reprint of 1705 tr. (London, 1967), 366a-7.

21. *Ibid.*, 367, as corrected in Albert van Dantzig, "English Bosman and Dutch Bosman: a Comparison of Texts – VII", *HA*, 9 (1982), 286-7.

22. CAOM, DFC, Côtes d'Afrique, no. 104, carton 75, "Relation du Royaume de Judas en Guinéé, De son Gouvernement, des moeurs de ses habitans, de leur Religion, Et du Negoce qui sy fait", 25.

23. *Ibid.*, 84.

24. Des Marchais' account can be found in two places. A French priest, Jean-Baptiste Labat, published a 4-volume work in Paris in 1730 titled *Voyage du chevalier Des Marchais en Guinée, isles voisines, et à*

Cayenne, fait en 1725, 1726 & 1727... It was based on a manuscript by Des Marchais titled "Journal du Voiage de Guinée et Cayenne Par Le Chevalier Des Marchais Capitaine Comandant La fregatte de la Compagnie des Indes, L'Expedition Pendant les Années 1724, 1725 et 1726..." The manuscript survives as Fonds Français 24223 in the Bibliothèque Nationale, Paris. Curiously, our information about first- and second-class royal wives at Whydah comes from Labat, who never set foot in Africa, not Des Marchais directly; conceivably the priest had a chance to question the mariner after his return to France, or had access to another, more detailed manuscript, now lost. Des Marchais had visited Whydah two decades earlier, and a journal dating from that period (Add. MSS 19560) is in the British Library, London. The British historian Paul Hair has advised me that it promises but fails to include material on Whydah, and he suggests that Labat may have had access to that missing portion.

25. Labat, *Voyage*, II, 79.

26. Labat and the Des Marchais MS. are in general accord on the police role of third-class wives. See *ibid.*, II, 96-8, 251, and Des Marchais, "Journal", folio 48 verso, folio 60 recto.

27. W. J. Argyle tells us that amazons sometimes carried out royal verdicts. If, for example, the head of a kinship lineage was guilty of a serious crime, they would kill him, tear down his compound and disperse or enslave his family. But the two sources Argyle cites for this information do not bear him out. Argyle, *Fon*, 82.

28. "[T]he Dahoman King must only condescend to live," Burton commented hyperbolically; "all, save what must necessarily be done by himself, is done for him." Burton, *Mission*, 149.

29. Law, "Further Light", 219.

30. Richard Lander, *Records of Captain Clapperton's Last Expedition to Africa*, 2 vols, reprint of 1830 edn (London, 1967), I, 124-5; Hugh Clapperton, *Journal of a Second Expedition into the Interior of Africa from the Bight of Benin to Soccatoo*, reprint of 1829 edn (London, 1966), 66-7, 72.

31. Lander, *Records*, II, 191-4.

32. Burton, *Mission*, 86 n. 2; "Notes on the Dahoman" in Richard Burton, *Selected Papers on Anthropology, Travel and Exploration*, ed. N.M. Penzer (London, 1924), 123.

33. Law, "Further Light", 217.

34. William Snelgrave, *A New Account of Some Parts of Guinea and the Slave-Trade*, reprint of 1734 edn (London, 1971), 34.

35. Albert van Dantzig, ed., tr., *The Dutch and the Guinea Coast 1674-1742: a Collection of Documents from the General State Archive at The Hague* (Accra, 1978), 296.

36. Antoine-Edmé Pruneau de Pommegorge (a.k.a. Joseph Pruneau), *Description de la Nigritie* (Amsterdam, 1789), 162.

37. Dalzel, *History*, xiii.

38. Robert Norris, *Memoirs of the Reign of Bossa Ahádee, King of Dahomy, an Inland Country of Guiney*, reprint of 1789 edn (London, 1968), 94.

39. *Ibid.*, 105-6.

40. Pierre Labarthe, *Voyage à la côte de Guinée* (Paris, 1803), 120, 122.

41. John M'Leod, *A Voyage to Africa with Some Account of the Manners and Customs of the Dahomian People*, reprint of 1820 edn (London, 1971), 38.

42. Norris, *Memoirs*, 130.

43. Dalzel, *History*, 205.

44. Norris, *Memoirs*, 130; Dalzel, *History*, 205.

45. Vicente Ferreira Pires, *Viagem de Africa em o Reino de Dahomé* (São Paulo, 1957), 79.

46. Dunglas, "Contribution à l'histoire du Moyen-Dahomey", tome 2, *ED*, XX (1957), 84 n. 1.

47. Répin, "Voyage", 99. Paul Hazoumé, Fon ethnologist and author of what has been called the first Dahomean novel, cites a tradition that a woman fired on Adandozan's supporters. *Doguicimi* (Paris, 1938), 184; *Doguicimi*, Eng. tr. Richard Bjornson (Washington, 1990), 128-9. See also Degbelo, "Amazones", 18-9.

48. Snelgrave, *New Account*, 126.

49. *Ibid.*, 124, 127-8.

50. *Ibid.*, 133-4.

51. Pruneau de Pommegorge, "Eclaircissemens sur le Commerce de la Compagnie des Indes à Juda...," carton 27 bis, série C6, Fonds des Colonies, Archives Nationales de France, p. 190. (This manuscript, dated to 1752, is chapter 8 of a 276-page "Mémoire sur le Commerce de la Concession du Sénégal.") See also I.A. Akinjogbin, *Dahomey and Its Neighbours, 1708-1818* (Cambridge, Eng., 1967), 87-8. He says Testefolle was taken to Abomey, sentenced to death and executed.

52. Herskovits, *Dahomey*, II, 84.

53. A.B. Ellis, *The Ewe-Speaking Peoples of the Slave Coast of West Africa...*, reprint of 1890 edn (Oosterhout, Netherlands, 1966), 183.

54. Law, "'Amazons'", 249.

55. Robin Law, "A Neglected Account of the Dahomian Conquest of Whydah (1727): the 'Relation de la guerre de Juda' of the Sieur Ringard of Nantes", *HA*, 15 (1988), 327.

56. *Ibid.*, 335 n. 17.

57. Snelgrave, *New Account*, 78. English surveyor William Smith, who visited Whydah just a month after Ringard, says the Dahomean army boys, some as young as seven or eight, were ordered to behead aged and wounded prisoners. *New Voyage*, 192.

58. Pruneau de Pommegorge, *Description*, 162.
59. *Ibid*.
60. *Ibid*., 181-2.
61. PRO, T 70/31, William Mutter to Committee, May 27, 1764; Joseph Dupuis, *Journal of a Residence in Ashantee*, 2nd edn (London, 1966), 237-9; R.S. Rattray, *Ashanti Law and Constitution* (London, 1929), 221; Adu Boahen, "Asante-Dahomey Contacts in the 19th Century", *Ghana Notes and Queries*, no. 7 (Jan. 1965), 1-2 and n. 9; Akinjogbin, *Dahomey*, 124 and n. 2; J.K. Fynn, *Asante and Its Neighbours, 1700-1807* (London, 1971), 96-7; Ivor Wilks, *Asante in the Nineteenth Century* (Cambridge, Eng., 1975), 320-3 and n. 51-77; Robin Law, *The Oyo Empire, c.1600 - c.1836* (Oxford, 1977), 170-1.
62. Norris, *Memoirs*, 108-9.
63. *Ibid*., 109.
64. Auguste Bouët, "Le royaume de Dahomey" (2nd of 3 parts), *L'- Illustration*, X, no. 491 (July 24, 1852), 62; Jean-Claude Nardin, "La reprise des relations franco-dahoméennes au XIXe siècle. La mission d'Auguste Bouët à la cour d'Abomey (1851)", *Cahiers d'Etudes Africaines*, VII, 1 (1967), 112.
65. Skertchly, *Dahomey*, 263.
66. *Ibid*., 264.
67. *Ibid*., 263.
68. Labarthe, *Voyage*, 148-9. Labarthe quotes from a report by de Montaguère without naming him.
69. Maire, *Dahomey*, 30-1, plate XI.
70. Dalzel, *History*, x-xi.
71. *Ibid*., 175-7.
72. Dalzel and/or Abson got their facts mixed up. Akinjogbin (*Dahomey*, 162 and n. 3, 163 and n. 1) has found solid evidence that the *Meu* died in 1779, not 1781, and that the attacks on Agouna preceded his death (PRO, T 70/1162, Day Book, William's Fort, Whydah, Jan. 2, 24 and 27, 1779). But he does not question the amazon role. See also Law, *Oyo*, 167 and n. 118.
73. Forbes, *Dahomey*, II, 88.
74. Pires, *Viagem*, 68.

Chapter 4: Why Dahomey?

1. Burton, *Mission*, 111-12.
2. *Ibid*., 254.
3. A.P.E. Wilmot, "Despatches from Commodore Wilmot Respecting His Visit to the King of Dahomey in December 1862 and January

1863", *IUP Series of British Parliamentary Papers, Colonies: Africa 50* (Shannon, 1971), 438.

Chapter 5: Recruitment

1. Le Hérissé, *Ancien royaume*, 72; Hazoumé, *Doguicimi*, (French) 130, (English) 88; Bay, "Royal Women", 143-4; Degbelo, "Amazones", 88. See also Chautard, *Dahomey*, 10; Antoine Mattei, *Bas-Niger, Bénoué et Dahomey* (Grenoble, 1890), 178 (who seems to copy Chautard).
2. Herskovits discusses the census at length (*Dahomey*, II, 74-9); his information is questioned by Argyle (*Fon*, 94-5, 97-9).
3. Pruneau de Pommegorge, *Description*, 165.
4. Labarthe, *Voyage*, 120.
5. Répin, "Voyage", 92.
6. Bouët, "Royaume" (2nd part), 60 n. 1; Nardin, "Reprise", 125.
7. T.B. Freeman, typescript of unpublished, untitled book, Methodist Missionary Society Archives, Biographical West Africa, Box 597, Library of SOAS, 326. This 524-page document will hereafter be referred to in the notes as Freeman typescript.
8. Blaise Brue, "Voyage fait en 1843, dans le royaume de Dahomey, par M. Brue, agent du comptoir français établi à Whydah", *Revue Coloniale*, tome VII, September 1845, 58.
9. Richard F. Burton, "The Present State of Dahome", *Transactions of the Ethnological Society of London*, III, new series, 1865, 406; *Mission*, 257. In the latter, earlier work, Burton phrased it "Xanthippes, who make men's eyes yellow".
10. Ellis, *Ewe-Speaking Peoples*, 183. See also Pierre-Bertrand Bouche, *Sept ans en Afrique occidentale. La Côte des Esclaves et le Dahomey* (Paris, 1885), 360.
11. Bay, "Royal Women", 148; Quénum, *Pays des Fons*, 21.
12. Foà, *Dahomey*, 256.
13. Adrien Djivo, *Guézo: la rénovation du Dahomey* (Paris, 1977), 81.
14. Burton, *Mission*, 229.
15. Edouard Dunglas, 'La première attaque des Dahoméens contre Abéokuta (3 mars 1851)", *ED*, I (1948), 15.
16. Burton, *Mission*, 257.

Chapter 6: Celibacy

1. Degbelo, "Amazones", 108.
2. Dalzel, *History*, xviii; John Adams, *Remarks on the Country Extending from Cape Palmas to the River Congo*, reprint of 1823 edn (London, 1966), 74-5.

3. Burton, *Mission*, 303.
4. Burton, "Notes", 121-2.
5. Ellis, *Ewe-Speaking Peoples*, 43.
6. M.-L.-E. Moreau de Saint-Méry, *Description topographique, physique, civile, politique et historique de la partie française de l'isle Saint-Domingue*, new edn, 3 vols (Paris, 1958), I, 52 (originally published in 1797).
7. *Ibid.*, I, 51.
8. Herskovits, *Dahomey*, I, 277-83.
9. *Ibid.*, I, 291-5, 299.
10. Quénum, *Pays des Fons*, 109.
11. Hunchbacks, dwarfs and albinos were among other organized groups. According to two French sources, even cannibals were regimented in Gezo's time. They were said to be descendants of anthropophagi captured in the early years of the monarchy and perpetuated solely to dine on captured enemy chiefs at the king's behest. Brue, "Voyage", 64; Guillevin, "Voyage dans l'intérieur du royaume de Dahomey", *Nouvelles Annales des Voyages, de la Géographie, de l'Histoire et de l'Archéologie*, 6th series, VIII, 2 (June 1862), 291. Guillevin's account appeared well after Gezo's death in 1858 but probably refers to an 1857 trip. See Cornevin, *République populaire*, 284.
12. Burton, *Mission*, 317. The districts apparently survived the French conquest. A French missionary who visited Abomey in early 1893 seemed to be referring to them when he wrote of "two quarters..., the absolute domain of crime that walked with its head high and *legally* demanded its wages, fixed by the prince [king] himself." Ignace Lissner, "De Whydah à Abomey" (4th of 5 parts), *MC*, XXVII, Sept. 13, 1895, 443.
13. Norris, *Memoirs*, 98.
14. Forbes, *Dahomey*, II, 95, 138, 246; PRO, FO 84/816, Beecroft to Palmerston, July 22, 1850. The citation is from p. 129 of a 150-page journal that Beecroft appended to his letter. It will hereafter be referred to as Beecroft's journal in the notes. In Forbes's journal, 72, 81, the women are twice called "public strumpets", wording his London editor may have considered indelicate.
15. Burton, *Mission*, 316-17, 335. See also Skertchly, *Dahomey*, 283-4.
16. Burton, *Mission*, 257 n. 8. See also Law, "'Amazons'", 256.
17. Guillevin, "Voyage", 292; Burton, *Mission*, 258 n. 10; "Present State", 406; Skertchly, *Dahomey*, 455.
18. Forbes, *Dahomey*, II, 82; Burton, *Mission*, 257; Skertchly, *Dahomey*, 154, 359, 455, 471; Ellis, *Ewe-Speaking Peoples*, 184; Alexandre L. d'Albéca, *La France au Dahomey* (Paris, 1895), 36.
19. Dalzel, *History*, 211.
20. Burton, *Mission*, 166-7.
21. Skertchly, *Dahomey*, 359.

22. *Ibid.*, 90.
23. Edmond Chaudoin, *Trois mois de captivité au Dahomey* (Paris, 1891), 322, 325-6. See also Maire, *Dahomey*, 51; Le Hérissé, *Ancien royaume*, 71-2.
24. Forbes, *Dahomey*, I, ix.
25. Burton, *Mission*, 258 n. 10.
26. Skertchly, *Dahomey*, 180.
27. Chautard, *Dahomey*, 10.
28. Laffitte, *Dahomé*, 90; PP, vol. 9 (1850), William Winniett's testimony, Apr. 30, 1849, before "the Select Committee.of the House of Lords appointed to consider the best Means which Great Britain can adopt for the final Extinction of the African Slave Trade", 69 (hereafter referred to as Winniett's testimony); Thomas C. Maroukis, "Warfare and Society in the Kingdom of Dahomey: 1818-1894", Ph.D. thesis, Boston U., 1974, 91.
29. Guillevin, "Voyage", 292.
30. Wilmot, "Despatches", 438.
31. Skertchly, *Dahomey*, 455.
32. Foà, *Dahomey*, 257-8.
33. Herskovits, *Dahomey*, II, 46.

Chapter 7: A Privileged Life

1. M'Leod, *Voyage*, 50.
2. Henry Veel Huntley, *Seven Years' Service on the Slave Coast of Western Africa*, 2 vols (London, 1850), I, 118.
3. Répin, "Voyage", 99.
4. Huntley, *Seven Years' Service*, 118.
5. Chaudoin, *Trois mois*, 269, 329.
6. Chautard, *Dahomey*, 13.
7. Maire, *Dahomey*, 72.
8. Bay, "Royal Women", 20. See also Bay's "Servitude and Worldly Success in the Palace of Dahomey" in Claire C. Robertson and Martin A. Klein, eds, *Women and Slavery in Africa* (Madison, 1983), 354.
9. Bay, "Royal Women", 21.
10. Répin, "Voyage", 100.
11. Exceptionally, Ellis tells of meeting a party of armed amazons led by a bell-ringing officer. He says they were *en route* to Whydah to fetch a chief who had offended the king and take him to Abomey. A.B. Ellis, *The Land of Fetish*, reprint of 1883 edn (Westport, Conn., 1970), 55, 58.
12. Skertchly, *Dahomey*, 384.

13. Burton, *Mission*, 123. See also John Duncan, *Travels in Western Africa, in 1845 and 1846*, 2 vols, reprint of 1847 edn (New York, 1967), I, 258; Skertchly, *Dahomey*, 110.

14. *Ibid..*, 168, 213.

15. CMS, CA2/016/34, Dawson's journal, 2, 24. Dawson was a native of Cape Coast in what is now Ghana, the son of an English father and a Fante mother. At Whydah he was first a Wesleyan missionary then a merchant. Later, in 1873-4, he served as an intermediary in his homeland between Britain and Asante.

16. Skertchly, *Dahomey*, 448, 457; G. de Wailly, "Un régiment sacré: Dahomey", *La Nouvelle Revue*, XII, no. 63 (March-April 1890), 391; Service Historique de l'Armée de Terre (Château de Vincennes), Dahomey, I, 14, "Campagne du Dahomey – relation anonyme", 87. (The latter document is a 108-page journal of the Franco-Dahomean war of 1892 that has been attributed to Foreign Legion Capt. Edouard Demartinécourt by Luc Garcia, *Le royaume du Dahomé face à la pénétration coloniale. Affrontements et incompréhension (1875-1894)*, [Paris, 1988], 159 n. 1. It will hereafter be referred to in the notes as Demartinécourt's journal.)

17. Burton, *Mission*, 123 n. 7. He noted specifically (p. 261) that each blunderbuss woman was accompanied by an "attendant" carrying ammunition.

18. Duncan, *Travels*, I, 230. Duncan had served in the Life Guards, a regiment that bears comparison to the amazons as Britain's first permanent military unit, formed in 1660 to protect the king. The Briton did not, however, remark on the parallel.

19. Foà, *Dahomey*, 255. He used the figure of 40 kilograms. But elsewhere (p. 106) Foà stated that a Dahomean woman, like a man, could headload 50 to 60 kilos (110 to 132 pounds) for several days' journey. Another French observer put the average headload in the country at 25 to 35 kilos (55 to 77 pounds). Marine Capt. Bertin, "Renseignements sur le royaume de Porto-Novo et le Dahomey", *Revue Maritime et Coloniale*, 106th tome (1890), 392.

20. Burton, *Mission*, 257.

21. Degbelo, "Amazones", 124.

22. Wilmot, "Despatches", 438, 427 (out of sequence).

23. Edouard Foà, "Dahomiens et Egbas", *La Nature*, XIX, 1st semester, no. 930 (March 28, 1891), 262-3 (2nd part of 2-part article).

Chapter 8: What They Wore

1. Dalzel, *History*, 169; Akinjogbin, *Dahomey*, 171. The trickle of freed slaves from Brazil to the Slave Coast swelled to thousands in the

mid-nineteenth century. Two typical Fon art forms, bas-reliefs and appliqué, have been attributed (impressionistically) to Brazilian inspiration.

2. F. Borghero, letter to Planque, Sept. 30, 1861, *APF*, XXXIV, no. 202 (May 1862), 222.

3. Burton, *Mission*, 227; Skertchly, *Dahomey*, 294; Henri Morienval, *La guerre du Dahomey. Journal de campagne d'un sous-lieutenant d'infanterie de marine* (Paris, 1893), 196; Foà, *Dahomey*, 257.

4. L. Brunet and Louis Giethlen, *Dahomey et dépendances* (Paris, 1900), 264.

5. Dalzel, *History*, vii, xvi.

6. Smith, *New Voyage*, 184; Des Marchais, "Journal", folio 62 recto–63 recto; Law, "Further Light", 219; Snelgrave, *New Account*, 80.

7. Snelgrave, *New Account*, 34.

8. Pruneau de Pommegorge, *Description*, 181.

9. *Ibid.*, 174.

10. Dalzel, *History*, plate II opp. p. 54, plate IV opp. p. 136.

11. Theophilus Conneau, *A Slaver's Log Book, or 20 Years' Residence in Africa* (Englewood Cliffs, NJ, 1976), 204.

12. Chaudoin, *Trois mois*, 321-2.

13. Degbelo, "Amazones", 122.

14. Thomas Birch Freeman, *Journal of Various Visits to the Kingdoms of Ashanti, Aku, and Dahomi in Western Africa*, 3rd edn, inc. reprint of 1844 edn (London, 1968), 262-3.

15. Duncan, *Travels*, I, 226. The amazon tunic is called many things in the literature, including jumper, doublet, chemisette, blouse, waistcoat, vest and jacket, and is almost always described as sleeveless.

16. *Ibid.*, I, 234.

17. Forbes, *Dahomey*, I, 78.

18. Burton, *Mission*, 243.

19. Foà, *Dahomey*, 257-8.

20. Winniett's testimony, 65. Forbes's journal, 61-2, says an amazon "regiment" begged him to convey their thanks to Victoria for the caps. This was left out of his book.

21. Burton, *Mission*, 332.

22. Herskovits, *Dahomey*, I, 283.

23. Chaudoin, *Trois mois*, 313-14.

24. Herskovits, *Dahomey*, I, 283.

25. Auguste Bouët, "Le royaume de Dahomey" (3rd part), *L'Illustration*, X, no. 492 (July 31, 1852), 71.

26. Mandirola and Morel, *Journal*, 77.

27. Burton, *Mission*, 285, 314.

28. Skertchly, *Dahomey*, 294.

29. Foà, *Dahomey*, 257.

30. Répin, "Voyage", 91.
31. Bouët, "Royaume" (3rd part), 71.
32. Burton, *Mission*, 246. He also (p. 285) saw "scouts coated in grass" dancing before Glele but did not specify their sex.
33. *Ibid.*, 155.
34. Skertchly, *Dahomey*, 140, 166, 254, 255, 263.
35. Foà, "Dahomiens et Egbas" (1st part), *La Nature*, XIX, 1st semester, no. 926 (Feb. 28, 1891), 202.
36. Vallon, "Royaume" (1st part), 345-6, 362; Burton, *Mission*, 262.
37. Burton, *Mission*, 163, 263.
38. Nardin, "Reprise", 110.
39. Bouët, "Royaume", *L'Illustration*, no. 490 (July 17, 1852), 39; no. 491, 61; Nardin, "Reprise", 109. Bouët also (*ibid.*, 111) saw an amazon "company" wearing "old-style light helmets". He doesn't say what they were composed of; animal skins are a possibility. Pruneau (*Description*, 173) mentions elephant-skin helmets worn by men soldiers. Chaudoin (*Trois mois*, 301) speaks of hats covered with black monkey skin, also worn by male troops.
40. Skertchly, *Dahomey*, 255, 256.
41. Norris, *Memoirs*, 112.
42. Vallon, "Royaume" (1st part), 345.
43. Forbes, *Dahomey*, II, 64.
44. Vallon, "Royaume" (2nd part), *Revue Maritime et Coloniale*, III (November 1861), 339.
45. Burton, *Mission*, 111.
46. *Ibid.* 228.
47. Skertchly, *Dahomey*, 251.
48. Nardin, "Reprise", 109-10.
49. Chaudoin, *Trois mois*, 322.
50. Burton, *Mission*, 243-4, 251.
51. Duncan, *Travels*, I, 225.
52. Burton, *Mission*, 228, 243, 244, 315.
53. Conneau, *Slaver's Log Book*, 204.
54. Répin, "Voyage", 92.
55. Beecroft's journal, 52.
56. Burton, *Mission*, 244.
57. Foà, *Dahomey*, 257; "Dahomiens" (2nd part), 263.
58. Duncan, *Travels*, I, 261.
59. Skertchly, *Dahomey*, 167.
60. Répin, "Voyage", 83.
61. Foà, *Dahomey*, 258.
62. Morienval, *Guerre*, 38.

Chapter 9: Their Weapons

1. E. Courdioux, "Côte des Esclaves", *MC*, VII, no. 336 (Nov. 12, 1875), 555. (From 1873 to 1878 Courdioux published many articles about Dahomey and its neighbors in this weekly organ of the Missions Africaines of Lyon under the general heading "Côte des Esclaves". After the initial reference they will be referred to in the notes by the number of the issue.)
2. Répin, "Voyage", 82, 91.
3. Snelgrave, *New Account*, 34.
4. Foà, *Dahomey*, 259.
5. Warren Moore, *Weapons of the Revolution...and Accoutrements* (New York, 1967), 59.
6. Ian V. Hogg and John H. Batchelor, *Armies of the American Revolution* (Englewood Cliffs, NJ, 1975), 57.
7. PRO, FO 84/1175, T.L. Perry to H.S. Freeman, Aug. 6, 1862. Euschart visited Abomey from June 28 to July 22, 1862. Perry, a British warship commander, wrote down the Dutchman's oral account after the trader's return to the coast, and sent it to the British governor in Lagos.
8. Ellis, *Land of Fetish*, 55. He saw an officer with a Winchester and some of her troops carrying British Enfields.
9. Forbes, *Dahomey*, II, 226, 236, 67. See also Beecroft's journal, 52, 55. Forbes's journal, 40, refers to the "seven-barrelled arquebuse" (harquebus) as "a 5 barrelled blunderbuss." Perhaps it was a mistake made in the heat of note-taking and corrected in the cool serenity of book-writing.
10. Nardin, "Reprise", 110.
11. Bouët, "Royaume", no. 492, 71-2.
12. Vallon, "Royaume" (November 1861), 339; Courdioux, no. 336, 555.
13. Nardin, "Reprise", 125.
14. Répin, "Voyage", 90.
15. Vallon, "Royaume" (1st part), 345.
16. Burton, *Mission*, 161 n. 36; Skertchly, *Dahomey*, 263.
17. Pruneau de Pommegorge, *Description*, 181; Norris, *Memoirs*, 94.
18. Freeman, *Journal*, 260, 263.
19. Chaudoin, *Trois mois*, 395-6.
20. Freeman, *Journal*, 263.
21. Répin, "Voyage", 91 (source of quote); Vallon, "Royaume" (1st part), 345.
22. *Ibid.*
23. Burton, *Mission*, 262.
24. Beecroft's journal, 58.

25. Nardin, "Reprise", 109.
26. Vallon, "Royaume" (1st part), 346.
27. Burton, *Mission*, 163-4.
28. Skertchly, *Dahomey*, 132.
29. Burton, *Mission*, 161; Skertchly, *Dahomey*, 254.
30. Vallon, "Royaume" (1st part), 338-9, 345.
31. Borghero, no. 206, 33; Mandirola and Morel, *Journal*, 77. Borghero thought both the handle and the blade were nearly a meter long.
32. Skertchly, *Dahomey*, 254.
33. Maire, *Dahomey*, 51. He says instances of such mutilation occurred during the Franco-Dahomean war of 1892 but gives no specifics.
34. Degbelo, "Amazones", 126. Ellis heard that amazons "mutilate[d] the wounded in a horrible manner" with their machetes, but did not elaborate. *Land of Fetish*, 55.
35. Burton, *Mission*, 161.
36. Archibald R. Ridgway, "Journal of a Visit to Dahomey; or, the Snake Country, in the Months of March and April, 1847", *The New Monthly Magazine and Humorist* (London), LXXXI, no. 323 (Nov. 1847), 303, 304 (the 2nd part of a 3-part article).
37. Vallon, "Royaume" (1st part), 355.
38. Skertchly, *Dahomey*, 281.
39. *Ibid.*, 20.
40. Foà, *Dahomey*, 258.
41. Brunet and Giethlen, *Dahomey*, 303.
42. Duncan, *Travels*, I, 226.
43. Bouët, "Royaume" (3rd part), 71.
44. Skertchly, *Dahomey*, 214.
45. *Ibid.*, 167.
46. Courdioux, no. 336, 555.
47. Jean Bayol, "Les forces militaires actuelles du Dahomey", *Revue Scientifique (Revue Rose)*, XLIX, no. 17 (April 23, 1892), 521.
48. Maire, *Dahomey*, 51.
49. Borghero, no. 202, 222.
50. Labarthe, *Voyage*, 122.
51. Répin, "Voyage", 92.
52. Brue, "Voyage", 63.
53. Burton, *Mission*, 262 n. 19.
54. *Ibid.*, 262.
55. *Ibid.*
56. Brue, "Voyage", 63.
57. Bayol, "Forces militaires", 521.
58. Conneau, *Slaver's Log Book*, 204.
59. Répin, "Voyage", 102.
60. Skertchly, *Dahomey*, 255.

61. Courdioux, no. 336, 550.
62. Le Hérissé, *Ancien royaume*, 60.
63. Pruneau de Pommegorge, *Description*, 181.
64. Burton, *Mission*, 155 n. 19.
65. Répin, "Voyage", 91.
66. Burton, *Mission*, 155 n. 19.
67. Le Hérissé, *Ancien royaume*, 71.
68. Nardin, "Reprise", 109.
69. Skertchly, *Dahomey*, 21.
70. Répin, "Voyage", 91.
71. Foà, *Dahomey*, 257.
72. Mandirola and Morel, *Journal*, 77.
73. King Béhanzin told a French mission to Abomey in March 1891 he had a factory that produced both firearms and gunpowder. He said the powder was made according to European methods but that he preferred to buy it from the whites. If the mission prolonged its stay, he said, he would send for his gunsmiths or their products, but the French soon left. In the absence of any evidence, Béhanzin's claim is dubious at best. CAOM, Dahomey, III, 2, J. d'Ambrières' journal; Aublet, *Guerre au Dahomey*, 98.
74. Herskovits, *Dahomey*, I, 126.
75. Duncan, *Travels*, I, 226.
76. Burton, *Mission*, 261.
77. Bayol, "Forces militaires", 521. Chaudoin (*Trois mois*, 301) mentions the use of "straw of *mandille*" for weaving bags; I have been unable to determine which spelling is correct.
78. Forbes, *Dahomey*, I, 23.
79. Burton, *Mission*, 156.
80. Skertchly, *Dahomey*, 166-7.
81. Duncan, *Travels*, I, 261.
82. Foà, *Dahomey*, 257.
83. Snelgrave, *New Account*, 27, 78.
84. Norris, *Memoirs*, 108.
85. Forbes, *Dahomey*, II, 39, 56, 222; Beecroft's journal, 60.
86. Skertchly, *Dahomey*, 281.
87. Burton, *Mission*, 187, 185.
88. *Ibid.*, 262-3.

Chapter 10: How Many Amazons?

1. Pruneau de Pommegorge, *Description*, 181.
2. Norris, *Memoirs*, 108-9; Dalzel, *History*, 176.
3. Pires, *Viagem*, 68.

4. Brue, "Voyage", 63.
5. Freeman, *Journal*, 260, 262, 263.
6. CAOM, SOM (Section Outre-Mer), D.3538, Pogla K. Glélè, "Le royaume du Dan-Hô-Min: tradition orale et histoire écrite", master's thesis, 78; Maire, *Dahomey*, 49.
7. Duncan, *Travels*, I, 227, 231.
8. Winniett's testimony, 65.
9. Ridgway, "Journal", 304, 408. The latter citation is in the 3rd part of the article, *New Monthly Magazine*, LXXXI. no. 324 (Dec. 1847).
10. Forbes, *Dahomey*, II, 55-6, 91, 226-7; Forbes's journal, 36.
11. Beecroft's journal, 42. On p. 45 he quotes Gezo as saying "a great number" of troops were away guarding the frontiers.
12. Burton, *Mission*, 263.
13. Richard F. Burton, *Abeokuta and the Camaroons Mountains*, 2 vols (London, 1863), I, 120 n. 1.
14. Bouët, "Royaume" (3rd part), 71; Nardin, "Reprise", 99, 125.
15. Répin, "Voyage," 91, 92; Vallon, "Royaume" (1st part), 343; "Royaume" (2nd part), 347.
16. Guillevin, "Voyage", 292.
17. Borghero, no. 202, 222.
18. Burton, *Abeokuta*, I, 124; Dunglas, "Contribution", tome 2, 108; Maroukis, "Warfare", 200.
19. PRO, FO 84/1175, Perry to Freeman, Aug. 6, 1862.
20. CMS, CA2/016/34, Dawson's journal, 21.
21. Wilmot, "Despatches", 438.
22. Burton, *Abeokuta*, I, 122.
23. Burton, *Mission*, 263-4.
24. Skertchly, *Dahomey*, 455.
25. Foà, *Dahomey*, 30.
26. Médard Béraud, "Note sur le Dahomé", *Bulletin de la Société de Géographie*, 5th series, XII, Nov. 1866, 380; CAOM, Gabon, I, 6b, Fleuriot de Langle to French Navy Minister, July 16, 1866; Bouche, *Sept ans*, 381-3; E. Courdioux, "Côte des Esclaves", *MC*, IX, no. 397 (Jan. 12, 1877), 23; Ellis, *Ewe-Speaking Peoples*, 198; Bernard Schnapper, *La politique et le commerce français dans le golfe de Guinée de 1838 à 1871* (Paris, 1961), 190. As late as 1863, 10,000 slaves are said to have been shipped from Dahomey to Cuba. Honorat Aguessy, "Le Dan-Homê du XIXe siècle était-il une société esclavagiste?", *Revue Française d'Etudes Politiques Africaines*, no. 50 (Feb. 1970), 81.
27. Patrick Manning, "The Slave Trade in the Bight of Benin, 1640-1890" in Henry A. Gemery and Jan S. Hogendorn, eds, *The Uncommon Market: Essays in the Economic History of the Atlantic Slave Trade* (New York, 1979), 117.

28. Edmond Chaudoin, "Au Dahomey", *L'Illustration*, no. 2563 (April 9, 1892), 302; *Trois mois*, 118-19; Alfred Barbou, *Histoire de la Guerre au Dahomey* (Paris, 1893), 94; C.W. Newbury, *The Western Slave Coast and Its Rulers* (Oxford, 1961). 130 n. 4. The last slave shipment out of Dahomey may have consisted of 500 persons embarked on a German steamer May 1, 1892. CAOM, Dahomey, I, 5a, Ballay to French Navy Minister, May 8, 1892.

29. Béraud, "Note", 378.

30. Leaving aside a wildly exaggerated estimate of 15 to 20,000 by Ellis (*Land of Fetish*, 41).

31. Frédéric Schelameur, *Souvenirs de la campagne du Dahomey* (Paris, 1896), 235.

Chapter 11: Where They Lived

1. Forbes, *Dahomey*, I, ix; Skertchly, *Dahomey*, 455; Foà, *Dahomey*, 258; Degbelo, "Amazones", 92; Bay, "Servitude", 352.

2. Nardin, "Reprise", 123.

3. Norris, *Memoirs*, 82.

4. Law, "Further Light", 217.

5. MAE, Mémoires et documents, Afrique, 51, J. Lartigue, "Relation du voyage à Abomey", Sept. 2, 1860, 10.

6. Burton, *Mission*, 326.

7. CAOM, Dahomey, III, 1, Angot to Bayol, Jan. 5, 1890, 10.

8. Emmanuel G. Waterlot, *Les bas-reliefs des bâtiments royaux d'Abomey (Dahomey)*, (Paris, 1926), 3.

9. Th. Constant-Ernest d'Oliveira, *La visite du Musée d'Histoire d'Abomey* (Abomey, 1970), 7.

10. Dalzel, *History*, xiii; Freeman, *Journal*, 258.

11. Burton, *Mission*, 136.

12. D'Oliveira, *Visite*, 4.

13. Waterlot, *Bas-reliefs*, 3.

14. Law, "Further Light", 217.

15. Dalzel, *History*, 190-1.

16. Law, "Further Light", 217.

17. Freeman, *Journal*, 268.

18. Duncan, *Travels*, I, 219.

19. Répin, "Voyage", 80.

20. Freeman, *Journal*, 270.

21. *Ibid.*, 259.

22. Guillevin, "Voyage", 285.

23. Quénum, *Pays des Fons*, 16.

24. Dalzel, *History*, xv; Guillevin, "Voyage", 285; Burton, *Mission*, 141.

25. Brue, "Voyage", 61.
26. Burton, *Mission*, 86 n. 2.
27. Pruneau de Pommegorge, *Description*, 172. "These individuals", he related, "are of no use to the king, except to satisfy his vanity," missing the point of rendering males safe for palace duty.
28. PRO, FO 84/886, Louis Fraser's journal, enclosure no. 1 in Beecroft to Palmerston, Feb. 19, 1852, 126. (This 163-page document will hereafter be referred to as Fraser's journal in the notes.)
29. Norris, *Memoirs*, 127-8; Dalzel, *History*, xiv.
30. Norris, *Memoirs*, 128.
31. Nardin, "Reprise", 99.
32. Skertchly, *Dahomey*, 385.
33. Borghero, no. 206, 25.
34. Burton, *Mission*, 175.
35. Skertchly, *Dahomey*, 385.
36. Borghero, no. 206, 25.
37. Répin, "Voyage", 80.
38. Burton, *Mission*, 136, 175.
39. Norris, *Memoirs*, 106-7.
40. Forbes, *Dahomey*, II, 34, 67; Forbes's journal, 19, 41; Beecroft's journal, 31, 62, 65.
41. Burton, *Mission*, 21 n. 39, 190-1.
42. *Ibid.*, 239 and n. 61.
43. Skertchly, *Dahomey*, 353-4.
44. Burton, *Mission*, 136.
45. *Ibid.*, 322.
46. Smith, *New Voyage*, 183.
47. Law, "Further Light", 217.
48. CAOM, Dahomey, III, 1, Angot to Bayol, Jan. 5, 1890, 10.
49. Le Hérissé, *Ancien royaume*, 27.
50. Dunglas, "Contribution", tome 1, 92.
51. Bay, "Royal Women", 162.
52. Degbelo, "Amazones", 91.
53. Law, "Further Light", 217.
54. Pruneau de Pommegorge, *Description*, 162.
55. CAOM, DFC, Côtes d'Afrique, no. 111, carton 75, "Réfléxions sur Juda par les Sieurs de Chenevert et abbé Bullet", 7.
56. Dalzel, *History*, xiv.
57. De Chenevert and Bullet, "Réfléxions", 7.
58. Norris, *Memoirs*, 94.
59. Forbes, *Dahomey*, II, 20, 43, 57, 65, 75.
60. Beecroft's journal, 101.
61. *Ibid.*, 127, 128; Forbes, *Dahomey*, II, 162, 163.
62. Vallon, "Royaume" (1st part), 336-7; Répin, "Voyage", 84, 100.

63. Argyle, *Fon*, 67.
64. Vallon, "Royaume" (1st part), 337; Répin, "Voyage", 84.
65. *Ibid.*
66. Vallon, "Royaume" (1st part), 336.
67. *Ibid.*, 336, 337.
68. Burton, *Mission*, 141.
69. Vallon, "Royaume" (1st part), 337. Répin ("Voyage", 83) describes him as "a sort of chamberlain charged with maintaining order at ceremonies, and imposing silence on spectators".
70. Skertchly, *Dahomey*, 446.
71. Blanchély, "Relation du deuxième voyage fait, en 1850, dans le royaume du Dahomé, par Blanchély aîné, en compagnie de M. Esprit Cases, nouvel agent de la factorerie française Régis aîné, de Whydah", 1st of 2 parts, *MC*, XXIII, no. 1172 (Nov. 20, 1891), 563.
72. Forbes, *Dahomey*, II, 18, 75; Beecroft's journal, 44.
73. Burton, *Mission*, 175.
74. Vallon, "Royaume" (August 1861), 337; Répin, "Voyage", 83-4; Burton, *Mission*, 141-2, 164.
75. Jules Poirier, *Campagne du Dahomey, 1892-1894* (Paris, 1895), 245. See also Freeman, *Journal*, 257, 258, 265; Fraser's journal, 49, 105, 136; Vallon, "Royaume" (1st part), 337; Répin, "Voyage", 84. A modern scholar, Boniface I. Obichere, has claimed that Kangbodé ("Cambode") was not a title but simply the name of Gezo's treasurer ("Change and Innovation in the Administration of the Kingdom of Dahomey", *Journal of African Studies*, I, 3 [fall 1974], 244). This is not the impression conveyed by the testimony of Freeman, Blanchély, Forbes, Beecroft, Fraser, Vallon, Répin, Burton and Skertchly, and twentieth-century authors generally accept Kangbodé as an office. According to Poirier (*Campagne*, 245), Béhanzin's "chamberlain" was named Ayenkuken and his Tononu Tossa. Both were members of a futile peace delegation the fugitive king sent to Paris in November 1893.
76. Burton, *Mission*, 141, 251; Skertchly, *Dahomey*, 212, 226. Forbes (*Dahomey*, II, *passim*) called the Tononu's female counterpart the *mae-hae-pah*, Burton (*Mission*, 141, 251) and Skertchly (*Dahomey*, 212, 226) the *Yavedo*.
77. Bay, "Royal Women", 191.
78. Burton, *Mission*, 86 n. 2.
79. Argyle, *Fon*, 69.

Chapter 12: Military Training

1. David Ross, "Dahomey" in Michael Crowder, ed., *West African Resis-*

tance: The Military Response to Colonial Occupation (New York, 1971), 154.

2. Bayol, "Forces militaires", 521-2. An incident during the Beecroft/Forbes visit to Abomey in 1850 indicates that if any weapon lacked honor it was the club. Five or six officers convicted of misconduct in the recent Atakpamé campaign were rearmed solely with clubs and relegated to the rank of junior executioners. In this case at least, the club was a symbol of disgrace. Beecroft's journal, 117; Forbes, *Dahomey*, II, 149; Forbes's journal, 78.

3. Foà, *Dahomey*, 259.

4. De Wailly, "Régiment sacré", 393.

5. Duncan, *Travels*, I, 240.

6. Vallon, "Royaume" (2nd part), 350.

7. Burton, *Mission*, 261. Burton was quoting (approvingly if not explicitly) from a letter by "the celebrated lion-hunter, M. Jules Gerard", who had attended Dahomean military exercises at Cana. The letter appeared in *The Times* of London on Aug. 18, 1864, and was added to the original edition of *A Mission to Gelele* as an appendix.

8. Skertchly, *Dahomey*, 166-7, 209, 457.

9. Law, "Further Light", 218-19.

10. *Ibid.*, 217.

11. Pruneau de Pommegorge, *Description*, 161.

12. Labarthe, *Voyage*, 122.

13. *Ibid.*, 148-9.

14. Dalzel, *History*, xi.

15. Conneau, *Slaver's Log Book*, 204.

16. Duncan, *Travels*, I, 231-3.

17. Winniett's testimony, 65.

18. Forbes, *Dahomey*, II, 123-6; Forbes's journal, 64-7; Beecroft's journal, 101-3.

19. Bouët, "Royaume" (3rd part), 71.

20. *Ibid.*

21. Nardin, "Reprise", 100.

22. Répin, "Voyage", 91; Vallon, "Royaume" (2nd part), 348-9.

23. Répin, "Voyage", 92.

24. Vallon, "Royaume" (2nd part), 350.

25. Foà, "Dahomiens" (2nd part), 263.

26. De Wailly, "Régiment sacré", 393.

27. Skertchly, *Dahomey*, 295.

28. Fraser's journal, 126.

29. Bayol, "Forces militaires", 521.

30. Wilmot, "Despatches", 438. It is tempting to link this report on apprentice amazons to Snelgrave's remark more than a century earlier (*New Account*, 78) about boys accompanying male soldiers.

31. Le Hérissé, *Ancien royaume*, 60-1.
32. Law, "Further Light", 217.
33. Snelgrave, *New Account*, 27, 77-8.
34. Labarthe, *Voyage*, 122.
35. *Ibid.*, 148-9.
36. Dalzel, *History*, xi.
37. Freeman, *Journal*, 263. See also Freeman typescript, 324.
38. Duncan, *Travels*, II, 281-3.
39. *Ibid.*, I, 240.
40. Wilmot, "Despatches", 429. Admiral Didelot, who headed France's West African naval squadron in 1861-3, heard through Wilmot that the Dahomean army's "military education has for some time been pursued with much more care than before: shooting has made great progress since the soldiers began target practice, they know how to shoulder and aim [their guns] unlike nearly all other blacks, for whom the noise is everything and who shoot from all positions taking great care to turn their heads away." MAE, Mémoires et documents, Afrique, 52, Didelot to Chasseloup-Laubat, Mar. 27, 1863.
41. Borghero, no. 106, 30.
42. Degbelo, "Amazones", 115.
43. Duncan, *Travels*, I, 240.
44. Wilmot, "Despatches", 427, 429, 438.
45. Skertchly, *Dahomey*, 209.
46. Foà, *Dahomey*, 256.
47. Adolphe Burdo, "Au Dahomey", *Journal des Voyages*, no. 682 (Aug. 3, 1890), 70 (2nd part of a 3-part article). Burdo seems to have obtained his information secondhand.
48. J. Bern, *L'expédition du Dahomey (août-décembre 1892): notes éparses d'un volontaire* (Sidi-Bel-Abbès, Algeria, 1893), 261.
49. Forbes, *Dahomey*, I, 23.
50. Skertchly, *Dahomey*, 167, 457.
51. Foà, *Dahomey*, 259.
52. Foà, "Dahomiens" (2nd part), 262.
53. Degbelo, "Amazones", 115.
54. Forbes, *Dahomey*, 61-2.
55. Vallon, "Royaume" (2nd part), 347.
56. Chaudoin, *Trois mois*, 186.
57. Foà, *Dahomey*, 256, 258.
58. Duncan, *Travels*, I, 225-6.
59. Beecroft's journal, 52.
60. Wilmot, "Despatches", 438.
61. Foà, "Dahomiens" (2nd part), 262.
62. Bayol, "Forces militaires", 522.

63. Degbelo, "Amazones", 99, 115.
64. At first sight, this might seem to contradict descriptions of the teenaged archeresses as the most light-footed amazons, but trained runners normally peak in their twenties.
65. Ibid., 113-15.
66. Bayol, "Forces militaires", 522.
67. Borghero, no. 202, 225.
68. Ridgway, "Journal" (3rd part), 408.
69. Skertchly, Dahomey, 18.
70. Quénum, Pays des Fons, 162.
71. Conneau, Slaver's Log Book, 204, 205.
72. Duncan, Travels, I, 240.
73. Winniett's testimony, 69.
74. Ridgway, "Journal" (3rd part), 408.
75. Wilmot, "Despatches", 427.
76. Freeman typescript, 322, 323.
77. Laffitte, Dahomé, 82, 86. Laffitte's first name sometimes appears as Irénée in the records, and his family name is sometimes written with a single f.
78. Buzon, "Une visite à la cour du roi de Dahomey en 1874", Revue Bleue (Revue Politique et Littéraire), LI, no. 24 (June 17, 1893), 754.
79. Ellis, Land of Fetish, 55.
80. Chaudoin, Trois mois, 186.
81. Foà, Dahomey, 258, 259.
82. Bern, Expédition, 192.
83. Georges Verdal, "Les amazones du Dahomey", L'Education Physique, new series, XXXII, no. 29 (Jan. 1934), 58.
84. Ibid.
85. Bouët, "Royaume" (3rd part), 71.
86. Burton, Mission, 154.
87. Ibid., 224.
88. Ibid., 154.
89. Ibid., 262.
90. Skertchly, Dahomey, 341.
91. Le Hérissé, Ancien royaume, 68.
92. Insensitivity training may have first been tested on male army apprentices. As cited earlier (ch. 3, n. 57), William Smith (New Voyage, 192) heard that after the 1727 conquest of Whydah, the Dahomean general "order'd all the Boys in the Camp; some of which were not above Seven or Eight Years of Age, to cut off the Heads of all the Aged and Wounded among the Captives that were unmerchantable."
93. Dalzel, History, 171-3.
94. Conneau, Slaver's Log Book, 205.
95. Beecroft's journal, 39-40; Forbes, Dahomey, II, 49-53; Forbes's journal,

23, 28-31, 104. Forbes says Beecroft saved one of the men by paying
$100 for him, but Beecroft himself tells of four victims being "pitched
over" by the amazons.

96. Burton, *Mission*, 166, 233.

97. Skertchly, *Dahomey*, 358, 415, 417.

98. Chaudoin, 'Dahomey", 302. An unreliable writer named J. du Vistre
– he pretends Glele attended school in Marseille when actually it
was two of his younger brothers – relates that when amazons had to
sacrifice a man, he was dressed in European clothes, and the women
danced madly round him before doing him in. Du Vistre's article
"Au Dahomey" in *L'Illustration*, XLVIII, no. 2455, Mar. 15, 1890,
is illustrated by an engraving of a photo purporting to show just
that. While there is no sign du Vistre ever saw Dahomey, the photo
is credited to "Choa", an apparent misprint for Foà, who did indeed
live in the area from 1886 to 1890. Coincidentally, *Le Figaro*'s weekly
Supplément Littéraire (XVI, no. 10, Mar. 8, 1890, 38) had, only a
week earlier, published a 30-year-old account of a visit to Abomey
by Jules Lartigue titled "Les sacrifices humains au Dahomey –
révélations inédites" which may help make some sense out of du
Vistre's report and Foà's photo. Lartigue (whose original 20-page
MS. is preserved as MAE, Mémoires et documents, Afrique, 51,
"Relation du voyage à Abomey", Sept. 2, 1860) said Glele, tired of
sending blacks to serve his late father Gezo, decided to offer "whites".
He had two African prisoners dressed à l'européenne, paraded them
through the town in hammocks, then dispatched them to the other
world by hanging, the white man's form of execution. Conceivably
Béhanzin did his father Glele the same sort of honor with amazon
assistance. See also PRO, FO 84/1175, Perry to Freeman, Aug. 6,
1862, on prisoners from Ishagga (ch. 18) being dressed as Europeans
before being beheaded.

99. Anonymous, *La France au pays noir, campagne du Dahomey, 1890-1892*
(Paris, 1895), 39, 46, quoting from A. Angot's "journal", which I
have not been able to locate; Jean Bayol, "L'attaque de Kotonou, 4
mars 1890, impressions et souvenirs", *Revue Bleue (Revue Politique et
Littéraire)*, XLIX, no. 18 (Apr. 30, 1892), 572.

100. Anon., *France au pays noir*, 46, quoting Angot's journal; Léonce
Grandin, *A l'assaut du pays des noirs. Le Dahomey*, 2 vols (Paris, 1895),
I, 163; Chaudoin, *Trois mois*, 351-2.

101. G.A. Robertson, *Notes on Africa; Particularly Those Parts Which Are
Situated Between Cape Verd and the River Congo* (London, 1819), 270.

102. Duncan, *Travels*, I, 240.

103. Forbes, *Dahomey*, I, 6.

104. Bouët, "Royaume" (2nd part), 61.

105. Bern, *Expédition*, 327-8.

Chapter 13: Building *Esprit de Corps*

1. Forbes, *Dahomey*, I, 24.
2. Skertchly, *Dahomey*, 214.
3. *Ibid.*, 18.
4. Vallon, "Royaume" (1st part), 346.
5. Borghero, no. 202, 222, 224.
6. Forbes, *Dahomey*, II, 242.
7. Skertchly, *Dahomey*, 18.
8. Forbes, *Dahomey*, I, 24.
9. *Ibid.*, II, 227. Forbes kept tabs on bands (and everything else) in processions. Women's bands varied from four to forty members – twelve was the most common size – but often it is not clear whether amazons were involved. Many bands were composed exclusively of one instrument, usually drums or elephant-tusk horns; the sole four-member group played long brass trumpets. One 12-member band had "calabash instruments", presumably rattles. *Ibid.*, II, 214-41; Forbes's journal, 103-26.
10. Nardin, "Reprise", 110; Bouët, "Royaume" (2nd part), 59.
11. Duncan, *Travels*, I, 230.
12. Burton, *Mission*, 249.
13. Some drums may also have been made of pottery. See Clément da Cruz, "Les instruments de musique dans le Bas-Dahomey", *ED*, XII (1954), 16, 19.
14. Forbes, *Dahomey*, II, 235; Beecroft's journal, 55.
15. Burton, *Mission*, 154.
16. Nardin, "Reprise", 110, 111.
17. Forbes, *Dahomey*, II, 235; Beecroft's journal, 55.
18. Da Cruz ("Instruments", 15, 18) lists wooden horns and others made of buffalo and antelope horns in his mid-twentieth-century catalogue.
19. Forbes, *Dahomey*, II, 232; Beecroft's journal, 53.
20. Nardin, "Reprise", 109; Bouët, "Royaume" (2nd part), 59.
21. Dalzel, *History*, xi n. 1.
22. Morienval, *Guerre du Dahomey*, 198.
23. Forbes, *Dahomey*, II, 230.
24. Beecroft's journal, 131; Bouët, "Royaume" (2nd part), 59.
25. Beecroft's journal, 53.
26. Skertchly, *Dahomey*, 19. Da Cruz ("Instruments", 16) mentions seeds, both tied to the net and inside the calabash, plus rattles of iron.
27. Skertchly, *Dahomey*, 19. See also da Cruz, "Instruments", 17.
28. Répin, "Voyage", 91.
29. Duncan, *Travels*, I, 224; Bouët, "Royaume" (2nd part), 59; Borghero, no. 202, 225; Ridgway, "Journal" (2nd part), 301; Répin, "Voyage", 91; Skertchly, *Dahomey*, 165; Laffitte, *Dahomé*, 91.

30. Quénum, *Pays des Fons*, 159. Another Dahomean, Clément da Cruz, agreed ("Instruments", 34) that local musicians had "no idea of harmony according to European rules of music but [were] experienced in the practice of cadence".
31. Vallon, "Royaume" (1st part), 346.
32. *Ibid.* (2nd part), 347.
33. Burton, *Mission*, 227.
34. Skertchly, *Dahomey*, 247.
35. Ridgway, "Journal" (3rd part), 408.
36. Forbes, *Dahomey*, II, 39.
37. *Ibid.*, II, 242. Forbes's journal, 127, 128, also mentions shield and bow-and-arrow dances.
38. Burton, *Mission*, 227-8.
39. Borghero, no. 202, 225.
40. Dalzel, *History*, xi n. 1.
41. Ridgway, "Journal" (3rd part), 408.
42. Forbes, *Dahomey*, II, 92; Beecroft's journal, 49.
43. *Ibid.*, 60.
44. Burton, *Mission*, 230 n. 44.
45. *Ibid.*, 224, 227, 262.
46. Ridgway, "Journal" (3rd part), 408.
47. Borghero, no. 202, 225.
48. Burton, *Mission*, 227-8.
49. *Ibid.*, 161.
50. Skertchly, *Dahomey*, 214.
51. *Ibid.*, 209-10.
52. *Ibid.*, 231.
53. Répin, "Voyage", 92-3.
54. Vallon, "Royaume" (1st part), 362; (2nd part), 349.
55. Forbes, *Dahomey*, II, 39; Beecroft's journal, 43.
56. Burton, *Mission*, 285.
57. Skertchly, *Dahomey*, 169, 201, 214, 219, 344.
58. Boniface I. Obichere, *West African States and European Expansion: the Dahomey-Niger Hinterland, 1885-1898* (New Haven, 1971), 75.
59. Forbes, *Dahomey*, II, 27. See also *ibid.*, II, 102, re sandals, and Beecroft's journal, 94.
60. Forbes, *Dahomey*, II, 154.
61. *Ibid.*, II, 110.
62. Duncan, *Travels*, I, 225.
63. Ridgway, "Journal" (3rd part), 408.
64. Forbes, *Dahomey*, II, 120.
65. *Ibid.*, II, 164.
66. Beecroft's journal, 128, 129, 132. See also Forbes's journal, 60.
67. Vallon, "Royaume" (2nd part), 349.

68. Bayol, "Attaque de Kotonou", 572.
69. Forbes, Dahomey, I, 23.
70. Beecroft's journal, 43.
71. Borghero, no. 206, 30; Mandirola and Morel, Journal, 74.
72. Wilmot, "Despatches", 438.
73. Duncan, Travels, I, 240.
74. Winniett's testimony, 65.
75. Le Hérissé, Ancien royaume, 67; Prévaudeau, Abomey-la-mystique, 94; Quénum, Pays des Fons, 57; Law, "'Amazons'", 257-8.
76. Paul Mercier, Civilisations du Bénin (Paris, 1962), 289.
77. Forbes, Dahomey, II, 96.
78. Skertchly, Dahomey, 232.
79. Ibid., 348.
80. Borghero, no. 206, 35-6; Mandirola and Morel, Journal, 80-1.
81. Fraser, Warrior Queens, 209, 331-2.
82. Forbes, Dahomey, I, 23, 134, II, 27, 119 (source of quotation).
83. Ibid., I, 134.
84. D'Almeida-Topor, Amazones, 80, quoting from Adrien Djivo, "Béhanzin et Ago-li Agbo", doctoral thesis, Paris I, 1979, 71. See also Forbes's journal, 58-9.
85. Degbelo, "Amazones", 168.
86. Bay, "Royal Women", 21, citing Paul Hazoumé, "Tata Ajachê soupo ma ha Awouinyan", La Reconnaissance Africaine, no. 1 (Aug. 15, 1925), 9.
87. Forbes, Dahomey, II, 108. In Forbes's journal, 59, this reads: "[W]e marched against Attahpam thinking them Men, we found them worse that [sic] women."
88. Burton, Mission, 162.
89. Skertchly, Dahomey, 232.
90. Burton, Mission, 259 n. 13.
91. Forbes, Dahomey, II, 95, 107-19, 150-1, 154, 167-8; Beecroft's journal, 92, 94, 99, 118, 120, 121, 132.
92. Wilmot, "Despatches", 427.
93. Ibid., 438.
94. Burton, Mission, 161.
95. Ibid., 164.
96. Ibid., 228.
97. Skertchly, Dahomey, 457.
98. Foà, Dahomey, 256; "Dahomiens" (1st part), 202.
99. Le Hérissé, Ancien royaume, 270.
100. D'Almeida-Topor, Amazones, 73-4. She gives M.A. Glélé's 1974 book, Le Danxome, as the source for this song, but it is not in it.
101. D'Almeida-Topor, Amazones, 79. This song too is mistakenly attributed to M.A. Glélé's book.

102. Alexandre Adandé, *Les récades des rois du Dahomey* (Dakar, 1962), 26.
103. Snelgrave, *New Account*, 126.
104. Pruneau de Pommegorge, *Description*, 181.
105. Norris, *Memoirs*, 109.
106. Freeman, *Journal*, 256.
107. Nardin, "Reprise", 117.
108. Burton, *Mission*, 131 n. 8.
109. Skertchly, *Dahomey*, 207, 255, 456.
110. Forbes, *Dahomey*, II, 227, 214.
111. *Ibid.*, II, 112.
112. Vallon, "Royaume" (2nd part), 338.
113. Snelgrave, *New Account*, 126.
114. De Chenevert and Bullet, "Réfléxions", 53.
115. Burton, *Mission*, 209.
116. Brue, "Voyage", 62.
117. Burton, *Mission*, 152.
118. *Ibid.*, 251.
119. Skertchly, *Dahomey*, 207.
120. Burton, *Mission*, 131 n. 8.
121. *Ibid.*, 263.
122. *Ibid.*
123. Skertchly, *Dahomey*, 15-16.
124. Ridgway, "Journal" (2nd part), 302.
125. Forbes, *Dahomey*, II, 218, 236.
126. Brunet and Giethlen, *Dahomey*, 304.
127. Courdioux, no. 336, 555.
128. Forbes, *Dahomey*, II, 38.
129. *Ibid.*, II, 67; Beecroft's journal, 61.
130. Bouët, "Royaume" (3rd part), 72.
131. Forbes, *Dahomey*, II, 56.
132. Beecroft's journal, 60; Skertchly, *Dahomey*, 281.
133. Beecroft's journal, 61.
134. Répin, "Voyage", 87; Vallon, "Royaume" (2nd part), 344.
135. Burton, *Mission*, 212, 224.
136. Degbelo, "Amazones", 129, 123.
137. CAOM, Dahomey, III, 2, Decoeur's journal, 5.
138. D'Almeida-Topor, *Amazones*, 80.
139. Skertchly, *Dahomey*, 357.
140. Chaudoin, *Trois mois*, 301.
141. Hazoumé, *Doguicimi* (French), 120, 210; (English), 79, 148.
142. Snelgrave, *New Account*, 37-8.
143. Dalzel, *History*, 165-6.
144. Duncan, *Travels*, I, 233-4.

145. *Ibid.*, I, 261.
146. De Wailly, "Régiment sacré", 392.
147. CMS, CA2/016/34, Dawson to Fitzgerald, May 2, 1862.
148. Burton, *Mission*, 317-8.
149. Foà, *Dahomey*, 260; Le Hérissé, *Ancien royaume*, 52; Herskovits, *Dahomey*, II, 95; M.A. Glélé, *Danxome*, 133.
150. Duncan, *Travels*, I, 234.
151. Bay, "Servitude", 356.
152. Skertchly maintains (*Dahomey*, 454) that when girls were recruited, "the most promising...children of the upper ten", meaning the highest social class, were "created...officers, while the lower orders were dubbed soldiers", but no one backs him up.
153. Duncan, *Travels*, I, 234.
154. Foà, *Dahomey*, 257; "Dahomiens" (2nd part), 263.
155. Bay, "Royal Women", 178.
156. Law, "Further Light", 219.
157. Conneau, *Slaver's Log Book*, 204.
158. Laffitte, *Dahomé*, 90-1.
159. Borghero, no. 202, 226.
160. Forbes, *Dahomey*, II, 121, 11. Forbes's journal, 6, adds gin to the stone wall mix, identifies the wine as "Hock", meaning white Rhine wine, and calls the lemonade "*Gaseuse*", or sparkling.
161. Burton, *Mission*, 360.
162. Maire, *Dahomey*, 53. See also Demartinécourt's journal, 89, on anisette.
163. D'Almeida-Topor, *Amazones*, 77. See also Garcia, *Royaume*, 135.
164. *Ibid.*
165. E. Nuëlito, *La guerre sous les tropiques* (Abbeville, 1901), 234-43. He tells the same story in an earlier version of his book, *Au Dahomey. Journal d'un officier de spahis* (Abbeville, 1897), 190-5.
166. Burton, *Mission*, 263 and n. 21.
167. Skertchly, *Dahomey*, 26.

Chapter 14: Earning a Living

1. Bay, "Royal Women", 160.
2. Forbes, *Dahomey*, I, 70, II, 178.
3. Nardin, "Reprise", 126.
4. Fraser's journal, 48.
5. Laffitte, *Dahomé*, 90.
6. Burton, *Mission*, 269.
7. Skertchly, *Dahomey*, 396.
8. Burton, *Mission*, 269.

9. Skertchly, *Dahomey*, 25.
10. Forbes, *Dahomey*, I, 70; II, 179.
11. Bay, "Royal Women", 160.
12. Laffitte, *Dahomé*, 90.
13. Hazoumé, *Doguicimi* (French), 129; (English), 87.
14. Burton, *Mission*, 269.
15. Bay, "Royal Women", 159-60.
16. Skertchly, *Dahomey*, 154, 52, 89.
17. Maire, *Dahomey*, plate 3, 14-15.
18. Forbes, *Dahomey*, I, 70.
19. Burton, *Mission*, 269; "Present State", 405.
20. Jacqueline Delange, *Arts et peuples de l'Afrique noire* (Paris, 1967), 70; Bay, "Royal Women", 158-9. See also Hazoumé, *Doguicimi* (French), 127-8, (English), 86.
21. Brue, "Voyage", 66.
22. Duncan, *Travels*, I, 264, II, 271.
23. Burton, *Mission*, 219 and n. 29, 190 n. 3; Skertchly, *Dahomey*, 215-17.
24. Burton, *Mission*, 131 n. 8.
25. Hazoumé, *Doguicimi* (French), 127-8; (English), 86.
26. Forbes's journal, 94. In Beecroft's journal, 148, the same statement is recorded as: "I cannot take my women to Plant Farms." See also Forbes, *Dahomey*, II, 185-8; Robin Law, "The Politics of Commercial Transition: Factional Conflict in Dahomey in the Context of the Ending of the Atlantic Slave Trade", *JAH*, XXXVIII, 2 (1997), 215.
27. *Ibid.*, II, 95; Beecroft's journal, 92.
28. Laffitte, *Dahomé*, 90; Foà, *Dahomey*, 269.
29. Degbelo, "Amazones", 92.
30. *Ibid.*, 93, 96.
31. *Ibid.*, 94; Bay, "Royal Women", 160.
32. *Ibid.*
33. *Ibid.*
34. Snelgrave, *New Account*, 36-7.
35. Forbes, *Dahomey*, I, 157-8.
36. E. Courdioux, "Côte des Esclaves", *MC*, X, no. 492 (Nov. 8, 1878), 538; Skertchly, *Dahomey*, 28; Dalzel, *History*, xii; Forbes, *Dahomey*, II, 183; Degbelo, personal communication, March 4, 1994.
37. Skertchly, *Dahomey*, 28.
38. Dalzel, *History*, xii, 214-15.
39. Gourg, "Ancien mémoire sur le Dahomey. Mémoire pour servir d'instruction au directeur qui me succédera au comptoir de Juda, par M. Gourg (1791)", *Mémorial de l'Artillerie de la Marine*, XX (1892), 769.

40. Forbes, *Dahomey*, II, 183-4; Burton, *Mission*, 283; Skertchly, *Dahomey*, 28.
41. Fraser's journal, 136.
42. Courdioux, no. 492, 538.
43. Winniett's testimony, 69.
44. Guillevin, "Voyage", 292.
45. Burton, *Mission*, 260.
46. CAOM, Dahomey, III, 2, d'Ambrières' journal, 27.
47. Bay, "Royal Women", 170; "Servitude", 356.
48. Garcia, *Royaume*, 133.
49. Bouët, "Royaume" (3rd part), 74.

Chapter 15: Making War

1. Foà, *Dahomey*, 26.
2. Argyle, *Fon*, 81.
3. Duncan, *Travels*, I, 266.
4. Dalzel, *History*, 216-21.
5. Djivo, *Guézo*, 72-3.
6. Duncan, *Travels*, I, 260.
7. Brodie Cruickshank, "Report...of His Mission to the King of Dahomey", Nov. 9, 1848, *IUP Series of British Parliamentary Papers, Colonies: Africa 50*, 243; Wilmot, "Despatches", 434. See also Forbes, *Dahomey*, II, 17, 32; Burton, *Mission*, 232, 313; Skertchly, *Dahomey*, 181, 462; Maroukis, "Warfare", 68-74; Law, "Politics", 219.
8. J. Huizinga, *The Waning of the Middle Ages* (Harmondsworth, Eng., 1976), 91 (originally published in 1924).
9. Dov Ronen, "On the African Role in the Trans-Atlantic Slave Trade in Dahomey", *Cahiers d'Etudes Africaines*, XI, 1st cahier (1971), 9-10, 13.
10. Richard F. Burton, *A Mission to Gelele, King of Dahome*, 2 vols. (London, 1864), II, 209. Burton made the statement in a chapter titled "Of 'The Negro's Place in Nature'" that was omitted from the 1966 edition that I use. In the same book, however, on p. 322 of the 1966 edition, he speaks of "the annual withdrawal of both sexes from industry to slave hunting."
11. Laffitte, *Dahomé*, 91. See also Chaudoin, *Trois mois*, 393.
12. CMS, CA2/016/34, Dawson's journal, 24, Dawson to Fitzgerald, Nov. 30, 1861.
13. Garcia, *Royaume*, 141.
14. Le Hérissé, *Ancien royaume*, 64; Dunglas, "Contribution", tome 1, 168-9.

15. Snelgrave, *New Account*, 9. See also pp. 121 and 149-50 re military intelligence.
16. Hazoumé, *Pacte de sang*, 24, 25; *Doguicimi* (French), 263-4, (English), 190; Djivo, *Guézo*, 59; Garcia, *Royaume*, 140.
17. Argyle, *Fon*, 84.
18. Hazoumé, *Pacte de sang*, 21-5.
19. Beecroft's journal, 125; Forbes, *Dahomey*, II, 156-7.
20. Le Hérissé, *Ancien royaume*, 65.
21. Laffitte, *Dahomé*, 92.
22. Hazoumé, *Pacte de sang*, 25-6. See also Cruickshank, "Report", 241; Bayol, "Forces militaires", 522; Le Hérissé, *Ancien royaume*, 65; Garcia, *Royaume*, 141.
23. Degbelo, "Amazones", 124.
24. Wilmot, "Despatches", 436.
25. Bernard Maupoil, *La géomancie à l'ancienne Côte des Esclaves*, reprint of 1943 edn (Paris, 1981), 164 and n. 1; Garcia, *Royaume*, 143.
26. Maupoil, *Géomancie*, 164.
27. Degbelo, "Amazones", 123.
28. Herskovits, *Dahomey*, II, 74-5.
29. J.F. de Monléon, "Le cap des Palmes, le Dahomey, Fernando-Pô et l'île du Prince, en 1844", *Revue Coloniale*, VI, May 1845, 66.
30. Norris, *Memoirs*, 18.
31. Burton, *Mission*, 174-5 n. 30.
32. Foà, *Dahomey*, 254.
33. Burton, *Mission*, 337-8.
34. *Ibid.*, 138 and n. 32; Ellis, *Ewe-Speaking Peoples*, 186.
35. Vallon, "Royaume" (1st part), 344.
36. Duncan, *Travels*, I, 224, 227, 231.
37. Forbes, *Dahomey*, II, 112-13.
38. Borghero, no. 202, 222.
39. Laffitte, *Dahomé*, 84.
40. J. Lombard, "The Kingdom of Dahomey" in *West African Kingdoms in the Nineteenth Century*, eds, Daryll Forde and P.M. Kaberry (London, 1967), 87.
41. Burton, *Mission*, 182; Skertchly, *Dahomey*, 164; Le Hérissé, *Ancien royaume*, 324; Quénum, *Pays des Fons*, 16; Dunglas, "Première attaque", 13; "Deuxième attaque des Dahoméens contre Abeokuta (15 mars 1864)", *ED*, II (1949), 49.
42. Degbelo, "Amazones", 123.
43. Quénum, *Pays des Fons*, 16.
44. Elet, the Dutchman who saw two women with muskets standing behind Agaja's throne in 1733, met the Migan ("Tamiga") and an official he called "the King's First and Supreme Councillor". Law thinks the latter was the Meu. Norris places both ("*Tamegan*" and

"*Mayhou*") in Agaja's reign. Van Dantzig, *Dutch and Guinea Coast*, 295; Law, *Slave Coast*, 86 and n. 86; Norris, *Memoirs*, 4-11. A year before Elet another Dutchman, C.T. Hoffmeester, mentioned the Gau ("General Agau"), and in 1724 Lamb seems to have been referring to the same officer when he told of meetings with Agaja's "great Captain of War, or General". Van Dantzig, *Dutch and Guinea Coast*, 281; Smith, *New Voyage*, 178. A French document of 1733 cites the Kposu ("Possou"). Akinjogbin, *Dahomey*, 105 and n. 2; Law, *Slave Coast*, 271 n. 40.

45. Le Hérissé, *Ancien royaume*, 62-3; Dunglas, "Contribution", tome 1, 90; Jean Pliya, *Histoire: Dahomey, Afrique Occidentale* (Issy-les-Moulineaux, France, 1970), 57, 59; P.K. Glélè, "Royaume", 65, 66, 68; Obichere, "Change and Innovation", 243, 246.

46. Law, *Slave Coast*, 85 and n. 81; Adam Jones, tr., ed., *West Africa in the Mid-Seventeenth Century: an Anonymous Dutch Manuscript* (Atlanta, 1995), 40 and n. 12.

47. Le Hérissé, *Ancien royaume*, 66.

48. Forbes, *Dahomey*, I, 22.

49. *Ibid.*, II, 62.

50. Herskovits, *Dahomey*, II, 91.

51. Djivo, *Guézo*, 53.

52. Maroukis, "Warfare", 95 and n. 22.

53. Herskovits, *Dahomey*, II, 91.

54. Le Hérissé, *Ancien royaume*, 66.

55. Duncan, *Travels*, I, 248, 232; Freeman, *Journal*, 257; Burton, *Mission*, 138 and n. 33.

56. Djivo, *Guézo*, 55, 70.

57. Van Dantzig, *Dutch and Guinea Coast*, 299-300.

58. Dalzel, *History*, 167, 185-8, 226.

59. Burton, *Mission*, 138 and n. 34, 139 and n. 39. See also Skertchly, *History*, 456, re the Fosupo.

60. Law, "'Amazons'", 255.

61. Vallon, "Royaume" (1st part), 344-6.

62. Borghero, no. 202, 222.

63. Foà, *Dahomey*, 258.

64. Burton, *Mission*, 262; Skertchly, *Dahomey*, 457.

65. *Ibid.*; Chautard, *Dahomey*, 11. Ellis thought that by 1890, the archeresses' 'company" had been 'extinct for some time". *Ewe-Speaking Peoples*, 187.

66. Burton, *Mission*, 243.

67. Maire, *Dahomey*, 49.

68. Ellis, *Ewe-Speaking Peoples*, 187.

69. Duncan, *Travels*, I, 236.

70. Degbelo, "Amazones", 120-1. See also Michel Dossou Sedolo, "Com-

ment fut décidée la deuxième et dernière expédition des Dahoméens contre la ville de Kétou", *Notes Africaines*, no. 57 (Jan. 1953), 24 n. 3.

71. Le Hérissé, *Ancien royaume*, 67.
72. Chaudoin, *Trois mois*, 397-8.
73. Argyle, *Fon*, 84, 86.
74. Beecroft's journal, 93; Forbes, *Dahomey*, II, 96.
75. Beecroft's journal, 132; Forbes, *Dahomey*, II, 168.
76. Beecroft's journal, 125.
77. Laffitte, *Dahomé*, 91; Skertchly, *Dahomey*, 447.
78. Degbelo, "Amazones", 122; d'Almeida-Topor, *Amazones*, 78.
79. Dunglas, "Contribution," tome 2, 85.
80. Herskovits, *Dahomey*, I, 123-4, II, 83.
81. Forbes, *Dahomey*, II, 123; Beecroft's journal, 123, 134.
82. Dunglas, "Contribution," tome 2, 121; "Deuxième attaque", 52.
83. The word appears in many variations: *kankies, kenkie, akanasan, akansan, akassa, akassas, acassas, akasand, akaras, arkasa.*
84. Skertchly, *Dahomey*, 490.
85. Burton, *Mission*, 286, 360.
86. Répin, "Voyage", 102; Vallon, "Royaume" (1st part), 344.
87. Duncan (*Travels*, II, 11) tells of a seven-month siege of a Mahi mountain stronghold during which the Dahomeans "were able to avail themselves of the crops and cattle on the plains". Skertchly (*Dahomey*, 448) says that after the Fon capture a town, "every goat, fowl, or duck that can be laid hold of is carried off."
88. Foà, *Dahomey*, 262.
89. Garcia, *Royaume*, 137.
90. Demartinécourt's journal, 32-3.
91. Degbelo, "Amazones", 123.
92. *Ibid.*
93. Snelgrave, *New Account*, 28-9.
94. PP, LXVI (1864), nos. 96 and 98, Wilmot to Walker, May 24 and 26, 1863.
95. Skertchly, *Dahomey*, 421-2, 447.
96. Chaudoin, *Trois mois*, 397.
97. Burton, *Mission*, 288.
98. Schelameur, *Souvenirs*, 118-19.
99. Demartinécourt's journal, 98-9. See also Garcia, *Royaume*, 173, for another officer's description of the same camp.
100. Foà, *Dahomey*, 260-1.
101. *Ibid.*, 261.
102. Le Hérissé, *Ancien royaume*, 65.
103. Noël Baudin, "L'orphelinat de Puerto-real", *MC*, VI, no. 243 (Jan. 30, 1874), 59; Hazoumé, *Doguicimi* (French), 99, (English), 64;

Blanchély, "Au Dahomey: premier voyage de M. Blanchély aîné, gérant de la factorerie de M. Régis, de Marseille, à Whydah (1848)", 2nd of 2 parts, *MC*, XXIII, no. 1171 (Nov. 13, 1891), 548; Djivo, *Guézo*, 53; Quénum, *Pays des Fons*, 21.

104. Duncan, *Travels*, I, 260; Bayol, "Forces militaires", 523; Burton, *Mission*, 289; Skertchly, *Dahomey*, 447; d'Albéca, *France au Dahomey*, 23; Quénum, *Pays des Fons*, 21; Dunglas, "Contribution", tome 1, 169; Maroukis, "Warfare", 125.

105. Foà, *Dahomey*, 261.

106. Duncan, *Travels*, I, 260.

107. Foà, *Dahomey*, 261.

108. Quénum, *Pays des Fons*, 21.

109. Smith, *New Voyage*, 192; Law, *Slave Coast*, 289, quoting a contemporary British document.

110. Dalzel, *History*, 165.

111. Forbes, *Dahomey*, I, 16.

112. Burton, *Mission*, 233.

113. *Ibid.*, 289.

114. Foà, *Dahomey*, 261.

115. Chaudoin, *Trois mois*, 398.

116. Burton, *Mission*, 289.

117. Skertchly, *Dahomey*, 447.

118. Blanchély, "Dahomey", 2nd part, 548; Cruickshank's report, 241-2; Duncan, *Travels*, I, 260-1; Laffitte, *Dahomé*, 93; Baudin, "Orphelinat", 59; d'Albéca, *France au Dahomey*, 23; Poirier, *Campagne*, 39; Le Hérissé, *Ancien royaume*, 66; Quénum, *Pays des Fons*, 21.

119. Ellis, *Ewe-Speaking Peoples*, 189.

120. Quénum, *Pays des Fons*, 21.

121. Foà, *Dahomey*, 263.

122. Wilmot, "Despatches", 439; Skertchly, *Dahomey*, 448; Bayol, "Forces militaires", 523.

123. Laffitte, *Dahomé*, 93.

124. Chaudoin, *Trois mois*, 398.

125. Foà, *Dahomey*, 263.

126. Burton, *Abeokuta*, I, 124-5.

127. Burton, *Mission*, 264.

128. Labarthe, *Voyage*, 122.

129. Conneau, *Slaver's Log Book*, 205.

130. Freeman, *Journal*, 263.

131. De Monléon, "Cap des Palmes", 66.

132. Duncan, *Travels*, I, 224.

133. Forbes, *Dahomey*, I, 132.

134. *Ibid.*, I, 132, 134. Sarah Tucker, an English Anglican lady who may have been the only woman to write anything about the amazons

of Dahomey before the twentieth century, touched briefly on the same subject not long after Forbes: "[W]e now know that among the daughters of Africa, for the most part so affectionate and full of pity, there exists at this present time a band of women, who, treading under foot every tender feeling, and setting at nought the ties of nature and of home, have enrolled themselves as an army of blood-thirsty female warriors. And we know too there is a nation that is not ashamed to suffer them to fight its battles, and a king who shrinks not from leading them to the conflict." Miss Tucker never visited Africa and seems to have obtained all her information from missionaries. *Abbeokuta; or, Sunrise Within the Tropics: an Outline of the Origin and Progress of the Yoruba Mission* (London, 1853), 204.

135. Répin, "Voyage", 88. Répin may have inspired a compatriot, Armand Dubarry, who in 1879 published a fictional account of a visit to Dahomey. "In trampling underfoot the alluring qualities of their sex", wrote Dubarry, the amazons "acquire the sanguinary appetites of panthers, their heart turns to stone, nothing human remains in their head, in their breast." *Voyage au Dahomey* (Paris, 1879), 140.

136. Burton, *Mission*, 259-60; *Abeokuta*, I, 121-2 n. 1.

137. Skertchly, *Dahomey*, 457-8.

138. Maroukis, "Warfare", 311.

139. Degbelo, "Amazones", 128-9.

140. Chautard, *Dahomey*, 11.

141. Vallon, "Royaume" (1st part), 346.

142. Nardin, "Reprise", 98.

143. Paul Merruau, "Le Dahomey et le roi Guezo", *Revue des Deux Mondes*, XII, Dec. 15, 1851, p. 1051.

144. Burton, *Mission*, 262 n. 20.

145. Degbelo, "Amazones", 129.

146. Maire, *Dahomey*, 53.

147. Demartinécourt's journal, 31, 32-3, 70.

148. Maupoil, *Géomancie*, 164.

149. Garcia, *Royaume*, 139.

150. Nuélito, *Guerre*, 246.

151. P.K. Glélè, "Royaume", 77 and n. 5. Laffitte (*Dahomé*, 93) says some wounded Dahomean soldiers "had recourse to our medical science" (presumably at the Catholic mission in Whydah) and claims that a majority were hit from behind, which "betrayed their lack of valor".

152. Saburi O. Biobaku, *The Egba and Their Neighbours, 1842-1872* (Oxford, 1957), 44.

153. Nardin, "Reprise", 98.

154. Ellis, *Land of Fetish*, 69-70.

155. Tucker, *Abbeokuta*, 218 n. 1. Anglican missionary Henry Townsend

reported that several prisoners of war killed their captors and "some of the worst [were] put to death", but he did not specify their sex. *Memoir of the Rev. Henry Townsend, Late C.M.S. Missionary, Abeokuta, West Africa*, ed., George Townsend (London, 1887), 83; PRO, FO 84/816, Townsend to Beecroft, March 20, 1851. See also E. Olympus O. Moore (penname of Ajayi Kolawole Ajisafe), *History of Abeokuta* (London, 1916), 57.

156. Samuel Johnson, *The History of the Yorubas from the Earliest Times to the Beginning of the British Protectorate*, ed. O. Johnson, reprint of 1921 edn (London, 1966), 362.

157. Burton, *Mission*, 257 and n. 7.

158. Mandirola and Morel, *Journal*, 183.

159. T.J. Bowen, *Adventures and Missionary Labours in Several Countries in the Interior of Africa from 1849 to 1856*, reprint of 1857 edn (London, 1968), 148, 149.

160. Pierre Verger, "Influence du Brésil au golfe du Bénin" in *Les Afro-Américains* (Dakar, 1952), 54-5, 93. See also Le Hérissé, *Ancien royaume*, 331. In the waning days of the Atlantic slave trade, Borghero saw six Whydah (male) natives who had been captured at Abeokuta, sold to Muslim slave dealers, and were being held for resale at the port of Epe, near Porto-Novo. F. Borghero, letter to Planque, Aug. 1866, 1st of 2 parts, *APF*, XXXIX, no. 231 (March 1867), 112-3; Mandirola and Morel, *Journal*, 159-61.

161. Nuëlito, *Guerre*, 239-41.

162. Verdal, "Amazones", 58.

Chapter 16: Early Amazon Battles

1. Snelgrave, *New Account*, 58. See also Akinjogbin, *Dahomey*, 82; Law, *Slave Coast*, 281-2.

2. Akinjogbin, *Dahomey*, 88-95, 107, 123-7; Law, *Slave Coast*, 292-4, 318-23.

3. Dunglas, "Contribution", tome 1, 146. See also Le Hérissé, *Ancien royaume*, 319; E.G. Parrinder, *The Story of Ketu, an Ancient Yoruba Kingdom* (Ibadan, 1956), 28.

4. Le Hérissé, *Ancien royaume*, 319-20.

5. *Ibid.*, 322; Dunglas, "Première attaque", 7; "Contribution", tome 2, 56-7; Parrinder, *Story of Ketu*, 29; Augustus A. Adeyinka, "King Gezo of Dahomey, 1818-1858: a Reassessment of a West African Monarch in the Nineteenth Century", *African Studies Review*, XVII, no. 3 (Dec. 1974), 544; Djivo, *Guézo*, 73-4; Law, *Oyo*, 271-2. Dunglas dates Oyo's defeat to *c.* 1820-22, Law to 1823, Parrinder and Adeyinka to 1827.

6. Hazoumé, *Doguicimi* (English), xxxii; Djivo, *Guézo*, 74-5.

7. Freeman typescript, 168. Freeman called Hounjroto Hungwiror. Dawson, who, as a onetime Wesleyan missionary, may have got some of his information from Freeman, says Gezo formed the amazons "when he lost the battle at Hundgwiss". CMS, CA2/016/34, Dawson's journal, 21.

8. Duncan, *Travels*, I, 245-6.

9. Ellis, *Ewe-Speaking Peoples*, 311.

10. Forbes, *Dahomey*, II, 65-7, 219; Beecroft's journal, 33, 56, 61.

11. Waterlot, *Bas-reliefs*, plate XIII-A; Paul Mercier and Jacques Lombard, *Guide du Musée d'Abomey* (Porto-Novo, 1959), 28. The latter authors think the *récade* represents *all* the amazons, which seems doubtful.

12. Répin, "Voyage", 88; Vallon, "Royaume" (1st part), 347.

13. Maire, *Dahomey*, plate XIV, 36-7.

14. Forbes, *Dahomey*, I, 16-17.

15. Beecroft's journal, 115.

16. Forbes, *Dahomey*, II, 93 n. 1.

17. *Ibid.*, II, 92-3.

18. *Ibid.*, II, 92-100, 136-49; Beecroft's journal, 91-6, 113a-17. Adandé (*Récades*, 27-9) says that without the heroism and bravery of the amazons, the Dahomean army would have suffered a crushing defeat at Atakpamé, and he gives us the words of a victory song.

19. Blanchély, "Relation du troisième voyage fait en 1850 dans le royaume du Dahomey, par M. Blanchély aîné, agent de la factorerie française de Whydah", *MC*, XXIII, no. 1174 (Dec. 4, 1891), 587.

20. Robert Cornevin, "Avec le lieutenant Plehn à la recherche d'un cercle du Moyen Togo", *ED*, IV (1950), 47.

21. Le Hérissé, *Ancien royaume*, 67.

22. Johnson, *History*, 228; Dunglas, "Première attaque", 8-9.

23. Beecroft's journal, 68; Forbes, *Dahomey*, I, 31, 68. See also Burton, *Mission*, 171.

24. Dunglas, "Première attaque", 9; "Contribution", tome 2, 77.

25. Le Hérissé, *Ancien royaume*, 324.

26. Duncan, *Travels*, II, 276-7.

27. Beecroft's journal, 109; Forbes, *Dahomey*, II, 133. Called Lah-maa cee-dug-bee by Beecroft and Seh-dong-hong-beh by Forbes, who says her name meant "God speaks true", she was the model for Forbes's classic portrait of an amazon holding a severed head in his first volume opposite p. 23.

28. Beecroft's journal, 99.

29. Le Hérissé, *Ancien royaume*, 325.

30. Dunglas, "Contribution", tome 2, 77.

31. Ellis, *Ewe-Speaking Peoples*, 311; Forbes, *Dahomey*, I, 21, II, 115 n.

1. Forbes mistakenly dates this defeat to 1848 and wrongly places it at Okeadon. He heard that an amazon "regiment" had been destroyed.
32. Moore, *History*, 44.
33. Dunglas, "Contribution", tome 2, 78.
34. Johnson, *History*, 296-7.
35. Bowen, *Adventures*, 110; Burton, *Abeokuta*, I, 118-19.
36. Ridgway, "Journal" (3rd part), 408.
37. Beecroft's journal, 108. In mentioning wounded amazons who were introduced to them, Forbes (*Dahomey*, II, 133) does not single out the Okeodan heroine, perhaps because he had earlier reported (I, 16) that the town had put up no resistance.
38. Tucker (*Abbeokuta*, 206) heard of 20,000 captives, Ellis (*Ewe-Speaking Peoples*, 312) of nearly 20,000, Bowen (*Adventures*, 114) of about 20,000 killed and captured. The figure seems highly inflated.
39. Le Hérissé, *Ancien royaume*, 324.
40. Bowen, *Adventures*, 114.
41. Forbes, *Dahomey*, II, 10; Beecroft's journal, 21. The quotation is from Forbes. The phrase "dreadful tragedy" was toned down from a remark in his journal (p. 6) that the attack on Okeadon was "one of the most cowardly acts that ever disgraced a Tyrant".

Chapter 17: Abeokuta 1851

1. PRO, FO 84/976, Campbell to Clarendon, Lagos, Feb. 15, 1855.
2. CMS, CA2/043, Gollmer to Straith, Oct. 25, 1850, cited in J.F. Ade Ajayi and Robert S. Smith, *Yoruba Warfare in the Nineteenth Century*, 2nd edn (Cambridge, Eng., 1971), 72.
3. See esp. Beecroft's journal, 92-4, 99; Forbes, *Dahomey*, II, 110-20.
4. Beecroft's journal, 132.
5. *Ibid.*, 99.
6. PRO, FO 84/816, Beecroft to Palmerston, July 22, 1850; Beecroft's journal, 149; Forbes, *Dahomey*, II, 189-90.
7. Bowen, *Adventures*, 116.
8. Townsend, *Memoir*, 75; Moore, *History*, 56.
9. A figure of 6,000 amazons, traceable to Bowen (*Adventures*, 118) and often copied, seems excessive. Foà (*Dahomey*, 24) raised the figure to 7-8,000, and Ellis (*Land of Fetish*, 69; *Ewe-Speaking Peoples*, 315) reduced it to 3,000. Burton (*Abeokuta*, I, 120) and Maroukis ("Warfare", 178) may have been closest to the truth with 4,000. Estimates of total Dahomean strength range from 8,000 (Ellis, *Land of Fetish*, 69) to 20,000 (PRO, FO 84/816, Townsend to Beecroft, March 20, 1851) and even to a wholly unrealistic 30,000 (Foà, *Dahomey*, 24).
10. Dunglas, "Première attaque", 13.

11. Townsend, *Memoir*, 74.
12. Tucker, *Abbeokuta*, 209-11; Burton, *Abeokuta*, I, 119; Ellis, *Ewe-Speaking Peoples*, 314-15; Johnson, *History*, 314; Dunglas, "Première attaque", 15, 16; "Deuxième attaque", 38.
13. Bowen, *Adventures*, 105-6.
14. Dunglas, "Première attaque", 16.
15. *Ibid.*
16. Bowen, *Adventures*, 118.
17. Townsend, *Memoir*, 75; PRO, FO 84/816, Townsend to Beecroft, March 20, 1851; Bowen, *Adventures*, 118.
18. *Ibid.*
19. Dunglas, "Contribution", tome 2, 86.
20. Burton, *Abeokuta*, I, 123.
21. Foà, *Dahomey*, 25.
22. Johnson, *History*, 315.
23. Dunglas, "Première attaque", 17.
24. Bowen, *Adventures*, 116 and n. 1.
25. Townsend, *Memoir*, 79-80.
26. *Ibid.*, 82.
27. *Ibid.*, 81.
28. Tucker, *Abbeokuta*, 213 n. 1; Burton, *Abeokuta*, I, 123.
29. *Ibid.*, 80, 81-2; PRO, FO 84/816, Townsend to Beecroft, March 20, 1851; Bowen, *Adventures*, 120.
30. Estimates of amazon dead range from "more than a thousand" (Dunglas, "Contribution", tome 2, 88) to an extravagant 4,000 (Foà, *Dahomey*, 26).
31. *Ibid.*
32. PRO, FO 84/816, Townsend to Beecroft, March 20, 1851; *Memoir*, 82.
33. Maroukis, "Warfare", 185.
34. Forbes, *Dahomey*, II, 156-7; Beecroft's journal, 125.
35. For details of the first battle of Abeokuta, see Tucker, *Abbeokuta*, 211-15; Bowen, *Adventures*, 117-20; Burton, *Abeokuta*, I, 118-24; Townsend, *Memoir*, 74-83; Ellis, *Land of Fetish*, 65-70; *Ewe-Speaking Peoples*, 314-16; Foà, *Dahomey*, 24-6; Moore, *History*, 56-7; Johnson, *History*, 313-16; Dunglas, "Première attaque", 13-19; "Contribution," tome 2, 84-9; Biobaku, *Egba*, 43-6; Ajayi and Smith, *Yoruba Warfare*, 37-51.

Chapter 18: Abeokuta 1864

1. Fraser's journal, 126-7, 128, 130.

2. Répin, "Voyage", 91, 92; Vallon, "Royaume" (2nd part), 347, (1st part), 343.
3. Répin, "Voyage", 88; Vallon, "Royaume" (2nd part), 347.
4. PRO, FO 84/1061, Campbell to Clarendon, March 3, 1858; Hazoumé, *Pacte de sang*, 110-2; Dunglas, "Contribution", tome 2, 91-2; Djivo, *Guézo*, 92, 94. Gezo's assassination was concealed long after his death. The official line was that he had died of smallpox; Burton (*Mission*, 146 n. 4) and Skertchly (*Dahomey*, 452) accepted it, and Law ("Politics", 227 and n. 100) is still inclined to accept it.
5. Baudin, "Orphelinat", 59.
6. Maroukis, "Warfare", 202, citing "Recent Intelligence – Yoruba Mission", *Church Missionary Intelligencer*, XIII (June 1862). See also CAOM, Afrique, IV, 9d, letter from Augustin Planque to Minister of Navy and Colonies, July 13, 1862.
7. CMS, CA2/016/34, Dawson to Fitzgerald, April 2 and May 2, 1862. Dawson also heard, purportedly in a message from Glele himself, that the Dahomeans had intended to attack Abeokuta but had instead responded to an unprovoked attack by Ishagga.
8. Moore, *History*, 69.
9. Baudin, "Orphelinat", 59.
10. E. Courdioux, "Côte des Esclaves", *MC*, X, no. 490 (Oct. 25, 1878), 514-5. A bas-relief in Glele's palace shows a severed Yoruba head attached to a horse's neck. Waterlot (plate XIX-A) says it represents slain Ishagga cavaliers and their mounts on the way to Abomey. Mercier and Lombard (*Guide*, 30) think it's the ex-ruler of Ishagga and his own horse en route to Whydah. See also CMS, CA2/016/34, Dawson to Fitzgerald, May 30, 1862.
11. PRO, FO 84/1175, Perry to Freeman, Aug. 6, 1862; Moore, *History*, 68-9; Dunglas, "Deuxième attaque", 42-3.
12. Degbelo, "Amazones", 127.
13. Baudin, "Orphelinat", 59-60; Courdioux, no. 490, 514-5. Borghero also bought enslaved men prisoners from Ishagga to work for his mission. Mandirola and Morel, *Journal*, 113-14.
14. Burton, *Mission*, 156.
15. Dunglas, "Deuxième attaque", 38, 40-1. Burton (*Mission*, 156) construed the skull cup as "a sign that [Oba Koko] ought to have given water to a friend in affliction".
16. PP, XXXVIII (1863), no. 512, "Memorial of the CMS to...the Duke of Newcastle...Secretary of State for the Colonies", Townsend letter, March 28, 1863, B2 verso; PP, LXVI (1864), no. 96, Wilmot to Walker, May 24, 1863; no. 98, Wilmot to Walker, May 26, 1863; Townsend, *Memoir*, 93-5 (he wrongly .dates this incursion to 1864); Moore, *History*, 72-3; Dunglas, "Deuxième attaque", 47; MAE,

Mémoires et documents, Afrique, 52, Didelot to Chasseloup-Laubat, March 27, 1863.

17. Wilmot, "Despatches", 434.

18. PP, XXXVIII (1863), no. 512, "Memorial of CMS to Newcastle", Wilmot to Townsend, Jan. 30, 1863, A4 recto.

19. Burton, *Abeokuta*, I, 68-70.

20. PP, LXVI (1864), no. 98, Wilmot to Walker, May 26, 1863. That the figure of 100,000 may not have been far off is suggested by a census count of 1911, which put the population of Abeokuta and the Egba hinterland at 264,814. Moore, *History*, 126.

21. Dunglas, "Deuxième attaque", 51.

22. *Ibid.*, 54; Degbelo, "Amazones", 128.

23. Laffitte, *Dahomé*, 87. He seems to have gotten his information from Borghero. See Mandirola and Morel, *Journal*, 184. In a compendium of several accounts of the battle and its aftermath published in the CMS's *Church Missionary Intelligencer*, XV (1864), 121-32, under the title "Attack on Abbeokuta, and Defeat of the Dahomian Army" it is said that the Egba also captured Glele's horse (pp. 124, 125-6). The report seems dubious. According to one of these accounts (p. 124), it was Egbe women (not amazons) who sang before the battle, and Egba men who threw their muskets in the air. This report, too, seems unlikely.

24. For details of the second battle of Abeokuta, see *ibid.*, 121-30; Burton, *Mission*, 359-64; "Present State", 407; "Notes on Dahoman", 112-13; Borghero, no. 231, 112, 126; letter to Planque, Aug. 1866 (2nd part), *APF*, XXXIX, no. 232 (May 1867), 233-4; Mandirola and Morel, *Journal*, 182-4; Ellis, *Ewe-Speaking Peoples*, 321-5; Johnson, *History*, 361-2; Dunglas, "Deuxième attaque", 49-57; "Contribution", tome 2, 119-25; Biobaku, *Egba*, 74; Maroukis, "Warfare", 202-6.

25. Djivo, *Guézo*, 77.

26. Townsend, *Memoir*, 96.

27. Skertchly, *Dahomey*, 281.

28. Townsend, *Memoir*, 73.

29. Moore, *History*, 82. See also Bouche, *Sept ans*, 358; Townsend, *Memoir*, 95; Dunglas, "Contribution", tome 2, 127-8; Maroukis, "Warfare", 216-17.

30. Townsend, *Memoir*, 95-8; Moore, *History*, 83; Johnson, *History*, 363 (he wrongly dates the event to 1873); Dunglas, "Contribution", tome 2, 129; Maroukis, "Warfare", 217-18.

31. Moore, *History*, 93-4; Johnson, *History*, 455; *Proceedings of the CMS for Africa and the East*, XCIV (1892-93), 20; Maroukis, "Warfare", 254.

32. *Ibid.*, 264.

33. Le Hérissé, *Ancien royaume*, 325.

Chapter 19: Years of Success

1. Paul Serval, "Rapport sur une mission au Dahomey", *Revue Maritime et Coloniale*, LIX (1878), 186.
2. Le Hérissé, *Ancien royaume*, 335-6.
3. Mercier and Lombard, *Guide*, 31.
4. Ernest-Marie Ménager, "La Guinée", *Bulletin de la Société de Géographie*, 6th series, tome 16 (July-Dec. 1878), 156.
5. PRO, CO 96/116, Strahan to Carnarvon, Nov. 22, 1875.
6. Newbury, *Western Slave Coast*, 101; Maroukis, "Warfare", 218.
7. Ellis, *Ewe-Speaking Peoples*, 327.
8. Degbelo, "Amazones", 135 and n. 1, 136 and n. 1.
9. Johnson, *History*, 463.
10. Ellis, *Ewe-Speaking Peoples*, 328-9.
11. PRO, CO 879/18, Part 1, "Notes of a Journey from Lagos by Lagoon to the Popo Country, and from Whydah to Dahomey, in the Interests of the Wesleyan Missionary Society, by the Rev. John Milum, from November 13th, 1880, to January 15th, 1881", 7-8.
12. MAE, Mémoires et documents, Afrique, 76, Ardin d'Elteil to MAE, Aug. 14, 1879. "As always", wrote the author, French consul at Whydah, "it's the Amazons who starred in this affair."
13. Le Hérissé, *Ancien royaume*, 333-4. See also Maroukis, "Warfare", 228-9.
14. Parrinder, *Story of Ketu*, 85-6. See also R.S. Smith, *Kingdoms*, 56-7, 83.
15. *Ibid.*, 30, 41; Waterlot, *Bas-reliefs*, plate XIV-B; Mercier and Lombard, *Guide*, 28.
16. Waterlot, *Bas-reliefs*, plate XX-A; Mercier and Lombard, *Guide*, 30.
17. Ellis, *Ewe-Speaking Peoples*, 327-8; Dunglas, "Contribution", tome 2, 131-3; Parrinder, *Story of Ketu*, 50-2; Maroukis, "Warfare", 225-7.
18. Ellis (*Ewe-Speaking Peoples*, 328), Johnson (*History*, 455), Parrinder (*Story of Ketu*, 60-1) and Dunglas ("Contribution", tome 2, 139) date this final war against Ketu to 1886. Another writer, Michel Dossou Sedolo, dates it to 1883 ("Considérations sur la guerre de Kétou Woto-to. II: Le siège et la prise de Kétou", *Notes Africaines*, no. 62 [Apr. 1954], 48). But citing contemporary archival documents, Maroukis ("Warfare", 229-34) proves that it took place in 1885.
19. Sedolo, "Comment fut décidée", 24 n. 4; Hazoumé, *Pacte de sang*, 20-1; Parrinder, *Story of Ketu*, 53. Exceptionally, Hazoumé says Arepa took part in two campaigns against Ketu.
20. Sedolo, "Comment fut décidée", 25.
21. Sedolo, "Considérations", 47.
22. *Ibid.*, 48.
23. Parrinder, *Story of Ketu*, 65. For more details on the second attack

against Ketu, see Sedolo, "Comment fut décidée", 24-5; "Considérations", 47-8; Parrinder, *Story of Ketu*, 53-61; Dunglas, "Contribution", tome 2, 139-42; Maroukis, "Warfare", 229-34.

Chapter 20: France vs. Dahomey, 1890

1. Akindélé and Aguessy, *Contribution*, 71, 72.
2. Barbou, *Histoire*, 79-82.
3. Grandin, *A l'assaut*, I, 255-6.
4. Bayol, "Attaque de Kotonou", 572.
5. Edouard Dunglas, "Contribution à l'histoire du Moyen-Dahomey", tome 3, *ED*, XXI (1958), 34. A Dahomean song improvised after the Battle of Cotonou credited the amazons with killing a white priest by biting his neck. Since no priests were involved in the fighting, it seems to refer to a European combatant who wore a beard, which the Fon associated with missionaries. The song is reproduced in Emmanuel Karl, *Traditions orales au Dahomey-Bénin* (Niamey, 1974), 411-13. Dunglas ("Contribution", tome 3, 53-4) says a black-bearded European soldier mistaken for a priest was slain in hand-to-hand combat, but he reproduces a song crediting the deed to Béhanzin himself. See also d'Almeida-Topor, *Amazones*, 135; Garcia, *Royaume*, 77.
6. Bayol, "Forces militaires", 523.
7. For details of the Battle of Cotonou, see Bayol, "Attaque de Kotonou", 570-2; Victor Nicolas, *L'expédition du Dahomey en 1890*, 2nd edn (Paris, 1893), 66-72; Anon., *France au pays noir*, 9-19; Grandin, *A l'assaut*, I, 270-2; d'Albéca, *France au Dahomey*, 38-9; Foà, *Dahomey*, 381-4; Brunet and Giethlen, *Dahomey*, 118-19; Dunglas, "Contribution", tome 3, 33-4; Maroukis, "Warfare", 245-9; Degbelo, "Amazones", 143-4; d'Almeida-Topor, *Amazones*, 134-6; Garcia, *Royaume*, 75-7.
8. For details of the Battle of Atchoupa, see Adolphe Burdo, "Au Dahomey" (3rd part), *Journal des Voyages*, no. 683 (Aug. 10, 1890), 90; Nicolas, *Expédition*, 106-12; J. De Riols, *La Guerre du Dahomey* (Paris, 1893), 34-6; Anon., *France au pays noir*, 22-5; Grandin, *A l'assaut*, I, 275-9; d'Albéca, *France au Dahomey*, 129-32; Jean Fonssagrives, *Notice sur le Dahomey* (Paris, 1900), 69-71; Dunglas, "Contribution", tome 3, 37-8; Maroukis, "Warfare", 252-4; Degbelo, "Amazones", 145-7; Garcia, *Royaume*, 79-81.
9. A. Pilgrim, "Les amazones au Jardin d'acclimatation", *Journal des Voyages*, no. 716 (March 29, 1891), 198.
10. *Journal des Voyages*, no. 809 (Jan. 8, 1893), 32.
11. Chaudoin, *Trois mois*, 118-19; "Au Dahomey", 302; MFO, Dahomey, I, 5a, Ballay to Navy Minister, May 8, 1892; Barbou, *Histoire*, 94;

Newbury, *Western Slave Coast*, 130 n. 4; Cornevin, *République populaire*, 348; Maroukis, "Warfare", 263-4; Garcia, 94, 98.
12. Demartinécourt (journal, 73, 89) and Garcia (*Royaume*, 167), citing Dodds, speak of 8-shot Winchesters, which would have been 1886 models. Maroukis ("Warfare", 301) thinks the carbines were 15-shot, or 1873 models. Perhaps both were used.

Chapter 21: France vs. Dahomey, 1892

1. CAOM, Dahomey, I, 5a, Ballay to Under-Secretary of State for the Colonies, April 22, 1892, includes message from Béhanzin to Ballot dated April 10.
2. Degbelo, "Amazones", 157.
3. MAE, Afrique, 126, Bayol to Etienne, Jan. 11, 1890, cited in Garcia, *Royaume*, 129 and n. 2. (I could not find this document in the MAE archives.)
4. See, for ex., Fonssagrives (*Notice*, 69), who carries the official report on the battle.
5. Chaudoin, *Trois mois*, 186, 394.
6. CAOM, Dahomey, III, 2, d'Ambrières' journal, 25.
7. See, for ex., CAOM, Dahomey, I, 8b, Dodds to Secretary of State for the Colonies, Aug. 8, 1892; CAOM, Dahomey, V, 6a, Dodds' "Rapport sur les opérations du corps expéditionnaire du Dahomey en 1892" (undated), 8; Bern, *Expédition*, 187; d'Albéca, *France au Dahomey*, 52; Fonssagrives, *Notice*, 103.
8. Garcia, *Royaume*, 130, 131. See also d'Almeida-Topor, *Amazones*, 40.
9. Demartinécourt's journal, 36-7.
10. Bern, *Expédition*, 154, 149.
11. For details of the Battle of Dogba, see Demartinécourt's journal, 29-37; Bern, *Expédition*, 144-61; Barbou, *Histoire*, 98-102; Maroukis, "Warfare", 275-9; Garcia, *Royaume*, 155-69.
12. *Ibid.*, 149. Demartinécourt (journal, 74-5) also mentions a captured Senegalese spahi whose body was found minus head, hands and lower legs, but he doesn't suggest an amazon role and dates the incident two weeks later.
13. Bern, *Expédition*, 149.
14. Barbou, *Histoire*, 124. He says this information was obtained from captured amazons.
15. Besides Bern's report on the reprisal executions, Demartinécourt (journal, 87) says that after a fruitless interrogation of two captured amazons, "they were secretly made to disappear". They may have been the same two mentioned by Bern. An unnamed French ser-

geant-major wounded at Dogba told the weekly *L'Illustration* (L, no. 2595 [Nov. 19, 1892], 420) that the few Fon wounded captured there had been "finished off". D'Albéca (*France au Dahomey*, 79) says the last shot of the Battle of Poguessa on Oct. 4 was fired by a Foreign Legionnaire dispatching a wounded amazon ("her head split in half...like an apple"). Abel Tinayre, war correspondent for the weekly *Le Monde Illustré*, reported ("Au Dahomey", XXXVII, no. 1869 [Jan. 21, 1893], 35) that three gravely wounded prisoners, including an amazon, apparently taken on the last day of fighting, were immediately shot because the French didn't even have enough "hammocks" to transport their own casualties. Referring to the Battle of Cotonou in 1890, Foà (*Dahomey*, 383) says a very young amazon found seriously wounded on the field "was finished off like all those [enemies] who were not found dead".

16. Demartinécourt's journal, 33-4; Barbou, *Histoire*, 101; Bern, *Expédition*, 188; Schelameur, *Souvenirs*, 104; Nuëlito, *Au Dahomey*, 166. The report on bullets passing through palms is from Schelameur. Demartinécourt says one projectile went through four men standing one behind the other. They are supported by a corporal in the expeditionary force's medical unit who saw a line of three or four Dahomean bodies killed by a single Lebel bullet that first transpierced a palm 50 cm. (*c.* 20 in.) in circumference. B. Szmigielski, "Histoire médicale de la campagne du Dahomey en 1892", M.D. thesis, Faculté de Médicine de Paris, 1897, 53.

17. Barbou, *Histoire*, 107; Bern, *Expédition*, 187; Morienval, *Guerre du Dahomey*, 151; Poirier, *Campagne du Dahomey*, 180; Nuëlito, *Au Dahomey*, 165.

18. Grandin, *A l'assaut*, II, 109.

19. Bern, *Expédition*, 186-7.

20. Grandin, *A l'assaut*, II, 106-7.

21. Bern, *Expédition*, 187; Grandin, *A l'assaut*, II, 107; Nuëlito, *Au Dahomey*, 169. Nuëlito says it was a Foreign Legionnaire, not a marine, and that the amazon was killed by his neighbor with a bayonet.

22. Poirier, *Campagne du Dahomey*, 179, quoting a fourth officer who was wounded there. Nuëlito (*Au Dahomey*, 165) repeats the story.

23. Schelameur, *Souvenirs*, 104.

24. Nuëlito, *Au Dahomey*, 166. For details of the Battle of Poguessa, see Demartinécourt's journal, 68-74; Bern, *Expédition*, 186-200; Morienval, *Guerre du Dahomey*, 149-56; Barbou, *Histoire*, 107-8; Grandin, *A l'assaut*, II, 106-11; Poirier, *Campagne du Dahomey*,179-80; Schelameur, *Souvenirs*, 103-4; Nuëlito, *Au Dahomey*, 165; *Guerre*, 200-7; Dunglas, "Contribution", tome 3, 72-4; Garcia, *Royaume*, 165-9.

25. A. Roques, "Le Génie au Dahomey en 1892", *Revue du Génie*

Militaire, VIII, 4 (July-Aug. 1894), 307, 311. See also Demartinécourt's journal, 46, 80-1, 83.

26. Nuëlito, *Au Dahomey*, 184.

27. D'Albéca, *France au Dahomey*, 82. See also Abel Tinayre, "Au Dahomey", *Le Monde Illustré*, XXXVII, no. 1867 (Jan. 7, 1893), 6. Curiously, Dodds himself (CAOM, Dahomey, V, 6a, "Rapport", 46) dates the first bayonet charge to Oct. 12; he seems to have been mistaken.

28. Nuëlito, *Au Dahomey*, 189.

29. Garcia, *Royaume*, 172. On p. 139 he says 433 amazons were involved and 417 fell. For details of the Battle of Adégon, see Demartinécourt's journal, 80-7; Roques, "Génie", 305-7; d'Albéca, *France au Dahomey*, 82; Nuëlito, *Au Dahomey*, 189; Brunet and Giethlen, *Dahomey*, 150; Dunglas, "Contribution", tome 3, 75; Maroukis, "Warfare", 281; Garcia, *Royaume*, 169-73.

30. Bern, *Expédition*, 259-61.

31. Morienval, *Guerre du Dahomey*, 180.

32. Bern, *Expédition*, 306.

33. Garcia, *Royaume*, 195. For details of the fighting from Oct. 12 to 27, see Bern, *Expédition*, 259-61, 306; Barbou, *Histoire*, 111-15; Morienval, *Guerre du Dahomey*, 180; Schelameur, *Souvenirs*, 206; Brunet and Giethlen, *Dahomey*, 155; Maroukis, "Warfare", 282-6; Garcia, *Royaume*, 173-201.

34. Dodds' general order no. 83, Nov. 12, 1892, quoted in Fonssagrives, *Notice*, 114.

35. Morienval, *Guerre du Dahomey*, 183.

36. CAOM, Dahomey, V, 6a, Dodds' "Rapport", 61.

37. *Ibid.*

38. Schelameur, *Souvenirs*, 113.

39. CAOM, Dahomey, V, 10, Dodds report of Oct. 6, 1892, quoted in Garcia, *Royaume*, 171. These were the same two amazons who, according to Demartinécourt (journal, 87), were 'made to disappear secretly" after refusing to talk.

40. Verdal, "Amazones", 58.

41. Demartinécourt's journal, 81; Bern, *Expédition*, 191; Schelameur, *Souvenirs*, 114; Garcia, *Royaume*, 169.

42. Dodds, "Rapport", 62.

43. Dunglas, "Contribution", tome 3, 82; Garcia, *Royaume*, 205.

44. For details of the three-day Battle of Cana, see Morienval, *Guerre du Dahomey*, 183-4; Barbou, *Histoire*, 116-18; Grandin, *A l'assaut*, II, 147-50; Fonssagrives, *Notice*, 114-15; Brunet and Giethlen, *Dahomey*, 157; Dunglas, "Contribution", tome 3, 81-2; Maroukis, "Warfare", 287-9; Garcia, *Royaume*, 201-6.

45. D'Albéca, *France au Dahomey*, 103; Dunglas, "Contribution", tome 3, 82.
46. Maroukis, "Warfare", 289.
47. Ross, "Dahomey", 163; Garcia, *Royaume*, 209.
48. Bern, *Expédition*, 191, 261.
49. Mathias-Jules-Pierre Tahon, *Carnets du général Tahon. Avec les bâtisseurs de l'empire* (Paris, 1947), 51.
50. Morienval, *Guerre du Dahomey*, 30, 156, 183.
51. Nuëlito, *Au Dahomey*, 170.
52. Schelameur, *Souvenirs*, 104.
53. Grandin, *A l'assaut*, I, 161, 162-3.

Epilogue

1. Degbelo, "Amazones", 156-7.
2. Ignace Lissner, "De Whydah à Abomey" (2nd of 5 parts), *MC*, XXVII, Aug. 30, 1895, 417.
3. Joseph Martin, "A travers le Dahomey" (1st of 4 parts), *MC*, XXVIII, Nov. 20, 1896, 563.
4. Rastignac, "Courrier de Paris", *L'Illustration*, LI, no. 2613 (March 25, 1893), 226; no. 2616 (April 15, 1893), 286; no. 2617 (April 22, 1893), 306.
5. Degbelo, "Amazones", 161, 178.
6. Le Hérissé, *Ancien royaume*, 68.
7. Degbelo, "Amazones", 161.
8. *Ibid.*, 162.
9. Maire, *Dahomey*, 95-6.
10. D'Almeida-Topor, *Amazones*, 136-7.
11. Geoffrey Gorer, *Africa Dances*, reprint of 1945 Penguin edn (Harmondsworth, Eng., 1983), 117.
12. Eva L.R. Meyerowitz, "'Our Mothers': the Amazons of Dahomey", *Geographical Magazine*, XV (1943), 446.
13. Personal communication, Oct. 16, 1996.

BIBLIOGRAPHY

As is evident in the body of this book and the endnotes, English-speaking students of the amazons of Dahomey are in luck. Although Dahomey fell squarely into the French sphere of influence in West Africa and French is still the official language of Dahomey's heir, the Republic of Benin, the most important works on the old kingdom were written in English.

Burton's *Mission to Gelele* and some of his other writings are cited no fewer than 150 times in the notes. Two other nineteenth-century British authors, Forbes and Skertchly, Burton's closest rivals for wealth of descriptive detail, are referenced around 100 times. For the eighteenth century the most useful published sources are Dalzel, Norris and Snelgrave. Among unpublished journals by visitors to Abomey, none compares in historical value with Beecroft's. And even in the twentieth century, Anglophone scholars like Herskovits, Law, Bay, Akinjogbin, Argyle, Newbury, Manning and Ross have been in the forefront of Dahomean studies.

Moreover, British and American publishers have, in the post-Second World War era, been much more willing than their French counterparts to put out reprints or new editions of significant but hard-to-find early works. Snelgrave, Norris, Dalzel, Freeman, Duncan, Forbes, Burton and Ellis are among authors thus made readily available to scholars. Indeed, of all the major contemporary English-language books treating the kingdom of Dahomey, only Skertchly's has, unaccountably, not been republished.

Students with a command of both English and French have access to more than 99 per cent of the source materials on Dahomey (including some translations from Dutch and Portuguese). The writings of the Frenchmen Dunglas, Foà, Vallon, Répin, Bouët, Le Hérissé, Laffitte and Courdioux, and of the Italian Borghero who wrote in French, give us valuable data on the amazons, as do twentieth-century French-language works by native Dahomeans (or Beninese), particularly Degbelo, Djivo, Garcia, Hazoumé and Quénum.

The Franco-Dahomean wars alone generated more than a score of books by Frenchmen, many of them participants, as well as a rush of

262

magazine and newspaper articles. Apart from a few English-language missionary reports on the battles of Abeokuta, these French writings provide us with our only eyewitness accounts of the amazons in action. Following are those books, articles, archival documents and university theses that were found most useful in writing this book. Other sources consulted are cited only in the notes.

Books

Adandé, Alexandre, *Les récades des rois du Dahomey* (Dakar, 1962).

Ajayi, J.F. Ade, and Smith, Robert S., *Yoruba Warfare in the Nineteenth Century*, 2nd edn (Cambridge, Eng., 1971).

Akindélé, A., and Aguessy, C., *Contribution à l'étude de l'histoire de l'ancien royaume de Porto-Novo*, reprint (Amsterdam, 1968).

Akinjogbin, I.A., *Dahomey and Its Neighbours 1708-1818* (Cambridge, Eng., 1967).

Albéca, Alexandre L. d', *La France au Dahomey* (Paris, 1895).

Almeida-Topor, Hélène d', *Les amazones: une armée de femmes dans l'Afrique précoloniale* (Paris, 1984).

Anonymous, *La France au pays noir, campagne du Dahomey, 1890-1892* (Paris, 1895).

Argyle, W.J., *The Fon of Dahomey: a History and Ethnography of the Old Kingdom* (Oxford, 1966).

Aublet, Ed., *La guerre au Dahomey, 1888-1893, d'après les documents officiels* (Paris, 1894).

Barbou, Alfred, *Histoire de la Guerre au Dahomey* (Paris, 1893).

Bern, J., *L'expédition du Dahomey (août-décembre 1892): notes éparses d'un volontaire* (Sidi-Bel-Abbès, Algeria, 1893).

Biobaku, Saburi O., *The Egba and Their Neighbours, 1842-1872* (Oxford, 1957).

Bosman, William, *A New and Accurate Description of the Coast of Guinea, Divided into the Gold, the Slave, and the Ivory Coasts*, new edn, intro. John Ralph Willis, notes J.D.Fage and R.E. Bradbury (London, 1967).

Bouche, Pierre, *Sept ans en Afrique occidentale: la Côte des Esclaves et le Dahomey* (Paris, 1885).

Bowen, T.J., *Adventures and Missionary Labours in Several Countries in the Interior of Africa from 1849 to 1856*, 2nd edn (London, 1968).

Brunet, L., and Giethlen, Louis, *Dahomey et dépendances* (Paris, 1900).

Burton, Richard F., *Abeokuta and the Camaroons Mountains. An Exploration*, 2 vols (London, 1863).

——, *A Mission to Gelele, King of Dahome*, ed. C.W. Newbury (New York, 1966).

Chaudoin, E., *Trois mois de captivité au Dahomey* (Paris, 1891).

Chautard, le Père, Le Dahomey (Lyon, 1890).

Conneau, Theophilus, A Slaver's Log Book or 20 Years' Residence in Africa (Englewood Cliffs, NJ, 1976).

Cornevin, Robert, La République populaire du Bénin des origines dahoméennes à nos jours (Paris, 1981).

Dalzel, Archibald, The History of Dahomy, an Inland Kingdom of Africa (1793, reprint London, with intro. by J.D. Fage, 1967).

Dantzig, A. van, ed., tr., The Dutch and the Guinea Coast 1674-1742: a Collection of Documents from the General State Archive at The Hague (Accra, 1978).

Djivo, Adrien, Guézo: la rénovation du Dahomey (Paris, 1977).

Duncan, John, Travels in Western Africa in 1845 & 1846, Comprising a Journey from Whydah, Through the Kingdom of Dahomey to Adofoodia, in the Interior, 2 vols, reprint in one volume (New York, 1967).

Ellis, A.B., The Land of Fetish, reprint (Westport, Conn., 1970).

——, The Ewe-Speaking Peoples of the Slave Coast of West Africa: Their Religion, Manners, Customs, Laws, Languages, &c., reprint (Oosterhout, Neth., 1966).

Foà, Edouard, Le Dahomey: histoire, géographie, moeurs, coutumes, commerce, industrie, expéditions françaises (1891-1894), (Paris, 1895).

Fonssagrives, Jean, Notice sur le Dahomey (Paris, 1900).

Forbes, Frederick E., Dahomey and the Dahomans, Being the Journals of Two Missions to the King of Dahomey and Residence at His Capital in the Years 1849 and 1850, 2 vols, reprint (London, 1966).

Fraser, Antonia, The Warrior Queens (New York, 1989).

Freeman, Thomas Birch, Journal of Various Visits to the Kingdoms of Ashanti, Aku, and Dahomi in Western Africa, 3rd edn, intro. Harrison M. Wright (London, 1968).

Garcia, Luc, Le royaume du Dahomé face à la pénétration coloniale: affrontements et incompréhension (1875-1894), (Paris 1988).

Glélé, Maurice Ahanhanzo, Le Danxome: du pouvoir aja à la nation fon (Paris, 1974).

Grandin, Commandant, A l'assaut du pays des noirs: le Dahomey, 2 vols (Paris, 1895).

Hazoumé, Paul, Doguicimi (Paris, 1938).

——, Doguicimi: the First Dahomean Novel (1937), tr. Richard Bjornson (Washington, 1990).

——, Le pacte de sang au Dahomey (Paris, 1956).

Herskovits, Melville J., Dahomey, an Ancient West African Kingdom, 2 vols (New York, 1938).

Johnson, Samuel, The History of the Yorubas from the Earliest Times to the Beginning of the British Protectorate, ed. O. Johnson, reprint (London, 1966).

Labarthe, P., *Voyage à la côte de Guinée ou description des côtes d'Afrique depuis le cap Tagrin jusqu'au cap de Lopez-Gonzalves* (Paris, 1803).

Labat, Jean-Baptiste, *Voyage du chevalier Des Marchais en Guinée, isles voisines, et à Cayenne, fait en 1725, 1726 & 1727*, 4 vols (Paris, 1830).

Laffitte, M. l'abbé, *Le Dahomé: souvenirs de voyage et de mission* (Tours, 1873).

Law, Robin, *The Oyo Empire, c. 1600-c. 1836* (Oxford, 1977).

——, *The Slave Coast of West Africa 1550-1750: the Impact of the Atlantic Slave Trade on an African Society* (Oxford, 1991).

Le Hérissé, A., *L'ancien royaume du Dahomey. Moeurs, religion, histoire* (Paris, 1911).

Maire, Victor-Louis, *Dahomey: Abomey – la dynastie dahoméenne. Les palais: leurs bas-reliefs* (Besançon, 1905).

Mandirola, Renzo, and Yves Morel, eds, *Journal de Francesco Borghero, premier missionnaire du Dahomey (1861-1865): sa vie, son journal (1860-1864), la relation de 1863* (Paris, 1997).

Maupoil, Bernard, *La géomancie à l'ancienne Côte des Esclaves*, reprint (Paris, 1981).

Mercier, P., *Civilisations du Bénin* (Paris, 1962).

Mercier, P., and Lombard, J., *Guide du Musée d'Abomey* (Porto-Novo, 1959).

M'Leod, John, *A Voyage to Africa with Some Account of the Manners and Customs of the Dahomian People*, reprint (London, 1971).

Moore, E. Olympus O. (pen name of Ajayi Kolawole Ajisafe), *History of Abeokuta* (London, 1916).

Morienval, Henri, *La guerre du Dahomey. Journal de campagne d'un sous-lieutenant d'infanterie de marine* (Paris, 1893).

Newbury, C.W., *The Western Slave Coast and Its Rulers: European Trade and Administration Among the Yoruba and Adja-Speaking Peoples of South-Western Nigeria, Southern Dahomey and Togo* (Oxford, 1961).

Nicolas, Victor, *L'expédition du Dahomey en 1890*, 2nd edn (Paris, 1893).

Norris, Robert, *Memoirs of the Reign of Bossa Ahádee, King of Dahomy, an Inland Country of Guiney. To Which Are Added, the Author's Journey to Abomey, the Capital; and a Short Account of the African Slave Trade*, reprint (London, 1968).

Nuëlito, E., *Au Dahomey. Journal d'un officier de spahis* (Abbeville, 1897).

Oliveira, Th. Constant-Ernest d', *La visite du Musée d'Histoire d'Abomey* (Abomey, 1970).

Parrinder, E.G., *The Story of Ketu, an Ancient Yoruba Kingdom* (Ibadan, 1956).

Pires, Vicente Ferreira, *Viagem de Africa em o Reino de Dahomé* (São Paulo, 1957).

Poirier, Jules, *Campagne du Dahomey, 1892-1894* (Paris, 1895).

Prévaudeau, Marie-Madeleine, *Abomey-la-mystique* (Paris, 1936).
Pruneau de Pommegorge, Antoine-Edmé (a.k.a. Joseph Pruneau), *Description de la Nigritie* (Amsterdam, 1789).
Quénum, Maximilien, *Au pays des Fons. Us et coutumes du Dahomey,* 3rd edn (Paris, 1983).
Samuel, Pierre, *Amazones, guerrières et gaillardes* (Grenoble, 1975).
Schelameur, Frédéric, *Souvenirs de la campagne du Dahomey* (Paris, 1896).
Skertchly, J.A., *Dahomey as It Is; Being a Narrative of Eight Months' Residence in That Country, with a Full Account of the Notorious Annual Customs, and the Social and Religious Institutions of the Ffons* (London, 1874).
Smith, Robert S., *Kingdoms of the Yoruba,* 3rd edn (London, 1988).
Smith, William, *A New Voyage to Guinea,* reprint (London, 1967).
Snelgrave, William, *A New Account of Some Parts of Guinea and the Slave Trade,* reprint (London, 1971).
Sobol, Donald J., *The Amazons of Greek Mythology* (South Brunswick, NJ, 1972).
Townsend, Henry, *Memoir of the Rev. Henry Townsend, Late C.M.S. Missionary, Abeokuta, West Africa, Compiled from His Journals by His Brother, Mr. George Townsend, of Exeter* (London, 1887).
Tucker, Miss, *Abbeokuta; or, Sunrise Within the Tropics: an Outline of the Origin and Progress of the Yoruba Mission* (London, 1853).
Tyrrell, William Blake, *Amazons: a Study in Athenian Mythmaking* (Baltimore, 1984).
Waterlot, Em. G., *Les bas-reliefs des bâtiments royaux d'Abomey (Dahomey),* (Paris, 1926).

Articles and chapters

Baudin, Noël, "L'orphelinat de Puerto-real", *MC*, VI, no. 243 (Jan. 30, 1874), 59-60.
Bay, Edna Grace, "Servitude and Worldly Success in the Palace of Dahomey" in Claire C. Robertson and Martin A. Klein, eds, *Women and Slavery in Africa* (Madison, 1983), 340-67.
Bayol, Jean, "Les forces militaires actuelles du Dahomey", *Revue Scientifique (Revue Rose),* XLIX, no. 17 (April 23, 1892), 520-4.
——, "L'attaque de Kotonou, 4 mars 1890, impressions et souvenirs", *Revue Bleue (Revue Politique et Littéraire),* XLIX, no. 18 (April 30, 1892), 570-2.
Béraud, Médard, "Note sur le Dahomé", *Bulletin de la Société de Géographie,* 5th series, XII, Nov. 1866, 371-86.
Blanchély, "Au Dahomey: premier voyage de M. Blanchély aîné, gérant

de la factorerie de M. Régis, de Marseille, à Whydah (1848)", 2 parts, *MC*, XXIII, nos. 1170-1 (Nov. 6 and 13, 1891), 534-7, 545-8.

——, "Relation du deuxième voyage fait, en 1850, dans le royaume du Dahomé, par Blanchély aîné, en compagnie de M. Esprit Cases, nouvel agent de la factorerie française Régis aîné, de Whydah", 2 parts, *MC*, XXIII, nos. 1172-3 (Nov. 20 and 27, 1891), 562-4, 575-6.

——, "Relation du troisième voyage fait en 1850 dans le royaume du Dahomey, par M. Blanchély aîné, agent de la factorerie française de Whydah", *MC*, XXIII, no. 1174 (Dec. 4, 1891), 587-8.

Borghero, F., letters to A. Planque from Whydah, *APF*, esp. XXXIV, no. 202 (May 1862) and XXXV, no. 206 (Jan. 1863).

Bouët, Auguste, "Le royaume de Dahomey", 3 parts, *L'Illustration*, X, nos. 490-2 (July 17, 24 and 31, 1852), 39-42, 59-62, 71-4. See also the Nardin listing below.

Brue, Blaise, "Voyage fait en 1843, dans le royaume de Dahomey, par M. Brue, agent du comptoir français établi à Whydah", *Revue Coloniale*, VII, Sept. 1845, 55-68.

Burdo, Adolphe, "Au Dahomey", 3 parts, *Journal des Voyages*, nos 681-3 (July 27, Aug. 3 and 10, 1890), 50-1, 69-71, 87-90.

Burton, Richard F., "The Present State of Dahome", *Transactions of the Ethnological Society of London*, III, new series, 1865, 400-8.

——, "Notes on the Dahoman" in Richard Burton, *Selected Papers on Anthropology, Travel and Exploration*, ed. N.M. Penzer (London, 1924), 109-33.

Coissy, Anatole, "Un règne de femme dans l'ancien royaume d'Abomey", *ED*, II (1949), 5-8.

Courdioux, E., "Côte des Esclaves", *MC*, esp. VII, no. 336 (Nov. 12, 1875), 555; IX, no. 397 (Jan. 12, 1877), 23; X, no. 490 (Oct. 25, 1878), 514-5; X, no. 492 (Nov. 8, 1878), 538.

Cruickshank, Brodie, "Report by B. Cruickshank, Esq. of His Mission to the King of Dahomey", Nov. 9, 1848, in *IUP Series of British PP, Colonies: Africa 50* (Shannon, 1971), 241-9.

Cruz, Clément da, "Les instruments de musique dans le Bas-Dahomey", *ED*, XII (1954), whole issue.

Dunglas, Edouard, "La première attaque des Dahoméens contre Abéokuta (3 mars 1851)", *ED*, I (1948), 7-19.

——, "Deuxième attaque des Dahoméens contre Abeokuta (15 mars 1864)", *ED*, II (1949), 37-58.

——, "Contribution à l'histoire du Moyen-Dahomey (royaumes d'-Abomey, de Kétou et de Ouidah)", 3 tomes, *ED*, XIX, tome 1 (1957); XX, 2 (1957); XXI, 3 (1958), whole issues.

Foà, Edouard, "Dahomiens et Egbas", 2 parts, *La Nature*, XIX, 1st semester, no. 926 (Feb. 28, 1891), 199-202; no. 930 (March 28, 1891), 262-6.

Guillevin, "Voyage dans l'intérieur du royaume de Dahomey", *Nouvelles Annales des Voyages, de la Géographie, de l'Histoire et de l'Archéologie*, 6th series, VIII, 2 (June 1862), 257-99.

Law, Robin, "Dahomey and the Slave Trade: Reflections on the Historiography of the Rise of Dahomey", *JAH*, XXVII, 2 (1986), 237-67.

———, "Problems of Plagiarism, Harmonization and Misunderstanding in Contemporary European Sources: Early (Pre-1680s) Sources for the 'Slave Coast' of West Africa" in Beatrix Heintze and Adam Jones, eds, *European Sources for Sub-Saharan Africa Before 1900: Use and Abuse* (Stuttgart, 1987), 337-58. (This book is vol. 33 of the annual *Paideuma*.)

———, "A Neglected Account of the Dahomian Conquest of Whydah (1727): the 'Relation de la guerre de Juda' of the Sieur Ringard of Nantes", *HA*, 15 (1988), 321-38.

———, "Further Light on Bulfinch Lambe and the 'Emperor of Pawpaw': King Agaja of Dahomey's Letter to King George I of England, 1726", *HA*, 17 (1990), 211-26.

———, "The 'Amazons' of Dahomey", *Paideuma*, 39 (1993), 245-60.

———, "The Politics of Commercial Transition: Factional Conflict in Dahomey in the Context of the Ending of the Atlantic Slave Trade", *JAH*, XXXVIII, 2 (1997), 213-33.

Lissner, Ignace, "De Whydah à Abomey", 5 parts, *MC*, XXVII, Aug. 23, 30, Sept. 6, 13, 20, 1895, 404-6, 416-19, 428-30, 442-4, 454-6.

Manning, Patrick, "The Slave Trade in the Bight of Benin, 1640-1890" in Henry A. Gemery and Jan S. Hogendorn, eds, *The Uncommon Market: Essays in the Economic History of the Atlantic Slave Trade* (New York, 1979), 107-41.

Mercier, Paul, "The Fon of Dahomey" in *African Worlds: Studies in the Cosmological Ideas and Social Values of African Peoples* (London, 1954), 210-34.

Monléon, de, "Le cap des Palmes, le Dahomey, Fernando-Pô et l'île du Prince, en 1844", *Revue Coloniale*, VI, May 1845, 62-82.

Nardin, Jean-Claude, "La reprise des relations franco-dahoméennes au XIXe siècle: la mission d'Auguste Bouët à la cour d'Abomey (1851)", *Cahiers d'Etudes Africaines*, VII, 1 (1967), 59-126. See also the Bouët listing above.

Obichere, Boniface I., "Change and Innovation in the Administration of the Kingdom of Dahomey," *Journal of African Studies*, I, 3 (fall 1974), 235-51.

Rastignac, "Courrier de Paris", *L'Illustration*, LI, nos. 2613, 2616, 2617 (March 25, April 15 and 22, 1893), 226, 286, 306.

Répin, A., "Voyage au Dahomey", *Le Tour du Monde*, VII, 2d semester (1863), 65-112. Extracts published in *ED*, III (1950), 89-95.

Ridgway, Archibald R., "Journal of a Visit to Dahomey; or, the Snake Country, in the Months of March and April, 1847", 3 parts, *The New Monthly Magazine and Humorist*, LXXXI, nos. 322-4 (Oct.-Dec. 1847), 187-98, 299-309, 406-14.

Roques, A., "Le Génie au Dahomey en 1892", *Revue du Génie Militaire*, VIII, 4 (July-Aug. 1894), 273-322.

Ross, David, "Dahomey" in Michael Crowder, ed., *West African Resistance: the Military Response to Colonial Occupation* (New York, 1971), 144-69.

Sedolo, Michel Dossou, "Comment fut décidée la deuxième et dernière expédition des Dahoméens contre la ville de Kétou", *Notes Africaines*, no. 57 (Jan. 1953), 24-5.

——, "Considérations sur la guerre de Kétou Woto-to, II, le siège et la prise de Kétou", *Notes Africaines*, no. 62 (April 1954), 47-8.

Tinayre, Abel, "Au Dahomey", *Le Monde Illustré*, XXXVII, nos. 1867, 1869 (Jan. 7 and 21, 1893), 6, 35.

Vallon, A., "Le royaume de Dahomey," 2 parts, *Revue Maritime et Coloniale*, II (Aug. 1861), 332-63; III (Nov. 1861), 329-58. Largely reproduced in L.-N. Veil, "Une mission au Dahomey en 1856", *L'Information Colonial*, I, no. 4 (Jan. 1936), 19; no. 5 (Feb. 1936), 18, and no. 7 (April 1936), 19.

Verdal, Georges, "Les amazones du Dahomey", *L'Education Physique*, new series, XXXII, no. 29 (Jan. 1934), 52-9.

Wailly, G. de, "Un régiment sacré: Dahomey", *La Nouvelle Revue*, XII, no. 63 (March-April 1890), 390-4.

Wilmot, A.P.E., "Despatches from Commodore Wilmot Respecting His Visit to the King of Dahomey in December 1862 and January 1863" in *IUP Series of British PP, Colonies: Africa 50*, 423-40.

Winniett, William, testimony before "the Select Committee of the House of Lords appointed to consider the best Means which Great Britain can adopt for the final Extinction of the African Slave Trade", April 30, 1849, PP, vol. 9 (1850), 61-71.

Archival Documents

ENGLAND

Church Missionary Society

CA2/016/34, extracts by C. Chapman from Dawson's journal and from his letters to F. Fitzgerald, Nov. 17, 1862. The CMS archives are housed in the Special Collections, Information Services, University of Birmingham.

Methodist Missionary Society

Typescript copy of unpublished book by T.B. Freeman, MMS Archives, Biographical West Africa, Box 597. The archives are housed in the Library of the School of Oriental and African Studies, University of London.

Public Record Office

PRO, FO 84/816, Beecroft to Palmerston, July 22, 1850, encloses Beecroft's journal.
PRO, FO 84/827, Fanshawe to Admiralty, July 19, 1850, encloses Forbes's journal.
PRO, FO 84/886, Beecroft to Palmerston, Feb. 19, 1852, encloses Louis Fraser's journal.
PRO, FO 84/1175, Perry to Freeman, Aug. 6, 1862, records Euschart's account of his visit to Abomey.

FRANCE

Bibliothèque Nationale

Fonds Français 24223, "Journal du Voiage de Guinée et Cayenne Par Le Chevalier Des Marchais Capitaine Comandant La fregatte de la Compagnie des Indes, L'Expedition Pendant les Années 1724, 1725 et 1726..."

Centre des Archives d'Outre-Mer

DFC, Côtes d'Afrique, no. 104, carton 75, "Relation du Royaume de Judas en Guinée, De son Gouvernement, des moeurs de ses habitans, de leur Religion, Et du Negoce qui sy fait." This document is undated but would appear to have been written between 1710 and 1715.
DFC, Côtes d'Afrique, no. 111, carton 75, "Réflexions sur Juda par les Sieurs De Chenevert et abbé Bullet", June 1, 1776.
Dahomey, III, 1, Angot to Bayol, Jan. 5, 1890.
Dahomey, III, 1, H. Decoeur's journal, April 3, 1891.
Dahomey, III, 2, J. d'Ambrières' journal, undated but covering the same mission to Abomey as Decoeur's journal, Feb. 9–March 25, 1891.
Dahomey, V, 6a, Dodds' "Rapport sur les opérations du corps expéditionnaire du Dahomey en 1892," undated.

Ministère des Affaires Etrangères

MAE, Mémoires et documents, Afrique, 51, J. Lartigue, "Relation du

voyage à Abomey", Sept. 2, 1860. Reproduced in *Le Figaro, Supplément Littéraire*, XVI, no. 10 (March 8, 1890), "Les sacrifices humains au Dahomey – révélations inédites", 38-9.
MAE, Mémoires et documents, Afrique, 52, Didelot to Chasseloup-Laubat, March 27, 1863.

Service Historique de l'Armée de Terre

Dahomey, I, 14, "Campagne du Dahomey – relation anonyme", an undated journal attributed to Edouard Demartinécourt.

Dissertations
Bay, Edna Grace, "The Royal Women of Abomey", Ph.D., Boston U., 1977.
Degbelo, Amélie, "Les amazones du Danxomè 1645-1900", master's, Université Nationale du Bénin, 1979.
Glélè, Pogla K., "Le royaume du Dan-Hô-Min: tradition orale et histoire écrite", master's, 1971 (CAOM, SOM, D.3538).
Maroukis, Thomas C., "Warfare and Society in the Kingdom of Dahomey: 1818-1894", Ph.D., Boston U., 1974.

INDEX

273